D0375631

I screamed out to the team, "Snipers! Snipers behind the tree to our front. Spider hole opening. . . ." Bullets tore over our heads as we went to ground. The loud cracks sounded like M-2 carbine fire on full automatic and close. Very close! None of us moved. Then Gary Woodruff, Burns, and I spread out into a firing line, low-crawling to the side where each of us had a lane to shoot down. The platoon behind us had hit the deck and stayed down to let us handle the problem.

Lafley whispered, "Wait till he comes up for another shot. Then we drill his ass together." The clicks of our safeties flicking off were drowned out by the rustling of our gear as we settled into position, our rifles trained and our sights on the base of a large tree. As Lafley had predicted, the cover of the spider trap moved and lifted. Seeking a target, the muzzle of a rifle poked from the hole.

Lafley yelled, "Now!"

By John J. Culbertson
Published by Ivy Books:

OPERATION TUSCALOOSA: *2nd Battalion, 5th Marines,*
at An Hoa, 1967

Books published by The Ballantine Publishing Group
are available at quantity discounts on bulk purchases
for premium, educational, fund-raising, and special
sales use. For details, please call 1-800-733-3000.

A SNIPER IN THE ARIZONA

2nd Battalion, 5th Marines,
in the Arizona Territory, 1967

John J. Culbertson

IVY BOOKS • NEW YORK

Sale of this book without a front cover may be unauthorized. If this book is coverless, it may have been reported to the publisher as "unsold or destroyed" and neither the author nor the publisher may have received payment for it.

An Ivy Book
Published by The Ballantine Publishing Group
Copyright © 1999 by John J. Culbertson

All rights reserved under International and Pan-American Copyright Conventions. Published in the United States by The Ballantine Publishing Group, a division of Random House, Inc., New York, and simultaneously in Canada by Random House of Canada Limited, Toronto.

Ivy Books and colophon are trademarks of Random House, Inc.

www.randomhouse.com/BB/

Library of Congress Catalog Card Number: 98-93522

ISBN 0-8041-1870-1

Manufactured in the United States of America

First Edition: March 1999

10 9 8 7 6 5 4 3 2

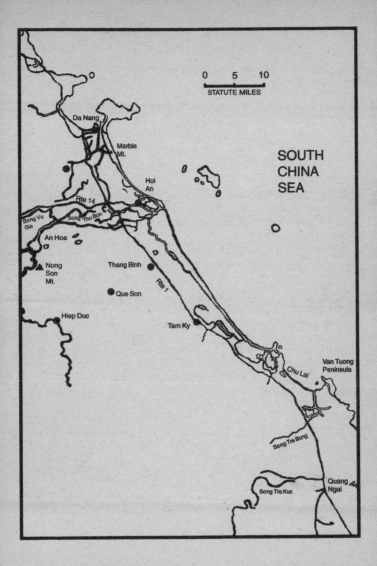

Prologue

In *Operation Tuscaloosa: 2nd Battalion, 5th Marines, at An Hoa, 1967*, I described how Hotel Company had destroyed the R-20th Main Force Battalion of the regular Viet Cong forces on January 26, 1967, at the river crossing over the Thu Bon River and in assaults against the VC/NVA regulars in the hostile villages of La Bac 1 and 2. Two hundred twenty-one enemy soldiers had been killed or wounded (body count) by the Marines of Foxtrot and Hotel Companies. By January 28, 1967, when Operation Tuscaloosa had been officially secured, the Marines of the 2nd Battalion, based at An Hoa Combat Base, twenty-five miles southwest of Marine headquarters at Da Nang, had sent a clear message to the Viet Cong high command to the north near the Laotian border: the U.S. Marines would press ahead with clearing the hamlets of I Corps of the indigenous Viet Cong terrorists who targeted its peaceful peasant South Vietnamese.

The peasants of South Vietnam themselves were the victims hardest hit by the violence sparked by the military dictatorship of Vo Nguyen Giap in North Vietnam's "People's Republic." For this reason, the Marines had chosen the sensible tactic of fortifying local hamlets using

1

U.S. Marine and South Vietnamese Army (ARVN) soldiers in civil action platoons (CAPs) to clear the countryside of the VC and NVA and to strengthen the local leaders so that they could maintain hegemony within their districts. Offensive strikes like Operation Tuscaloosa were designed to defeat large Communist military units and maintain U.S. superiority on the battlefield. However, victory in large-scale battles like Operation Starlight and Operation Prairie were simply not solely capable of stopping large-scale enemy infiltration into South Vietnam via the Ho Chi Minh trail (particularly into the DMZ, the A Shau Valley, and the Arizona Territory, west of Da Nang).

Operation Prairie I, which ended on January 31, 1967, had lasted 187 days and compiled some significant statistics: a buildup of Marines to over sixty thousand combat and support troops in I Corps; an expansion of U.S. Marine tactical area of responsibility from eight square miles in the beginning of 1966 to one thousand eight hundred square miles at the beginning of 1967; one hundred and fifty combat engagements with enemy forces of at least battalion or regimental strength; the destruction of several enemy battalions (as in Operation Tuscaloosa); the deaths of seven thousand three hundred (body count) enemy soldiers in major operations, with an additional four thousand enemy killed in action (KIA) as a result of over two hundred thousand Marine combat patrols. U.S. Marine losses during the period were one thousand seven hundred KIA and nine thousand wounded.

Despite the enemy's catastrophic losses, infiltration into South Vietnam did not let up during 1967; on the contrary, it intensified.

In order to control and pacify the eleven thousand

hamlets in South Vietnam, the U.S. and ARVN joint strategy was to present a strong presence by patrolling and village fortification and through the development of the Regional and Popular Forces that comprised the South Vietnamese National Guard. During the early months of 1967, the 2nd Battalion, 5th Marine Regiment, patrolled the Arizona Territory to win the hearts and minds of the local populace. The local populace, on the other hand, would just as soon have sent us on our way back to America, as the war by then had orphaned and widowed many of them. In Hotel Company the grunts still thought the United States could kick Charlie's butt (*Victor Charlie*, i.e., the Viet Cong, our enemy in the Arizona Territory) and win the war.

A Sniper in the Arizona is a true story of the events surrounding Hotel Company and its sister companies in the 2nd Battalion, 5th Marine Regiment, 1st Marine Division. 2/5 was garrisoned at An Hoa combat base at the southern periphery of the huge rice basin that covered the several hundred square miles in Quang Nam Province, South Vietnam, known as the Arizona Territory. Hotel Company, with the aid of Foxtrot, had just survived a near massacre on the sandbar wastelands of the Thu Bon River during Operation Tuscaloosa. After heavy fighting and maddening losses, the Marines had destroyed their foe in two frontal assaults.

CHAPTER ONE

Tuscaloosa Aftermath

The early weeks of February 1967 brought constant patrolling by Hotel and Foxtrot Companies along the meandering tributaries of the Thu Bon River (Song Thu Bon) deep into the Arizona Territory. The Communist high command in Hanoi was diverting new infantry and support battalions south to press the overall assault on the free Republic of South Vietnam. The invaders were entering South Vietnam through I (Roman numeral for "one") Corps, the northernmost of the four military sectors (formally called Corps Tactical Zones or CTZs) of Vietnam controlled by the Allied Forces.

The peasants had seen the 2nd Battalion, 5th Marine (2/5), troops file through the dusty earthen streets of their villages on many occasions in previous months. Yet the old men and mamma-sans were oddly withdrawn and agitated. Something was undercutting the general kindliness the village communities had earlier directed at the Leathernecks. Subtle changes in the mood of the people were important to note in the ever-shifting drama of the jungle war.

Reports of village unease and unfriendliness reached the battalion's commanding officer at his headquarters at An Hoa. Lieutenant Colonel Jackson had replaced Lieutenant Colonel Airheart as the battalion CO. Colonel Jackson immediately ordered 2/5's patrols to take Army of the Republic of Vietnam (ARVN) interpreters along on any mission through Arizona hamlets expressing hostility toward the Marines.

John Lafley, Luther Hamilton, John Jessmore, and I saddled up for a long patrol that would keep Hotel's 3rd Platoon in the bush for several weeks. In Hotel Company, we wore flak jackets and carried small Marine haversacks high on our upper backs. Helmets were worn unstrapped at the chin but low over the eyes to cut down the horrendous glare of the morning sun as it filtered through the trees. Except for FNGs ("fuckin' new guys"), helmet covers were faded camouflage. Our packs contained extra 7.62mm NATO rifle cartridges for our M-14 rifles, socks, cigarettes, and extra C-ration meals. Our jungle boots were white from constant immersion in the water of the paddies that made the Arizona Territory one of the most productive rice-producing valleys in Asia. Our M-14s were spotless. They rested in the crooks of our arms or over the flak-jacket padding of our shoulders. We wore bandoliers of ammo crisscrossed over our chests. Bayonets and K-bar knives hung loosely at the hip.

The Marines of Hotel Company were the victors of Tuscaloosa, which had matched them against the VC in one of the bloodiest battles yet in the Marine Corps' Vietnam experience, and they had the cold eyes and the swagger of seasoned professionals. When the men of 3rd Platoon crossed the perimeter wire of An Hoa combat base to enter the paddies leading into the Arizona Territory, we took on the frame of mind of a band of hardened killers; too many of our brothers had been killed and wounded on Operation Tuscaloosa.

Gerald Burns swaggered into the gaggle of Marines swarming through the double-apron barbed wire and forming into a long column heading northwest into the Arizona. Burns wore a filthy flak jacket. His M-14 was draped across one massive arm the way a quail hunter would carry a shotgun back home. A half-finished Camel cigarette hung from the redhead's lip. Burns's helmet was tilted back on his head nonchalantly, and the cigarette smoke eddied around the helmet-visor lip with each puff. Lafley glanced at Burns as he passed, joining the column winding along the red-clay trail that served as the main road. Something drew Lafley's attention toward the front of the column and then back to Burns.

"Hey, numbnuts, what the hell are you doing with *that* flak jacket on? Boy, are you crazy or something!" Lafley stammered in disbelief as Burns turned toward him and stepped out of the column. His reply was a sneer combined with that peculiar brand of sarcasm that made Burns the platoon joker. But his humor mirrored an utter ruthlessness and total disregard for his personal safety in combat; Burns was the epitome of the combat Marine. "I took this jacket off Lieutenant Smith's body after Tuscaloosa, Lafley. I figured the son of a bitch had so many bullet holes in it that they'll never kill old Private Burns in this rig. I even drew a bull's-eye on the burst of rounds that tore through the back and killed the lieutenant. Fuck the VC if they can't take a joke! They killed my brother over here, and that damn sure ain't no joke to me. Lafley, when I've finished my tour in this shithole, some gooks are gonna remember old Private Burns real good; he killed their sons and brothers, too, by God!"

Lafley shook his head as Burns rejoined the column, by then spread out and moving fast, looking for signs of the enemy.

CHAPTER TWO

Winning the Villagers' Hearts and Minds

The patrol cut off the main road from An Hoa to Phu Loc 6 firebase. Phu Loc 6 was manned around the clock by a platoon from 2/5 to provide fire support (artillery fire missions) and patrol the northern flatlands six miles north of An Hoa. A platoon from Echo Company manned the small, two-hundred-foot-tall graded knob that served as An Hoa's northern sentinel outpost. Worn and torn sandbagged bunkers outcropped around the perimeter of the Spartan earthworks that provided the only safety for thirty or so Marines. From the main road, a dirt track meandered up the two-hundred-foot grade to Phu Loc 6. The gradual ascent to the entrance to Phu Loc 6 would draw potential attackers upslope and into the interlocking fires of machine gun positions on both sides of the perimeter's double apron of barbed wire.

Just before the trail rose into the bunkers surrounding Phu Loc 6, the 3rd Platoon point scout stepped out into the grass-covered plain that descended toward the Song Thu Bon, which flowed through the quiltlike maze of rice paddies along the southern boundary of the enemy territory that the Marines had nicknamed "The Arizona Territory." The Arizona was so named because, like the Arizona Territory of the Old West, all men in it were presumed to be gunfighters. The names given to areas of the Arizona were out of cowboy legend: Tombstone, Dodge City, and the Coal Mines marked Marine battles past and future with the Viet Cong and NVA. Because the Marines were determined to pacify the hamlets of the Arizona and Quang Nam Province in southern I Corps, the commanding officers of the 5th Marine Regiment ordered daily patrols to intimidate the enemy. At the same time, the Viet Cong and the NVA were flooding the Arizona with fresh infantry companies to contest the Marine and ARVN presence and to force the village leaders into compliance with the Communist scheme for the overthrow of South Vietnam. All village chiefs or elders who resisted the Viet Cong's efforts at infiltration and control were marked for execution.

The Marine mission was clear. Support of the status quo in the network of villages was to be maintained using CAPs, Marine infantry troops combined with South Vietnamese (ARVN) soldiers, to fortify villages and protect the villagers from Viet Cong attacks. Secondly, Marine patrols, from squad to company strength, were fielded daily to project a physical presence in the Arizona Territory and try to make contact with Viet Cong units menacing the countryside. The main problem in closing with the VC was their ability to hide during daylight hours, when Marine air power was on station, and limit most of their movements to nighttime when detection was limited.

The patrol from Hotel entered the first section of rice fields stretching away from Phu Loc 6 toward the river. The point scouts had to be especially vigilant; the frequency of encountering booby traps and mines increased greatly once they were off the main road. The paddies west of Phu Loc 6 had already claimed their share of Marine casualties. In mid-January of 1967, a patrol of Marines had taken the western route off Phu Loc 6 toward the paddies flanking the Song Thu Bon. The platoon leader, Lt. Jim Kirschke from Pennsylvania, had triggered a land mine, later believed to be a rocket or mortar round, that had been buried and equipped with a trip wire and detonating fuse. The explosion blasted the young platoon leader's legs so badly that he was turning gray from blood loss by the time the medevac helicopter spun down from An Hoa. Lieutenant Kirschke eventually lost both legs; Hotel Company lost a fine leader. Subsequent patrols off Phu Loc 6 into the Arizona proceeded with extreme caution.

The Viet Cong were very skillful in the application of both passive and aggressive measures aimed at the Marines invading their country. To the average Marine infantryman, the Charlies (VC soldiers) seemed to be a chicken-livered bunch who would rather shoot Marines in the back than face them in battle. And with good reason; locally, Operation Tuscaloosa had proved who the best gunfighters in the Arizona were. Even so, few Marines wanted another pitched battle with the Main Force Viet Cong who had decimated our ranks at the river crossing on January 26, 1967.

The point scout called back to Gunnery Sergeant Jones who had replaced 3rd Platoon's Lieutenant Smith when the latter was killed on Tuscaloosa while crossing the sandbar. The point had sighted the first large village across an immense rice paddy flanked by dense tree lines. As 3rd Platoon broke into the open paddy and took the trail leading toward the village, machine gun fire exploded on our starboard (right) flank, raking the column of Marines from the point back to the tree line. Patches of grass and dirt were ripped off the dike walls as the bullets fell around the exposed Marines. The villagers rarely failed to pass the word about Marine patrols to the enemy before the patrol left An Hoa. For fear of compromising the safety of his Marines, Captain Doherty, who had skillfully commanded Hotel Company from 1966 through Operation Tuscaloosa in January 1967, had even refused to disclose Hotel's patrol routes to ARVN commanders on joint patrols or operations.

As the Viet Cong bullets continued to fall in a beaten zone on top of the now prostrate Marines, it was obvious to Gunny Jones and my squad leader, Luther Hamilton, that the ambush was no coincidence. Lafley yelled out in the first seconds of the contact, "Find some cover, boys! Put some fire into that tree line. Get a gun up here on the double! Even these assholes will hit somebody eventually." Gary Woodruff, an average-size Marine with the clean-cut face that made him look like the boy next door, was a Michigan boy, and in my experience, all Wolverines are hunters. Woody had fought through vicious close-quarter combat on the DMZ with Hotel 2/5. He had also survived the two-hour ambush on the sandbar during Operation Tuscaloosa. Woody had seen his friends shot to pieces, and if he had learned any lessons in Vietnam at all, he had learned that the answer to breaking the grip of an ambush was putting out return firepower. Immediately, if not sooner!

Woodruff rose from the filth and muck of the rice paddy where all the members of Hotel's 3rd Platoon had gone to ground when the initial burst of enemy fire slapped into the mud around us. Woody shouldered his M-14 with the selector on full automatic and fired three-round bursts into the tree line where the VC's muzzle flashes could be seen. I rose from my knees in the water and stood next to Woodruff and fired a sustained slow-fire volley of tracers into the enemy position from left to right. Stephen Gedzyk quickly had his M-60 machine gun up to Gary Woodruff's side and threw the gun onto the top of the paddy dike, the bipod thrust into the dirt. John Jessmore fed the belt into the gun and snapped the top-loading cover shut as Gedzyk squeezed the trigger. A stream of red tracers flowed into the Viet Cong position. Gedzyk's short bursts were methodical as he raked the tree line with deadly, grazing fire from side to side along its length. Meanwhile, the gunny had gotten our 60mm mortar team set up and into action. The heavy *thump* of the rounds leaving the tube added a special resonance to the staccato notes from the M-60 machine gun. A moment passed, and Tom Jiminez stepped up with one jungle boot on the dike. Jiminez shouldered his M-79 grenade launcher and lobbed 40mm rounds into the tree line to his front. The 60-Mike-Mike mortar rounds impacted directly in the center of the tree line. The high explosive (HE) mortar rounds bracketed the enemy trench line as Tom Jiminez's M-79 rounds spiraled into the fire and chaos. Balls of black and red death exploded in the Viet Cong trench as the Marine small arms fire continued to cut into the enemy hiding in the jungle foliage.

As our last mortar rounds impacted on top of the enemy trench, Gunny Jones ordered the platoon into the attack before Charlie could recover and regroup. Lafley and Woodruff leaped out of the paddy and over the dike, leading us forward in an assault line, two squads in width. Gunny Jones and his radioman brought up the rear with the 60mm mortar team. We advanced through the knee-deep paddy, firing M-14s from the hip into the dense vegetation of the tree line to our front. No enemy fire sought us out as we slogged across the squares of earth cupping murky brown water in the shimmering field of rice.

It seemed as if all of us reached the enemy trench line together. I was next to Gerald Burns as the redhead threw his heavy frame into the middle of a pile of enemy corpses sprawled in the bottom of the trench. The mortar attack, along with the M-79 fire of Tim Jiminez, had impacted with such accuracy that the VC had bugged out of the trench line without taking their dead. The VC often used crude wooden "body hooks" to drag off fallen comrades to confuse Marine body-count assessments. This time, instead of the usual drag marks and blood trails, all the Marines found were gunshot, tattered bodies with contorted faces. One wounded Viet Cong rose to his knees and gibbered away in singsong Vietnamese, but none of us understood anything he said. His black shirt and khaki trousers, sandals, and soft cloth jungle cap marked him as one of the Viet Cong guerrillas who harassed the South Vietnamese in the area. His eyes wide with fear, the Viet Cong clasped his hands over his head.

By the time Gunnery Sergeant Jones had reached our position in the trench line, we were forming into a column to march into the village not two hundred meters distant. Lafley and I assumed the point as Gunny Jones marched past the dead in the trench. Hamilton reported to the gunny that eight enemy bodies had been found in the bottom of the trench. Gunny Jones, who had served in the Chosin Reservoir defense with the 1st Marine Division in Korea in 1950, was no stranger to death. The 1st Marine Division grunts had killed Communist Chinese by the thousands in the ice and snow. Small engagements like this one were not earthshaking to Gunny Jones, but they did send a clear message to the Viet Cong in the local area: Ambush the 5th Marines and you will die like your buddies in the trench. As the troops filed back onto the paddy dikes toward the village, the gunny said, "Men, *that* is the Marine Corps way, take the fight to the enemy. Remember: gain fire superiority; hit Charlie with artillery or mortars; then assault under the curtain of small-arms fire. Remember on Tuscaloosa, when we all thought we had bought the farm? The artillery came in, and we assaulted, destroying the enemy. It never fails! Marines, I'm proud of you today. This was a righteous kill!"

As the column's point stepped out, taking the trail leading into the village, Burns spoke in a muted tone to my rear, "Stick with me, Culbertson. I'm starting to think you'll make a good trooper. Private Burns never lets any of these fuckers skate. You should only have to kill Charlie once. Know what I'm talkin' about?" I knew what Burns was talking about, and the scary part was that I was starting to agree with him.

CHAPTER THREE

Snipers in the VC Village

As Lafley and I approached the last hundred meters toward the grass-roofed huts on the edge of the village compound, rifle shots flashed from a ditch that ran in front of the length of huts that curved to our flanks along the paddies. Lafley was first into the paddy that bordered the trail, and I was barely a second behind. "Snipers!" came the shout from the squad leader to our rear. "Point, lay down some fire on the huts to your front."

Lafley brought up his M-14 and sighted in on the muzzle flashes twinkling behind the ditch at the village's front. He placed slow-fire, aimed shots along the top of the earthen trench. As I watched the dirt kick high in the air from the impact of the 150-grain bullets, I shouldered my weapon. The rest of the first fire team was kneeling in the paddy muck at our sides. Woodruff, Jiminez, Blocker, and the ever-bloodthirsty Private Burns clicked their rifles off safe and fired low, grazing shots into the top of the enemy trench. Gedzyk had the M-60 set up on the fire team's flank a moment after the first shots were fired. Jessmore ran a new belt into the gun. Gedzyk opened fire, first sending bursts into the ditch, then shifting his aim from flank to flank like a gardener hosing down his flower beds.

Gunney Jones got on the radio to An Hoa. "Steel Curtain, this is Hotel Leader. Over."

"Hotel Leader, this is Steel Curtain. I have you six by six. Over."

"Steel Curtain, Hotel Leader in contact with enemy snipers east side of village Le Nam 3 at AT 953513. My troops are one hundred meters east of village in paddy returning fire. Give me one Willy Peter (white phosphorus) targeted center of village. Hotel Leader will adjust. Over."

"Hotel Leader, this is Steel Curtain control. Fire mission. One round 105-Mike-Mike. Willy Peter. Fire center of village Le Nam 3 at AT (artillery target) 953513. Hotel Leader will adjust. Running fire mission. Over."

The Marines of 3rd Platoon heard a single report faintly across the rice fields toward An Hoa. The artillery shell had spun from the muzzle of the single gun in its revetment back at the artillery gun pits at An Hoa. Arcing through the light, midday clouds over the Arizona, the round turned down toward its target in the rice fields of Le Nam 3. The shriek of the shell startled the Marines as they returned fire at the sniper team of three VC and a cell of guerrillas armed with AK-47s. When the white phosphorus shell burst in the center of the small village, it showered the huts with smoking shards of white-hot phosphorus, and trails of black and white smoke quickly intertwined as white phosphorus from the shell flared into a flowing collage of burning death over the grass roofs.

The gunny was quickly back on the radio net to fire direction center at An Hoa with his fire mission request.

"Drop five-zero meters and fire for effect. Say again, drop five-zero meters and fire for effect. Hotel Leader, out."

The six 105-millimeter howitzers at An Hoa fired white phosphorus shells into the rice valley of the Arizona Territory. Immediately, the gunners of the 11th Marine regiment reloaded guns one through four and pulled the lanyards, sending an additional four shells. The ten rounds of WP shells slammed into the wood and thatch of the village main street and burst in silver-white petals of fiery metal. The entire village was soon cloaked in a curtain of black-and-white smoke, and geysers of molten phosphorus painted hellish arcs in the sky directly over the flaming huts.

The gunny secured the fire support, then turned to Burns and Lafley who had risen from their firing positions to receive assault orders from their platoon commander. "No need to enter that village, boys! There won't be anything left alive after the Willy Peter burns itself out!"

Burns stared at the village as if he was caught up in a bad dream and could not wake up. "God Almighty, Lafley, once that Willy Peter gets on a man, it just burns on and on. Remember that gook on Tuscaloosa that had the big char holes burnt in his back trying to run from the WP? It don't do no good to run. You just can't put that shit out. Well, Lafley, better them than us. Where's Culbertson?"

I was listening when Burns called my name through the drifting smoke. I was still hunkered in our firing position along the rice-paddy dike wall facing the burning village. I hoped an enemy soldier or two would be flushed out into the open paddy by the fires that raged in the village. The gusts of wind fanning the paddies carried burning sheaves of thatch and roofing into the air, filling the scene to the front with smoke trails that looked like children's chalky scribbling across a grade school blackboard. No Viet Cong ran out into my rifle sights, and I rose from my soggy sniper's lair, disappointed but still hopeful. The sun showed around 1400 hours, and the day might still yield me some opportunities to shoot.

Burns glanced hard at me through the smoke. "Culbertson, you are the trigger-happiest bastard in the 5th Marines. You'd sit on your mess kit all day just to kill one little dink."

"I've been breaking Culbertson in just fine without all your bullshit for help, Burns!" Lafley said. "Leave Culbertson to me. I'm turning the dude into a heartbreaker and a life-taker. Ain't that so, Oklahoma boy!"

I just nodded. When I got in the middle of an argument between Burns and Lafley, I never knew if the objective was military or theatrical. Maybe both! But I did feel that I was changing and becoming the kind of lean, green, mean machine the Marine Corps was renowned for. I probably would have sat there all day just to kill one VC. So would Burns and Lafley and any other trooper worth his salt!

The gunny cut my daydreaming short. "Lafley and Culbertson, get your butts on the point and skirt this village wide until we pick up the main trail to the next village. Move out and watch close for booby traps and mines."

CHAPTER FOUR

Casualties
Strewn in Le Nam 3

Lafley and I picked up the first dike trail that skirted the burning Le Nam 3. The white phosphorus shells had engulfed the wood-and-thatch village hootches in a swirling, crackling storm of whipping flames. Clouds of smoke eddied from the edge of the village in suffocating curtains that choked our small column of Marines working east around the rear of the village. Lafley coughed, ten paces to my front. "Culbertson, we got to double-time through this smoke. Man, I can hardly see, and the gooks could be lying in ambush up ahead. Pass the word to step up the pace until we reach that far tree line."

I passed the word to Blocker who shouldered the 3.5-inch rocket launcher ten paces to my rear, then I turned and began a quickstep behind Lafley toward the safety of the tree line a hundred meters ahead. No enemy shots were fired while thirty-five Marines ran double time along the dike dividing the village's rice fields. Every Marine held his helmet in one hand and his rifle or crew-served weapon in the other. Packs, canteens, bayonets, and bandoliers of ammo slapped and rustled against our Marine bodies as we snaked ahead.

Twenty meters farther brought the column past the smoke. Looking to our starboard flank, we saw the rear of the village exposed where the first artillery rounds had slammed home into the village main street. Lafley and I gazed upon a sight so horrible that we stopped the column and knelt down facing the remains of the charred huts. Slender wisps of smoke still twisted into the air from the blackened stumps of the remaining lodge poles. All the thatch was burnt away, and the insides of the hootches were exposed through skeletal frameworks. The carcasses of pigs, buffalo, and people fought for space on the bare earthen street of the village's main thoroughfare. The bodies of the animals were charred and still smoking. In death, the eyes of the buffalo protruded like giant eggs thrust from the tormented faces of the beasts. One huge pig was sliced practically in two, and from the gaping wound, entrails spilled out into the dusty street that sponged up the blood and gore. Lafley and I turned our attention to the rear of a partially collapsed hut. Two old men strode through the dissipating smoke of the dying firestorm. The old, white-bearded farmers supported a wide board that looked like a wooden door between their frail arms. Several village women in black pajamalike trousers and dirty, smoke-laced smocks—their straight black hair tied up in colorful cloths—followed the old farmers reverently carrying the palanquin between them. Lafley and I rose and strode toward the farmers as they rounded the trail between Marine squads kneeling in the paddy and searching the village.

When Lafley and I had closed to within ten meters of the farmers, the object of their concern became obvious. A young child lay on his back, naked from head to toe. His belly protruded grotesquely like a watermelon. The boy's chubby legs were covered with charred sores from which a yellowish pus had flowed, coating his inflamed limbs. As we drew closer, I saw that a trickle of blue liquid ran from his navel as though he had been doused in antifreeze. The child was writhing in agony with each step the farmers took, and he was whining when the bearers passed us. His eyes were glazed.

"God Almighty, that's the most pitiful bastard I ever laid eyes on!" Unnoticed, Burns had joined the small group of us watching the procession. "Well, it's a cinch he'll never grow up to be no VC like his daddy. Personally, I hope I get a shot at his old man later today." In his own way, Burns expressed the anger that veteran Marines developed in Vietnam as a mechanism to protect their emotions from the everyday horrors we were all exposed to. No one really wanted to see villagers, especially kids, suffer. However, in Vietnam as in all wars, fate did not discriminate when pain and suffering were apportioned.

Gary Woodruff joined our group and gazed in disbelief as the wounded child passed. "This war is really tough on Charlie, but I think it's a hell of a lot tougher on these peasants. What the hell did they do to deserve this shit? Those VC snipers probably weren't even from this village!"

Lafley broke the silence. "No, Woody, the VC snipers were on their way to hell. We just helped 'em along, that's all!" We stood there nervously and laughed at Lafley's joke. Lafley was usually funny as hell, and I think he and Burns kept us from sliding into depression. But the sight of the wounded boy was just too jarring. . . .

The mood of the troops of 3rd Platoon was jerked back into reality when the gunny ordered us back on the trail and on the march to the next village.

CHAPTER FIVE

The Old White Beard

As Lafley and Woodruff led the 3rd Platoon of Hotel Company down the levee road toward the next village in a chain of small hamlets in the floodplain of the Song Thu Bon, a throng of villagers appeared at the road's end. Gerald Burns and I took up positions behind Lafley and Woodruff, facing outward into the rectangles of rice sheaves that ran hundreds of meters in both directions from our main trail approaching the village. By the time Lafley and Woodruff had closed on the village entrance and the group of milling peasants waiting there, the rest of Hotel's Third Herd was spread out along the dike. All of us were tense and weary, and expecting sniper fire to pour out of the village at any moment. But no enemy troops presented themselves, probably because the Viet Cong had lost a platoon of soldiers in the trench-line firefight and again in the white phosphorus artillery barrage on Le Nam 3.

Lafley paused ten paces from the large group of peasants and he and Woodruff passed the word back to Gunny Jones that we had a welcoming committee. One white-bearded old man pushed his way through the cordon of Vietnamese who were smiling nervously at the Marines as they gathered at the trail's junction at the village gate. The old man raised his skinny arm and waved across the column of Marines and spoke in excited gushes of clipped Vietnamese. He folded his hands together and, touching his forehead, made a dignified bow to Lafley, Woodruff, Burns, and myself. As we stood in astonishment, the gunny strode up and spoke to Lafley. "What the hell is going on here? I want the men spread out in a perimeter. Jesus, one grenade would kill us all!"

Realizing that something unusual was taking place, Lafley spoke up. "Gunny, that old man is the same geezer that told the colonel about the VC before Tuscaloosa. He's got balls on him, and he hates the Viet Cong."

As Lafley finished identifying the old man, our Kit Carson scout came forward and exchanged some words with the old man. The scout looked at the gathering of Vietnamese villagers in black pajamas and smocks—women holding infants naked to their breasts; old men in loose white robes and carrying walking sticks. The villagers had dry, wrinkled skin, and constant exposure to the equatorial sun made even thirty-year-old mothers appear thirty years older. Those people were not Communists, they were the heart and soul of South Vietnam, respectable, honest rice farmers who fed the rest of the country. They were also prey for the Viet Cong military and political machine that robbed them of their sons, their rice, and frequently their lives under the disgusting lie of "People's Liberation."

The Kit Carson scout turned to the gunny and spoke in pidgin English. "The chief say whole village thanking Marines who killed many, many Viet Cong soldiers at river two weeks ago. These people are refugees. They run away from their village when battle start. Now can grow rice. Raise family again because Marines kill Viet Cong. Viet Cong soldiers say after battle they are beaucoup afraid of Marines. Viet Cong commander, he say many Marines die on sandbar, but more come ahead to die. Viet Cong never fight soldiers like these Marines. They say you Marines are crazy and do not fight like other U.S. soldiers. Viet Cong take wounded comrades to mountain hospital. No more fighting against Marines for long time. The old man say Marines free the people. They honor you!"

Woodruff faced me and shared what was on everyone's mind. "It's hard to believe after all this shit we've gone through that someone actually appreciated what we did on Tuscaloosa."

Burns spoke up from the rear of the platoon. "Gunny, we need to get the directions to that fucking gook hospital where all those bastards are laid up wounded. A B-52 strike or two would pretty much guarantee that we would never run into those assholes again!" Burns's expression of his usual compassion toward our enemies was, frankly, starting to make perfect sense to me.

The gunny had our Kit Carson scout thank all the villagers. We were then led into the village where three or four of us assembled in each thatch-roofed hut and were feted with a savory pork-and-rice meal by the villagers. Seated with crossed legs on the earthen floor of the huts, we ate in total silence. The peasants were pleasant and kind, and dumbfounded at our good luck, we nodded our thanks to the villagers and lit up cigarettes.

As the gunny passed the word to saddle up and resume

the patrol along the river, where we were to pick a defensive position to set in for the long night ahead, a rain squall broke and pelted the thatch roofs of the huts in a torrent.

CHAPTER SIX

Night Perimeter Along the River

Third Platoon meandered along earthen trails that cut across fallow paddies. In the rain, the footing along the dikes became especially muddy and treacherous. Occasionally, a Marine with overloaded pack would slip from the slick mud-cake on top of a dike and slide into the filthy paddy water. Marine Corps tradition dictated that exhibitions of stupidity or spasmodic losses of coordination be rewarded by general ridicule in the ranks. As we rounded a sharp corner in a large paddy, a lone Marine clutched for a marker stake thrust into the trail as one dike path climbed to join another. The Marine's grip slipped off the muddy stake as he tilted to his side, then fell into the paddy. A derisive cheer rose from the men following the hapless trooper, who by that time was floundering under the weight of a haversack loaded down with 60-Mike-Mike mortar rounds in black cardboard tubes. Burns and Lafley turned around and stared at the Marine as he tried to extricate his torso and legs from the firm grip of the paddy's muddy embrace.

Burns grinned at Lafley and spoke in a tone plenty loud enough for all hands to hear. "Lord Almighty! Another new rifle pogue (Marine slang for FNG) breaking himself in for point. Son, you just better pass them mortar rounds to some real Marines to haul until old Private Burns can school your ass a bit! Jesus, Lafley, this FNG's bullshit is enough to make Culbertson look salty!"

I just kept on humping the dikes with my mouth shut; Lafley, Burns, and even Gunny Jones thought I was coming along fine in my training to become a real combat Marine. In the Marine Corps, more than any other branch of the United States armed forces, a new trooper never won his spurs with the veterans until he passed the "Test of Blood." World War II and Korean "salts" never respected us Vietnam-era Marines until we had proved our courage in battle, the test of a true field Marine, a heartbreaker and a life-taker who rises to battle when the lead gets hot. I knew I had proved on Tuscaloosa that I could face enemy small-arms fire and mortars and still keep my shit wired tight. Burns was just reminding the new Marine that he had yet to prove himself to the veterans in the platoon. The rite of passage in becoming one of Uncle Sam's bullet stoppers was an unofficial honor, but all the Marines in 3rd Platoon knew who the real warriors were and who would stand under fire when the shit hit the fan. Some branches of the U.S. armed services seemed to send their men to school forever; the Marines' training school was in combat action against the regular Viet Cong or North Vietnamese infantry units. Marine commanders were certain their troops would learn faster under life and death curricula. As one old salt liked to brag about his Marine Corps training, "They broke my young ass in at the Frozen Chosin. After that I was seventeen going on thirty!"

In the near distance, a group of small hillocks broke the skyline. Lafley and Burns resumed the march toward the hills where we would dig fighting holes into the moist ground in a shallow ellipse and set in for the long night ahead. My pack straps had cut into my shoulders, and I wearily anticipated the pause in our march.

John Lafley and I teamed up and began digging our foxhole about ten meters from Burns and Woodruff. In the field, we dug our holes in closer proximity to our neighbor's position than on the permanent lines at Phu Loc 6 firebase and at An Hoa. In the field, we did not have barbed-wire obstructions to slow the enemy advance or sandbag reinforcements to protect us from enemy fire. In the bush, we were more likely to be probed or hit by the enemy, who always shadowed our patrols. Lafley took one of our few claymore mines from a canvas bag and embedded the four metal spiked legs in the earth in front of a dike ledge twenty meters to our front. He uncoiled the black detonation wires and ran them along the ground into our hole. He put the detonator on the front berm of our hole's shallow parapet. "You can always tell when the Marine Corps is looking after us, Culbertson! We got four claymores in the whole platoon to set out tonight. If we get hit by a company or more, we're in extra-deep shit! The army has so many of these fucking mines the whole gook army couldn't bust into one of their perimeters. The next thing they'll do is take away our M-14s and give us those toy guns. Plastic pieces of shit that shoot .22 bullets."

I agreed with the Cowboy on all counts. "Lafley, we got half of a platoon left that has any real combat experience after Tuscaloosa. Man, we lost Mexico, Cross, Lieutenant Smith, Sergeant Hooley, and Holloway. And Captain Doherty rotated home. I just don't understand how the Corps can take away the best combat leaders and expect Woodruff and Hamilton, and Burns, Jessmore, and Gedzyk to lead the whole company. I'm just glad Gunny Jones is here. That salty old bastard knows everything!"

"Gunny Jones is a cool dude! He don't give two shits about spit and polish. He's a field Marine for sure. I heard the old gunny has five rows of ribbons. He fought with the 5th Marines in Korea. So did Gunny Gutierrez. We are getting a new sergeant from the 5th Marines in Korea named Wadley. Crazy bastard joined up again after fourteen years out. Gunny Jones says Wadley won the Bronze Star on Outpost Vegas in Korea. Wadley and his squad killed thousands of Chinese making human wave assaults for ten straight days. Wadley's a real hard-core Marine."

Lafley and I settled into our hole as the last traces of winter sun sparkled through the tree lines surrounding the iridescent paddies that mirrored the placid evening sky. A few small clouds drifted by, but the night would be clear and cold. We checked the magazines of our M-14 rifles and laid out the extra mags with all our available grenades along the firing ledge of our dugout. Darkness slowly enveloped the landscape as Lafley kept his gaze focused to our front. Gary Woodruff and Burns were to our starboard flank. Woody nodded at Lafley and pointed at the closest thicket of trees as the most likely avenue of approach an enemy would make into our positions. Gedzyk and Jessmore had their M-60 covering the same tree line, and the grunts in the surrounding holes passed their cardboard and canvas boxes of machine gun ammo over to Jessmore.

On the other side of the Marine perimeter, Gunny Jones had continued the ring of holes ten meters or so apart with the machine-gun squad of Phil Fish and his assistant gunner Private First Class Fink. L. Cpl. Eugene Rasmussen, better known as "Russian," and Bert Romans added some salt to the combat experience of the platoon. Bert Romans and Russian had fought with the legendary original Hotel Marines on the DMZ at Con Thien. They remembered Kent Frazelle, Dale Pappas, Charlie Lightfoot, Terry O'Conner, and Keith Wright, combat heroes who had rotated back to the United States after their thirteen-month tours of duty were over. Romans thought that Hotel could really use the guidance of the old veterans from the DMZ, but what the hell, Burns, Lafley, Jessmore, and Culbertson had been hard-core on Tuscaloosa. They would learn the tricks of the trade in time, but just then, it was Bert Romans's job to steady the ship and provide some leadership.

The night passed without incident as the Marines stood two-hour watches, trading shifts at each even hour of the clock. Around midnight, Woodruff heard footfalls along the far paddy dike. He nudged Burns awake and into a firing position along the front of their fighting hole's parapet. I scanned the field to the front and saw that Burns and Woodruff were searching the paddy. As my vision cleared I saw a dozen small forms moving slowly, bent double, fifty meters toward the closest tree line to our front. As the word was passed from bunker to bunker that we had visitors, Marines stirred awake to take up positions facing outward into the rice fields to our front. Somewhere in the far tree lines, the Viet Cong had set up mortar tubes and roughly gauged the yardage to our perimeter, and the Viet Cong squad to our front opened fire at the exact moment their mortar crews dropped the first rounds down the tubes of the hidden mortars. The green tracers from the prone Viet Cong riflemen slapped into the dirt parapets of our bunkers and ricocheted skyward, trailing green phosphorus tails into the night sky. All the Marines on the perimeter were silhouetted by the enemy muzzle flashes at close range. The mortar rounds turned downward from the black expanse of sky over the Marines who were now returning fire. Then the mortar rounds burst in the perimeter as the Viet Cong tilted the mortar tubes slightly forward to walk shells completely through the Marines' lines.

After a dozen mortar shells burst across the Marine perimeter, Lafley yelled out, "Get ready to toss grenades if they rush us." I grabbed a grenade and straightened the safety pin, making it easier to pull and arm. Lafley and I looked at each other and, without any more communication, pulled the grenade pins and prepared to throw. Burns and Woodruff had the same thought. As Lafley and I tossed our grenades as far as we could, we heard the spoons fly and the fuses ignite on two grenades from the bunker next door. The four grenades exploded in the blackness, creating short-lived flashes of blinding light in the direction of the enemy rifle fire. Now the Marine lines erupted in interlocking bursts of rifle fire interspersed with streams of reddish tracers that drew arcing lines across the paddies where the enemy had opened fire. After a couple of minutes, the gunny yelled out, "Cease-fire. Cease-fire!"

The gunny got on the radio to An Hoa and called in a fire mission from the 155-millimeter howitzer battery for an illumination barrage to light up the front of 3rd Platoon's position.

"Hotel Leader. This is Steel Curtain Control. Roger your situation. Steel Curtain relaying status to 2/5 Battalion Actual. Fire Mission. Fire 155-Mike-Mike with illumination over AT 955514. Hotel Leader will adjust. Stand by Hotel Leader. Steel Curtain can deliver 105-Mike-Mike firing for effect with HE rounds. If enemy attack continues, Steel Curtain can fire for effect, "danger close." Hotel Leader must adjust primary fire mission. Steel Curtain, out."

The gunny strained his ears toward An Hoa about seven miles to the southeast. A single howitzer hurled its missile over the rice fields that quilted the landscape all the way to the Thu Bon River and the positions of 3rd Platoon. The huge canister split with a loud *pop* over the heads of us grunts hunkered in our dirt-caked holes. A brilliant filament spiraled down over the perimeter. The burning illumination charge swung to and fro, suspended by its parachute, splattering the paddies and the bunkers of 3rd Platoon in eerie swatches of false light. The illumination reached out into the darkness and sought out the bodies that lay disjointed to Hotel's front.

"Jesus, man, it looks like we got at least half a dozen of those bastards," Gary Woodruff said. "Don't look like any other Cong hung around. I think they beat feet out of there when the machine guns ripped up those paddies."

The gunny spoke up from the center of the perimeter. "Lafley, I want your team on full alert until 0400 hours. We have to guard against attack by a larger force later tonight or in the early morning. Stay alert and on guard. Squad leaders, I want your sitreps and names of any wounded Marines. Carry on!"

The gunny took the handset from Vic Peterson, his radio operator. "Steel Curtain, this is Hotel Leader. Your 155-Mike-Mike illumination round shot was on target. Give me one 155 illumination on positions at AT 955514 every quarter hour. Repeat, one round 155-Mike-Mike illumination every one-five minutes over AT 955514. Full battery 105-Mike-Mike drop one-five-zero meters to AT 955514 and fire for effect—danger close when requested. Hotel Leader, out."

Peterson listened to the radio static as Steel Curtain came back on the net for Gunny Jones. "Hotel Leader. This is Steel Curtain Control. Roger Hotel Leader's 155-Mike-Mike illumination mission every one-five minutes on AT 955514. Hotel Leader can request full battery 105-Mike-Mike, firing for effect, HE fuses, drop one-five-zero meters to AT 955514. Hotel Leader may call 105-Mike-Mike, HE concentration on Button Hotel UMBRELLA, danger close. This is Steel Curtain running illumination mission. Out."

We nestled in our foxholes, but we kept our rifles next to us with a round in the chamber. If Charlie was fool enough to attack again, we were ready. Besides, nobody ever got much sleep after being jolted awake by a mortar attack in the middle of a dark night. The things that scared me the most were things I couldn't see or prepare for in advance. A nighttime mortar attack represented the worst case in both surprise and terror.

CHAPTER SEVEN

Force March
to An Hoa

At first light, the troops were saddled up ready to make a force march back to An Hoa. During the Viet Cong mortar attack, several of us, including Gedzyk and Jessmore, had been slightly wounded by mortar fragments. One shell had fallen so close to Gary Woodruff that his helmet had shrapnel gouges. Fortunately, the majority of the round had plowed into the mud and burst harmlessly. Several Marines had been nicked and cut, missing death by inches. But when the first light of dawn spread over the paddies, there were no dead Leathernecks.

A tight knot of dead enemy soldiers lay in a contorted pile seventy meters to the platoon's front. The Viet Cong wore khaki shirts and trousers with sandals and floppy French-style bush hats. They had carried SKS carbines and packs full of American grenades and several 3.5-inch rocket rounds rigged with trip wires for booby traps. This group had been part of a larger Viet Cong guerrilla sapper force. Their intention was to probe our positions to determine the number and direction of fire of our automatic weapons. Then, in a squad rush, cover part of the distance shielded by their mortar attack. The sapper team would then advance to our perimeter and initiate a grenade and small-arms attack while placing their booby-trapped rocket charges around Marine fighting holes in the hopes we would counterattack as they fell back. Their attack was foiled by the alertness of Lafley, Burns, Woodruff, and myself. Our initial grenade toss had blinded and confused the attacking sappers, and our small-arms fire had cut them down as they milled about helplessly in front of our gun sights.

Lafley and Woodruff had experienced exactly this sort of nighttime attack as Hotel stood midnight watches near Con Thien on the DMZ the previous fall, in 1966. Woodruff faced the weary squad and silently eyed the younger warriors of Hotel Company's 3rd Platoon. Woody began his analysis slowly for the sole benefit of the "new guys." "Fellas, everyone did all right last night. Thanks to the fact that the gooks came straight into our line of fire. Never think Charlie does anything by accident. Charlie wanted you shitheads to sit up high in your bunker or stand up to aim better. That's when the fucking mortar shells come tearing in here. Once the mortar fire lifts, Marines are confused, scared, and most important, you lost your night vision. How you going to hit Charlie as he runs by your hole and drops in a couple of grenades for a keepsake, and all you see are bright flashes and stars where your night vision is supposed to be? Jesus, Lafley and me told you rookies never underestimate your enemy. These Viet Cong may not be big and tough like us, but most of the vicious little bastards have forgotten more combat than you're ever likely to see. If you were on Tuscaloosa, then you know what the hell I'm talking about. Just ask Culbertson how many times they shot holes in his canteen, rifle, and britches. These little VC are gunfighters, and if you let 'em pin you down, they will—by God—kill every one of us!"

Lafley broke into Woodruff's lecture for effect. "You new boys listen good to what Woody says. These here Viet Cong are the same breed of soldier that killed the French at Dien Bien Phu in the 1950s. The French troops they fought wasn't their REMFs, but they was Airborne and Foreign Legion troops. They were hard-core badasses, probably better than us. Shit, any of you men who take these VC sappers for amateurs and laydowns are going to get a ticket home in a fucking body bag. You got that?"

The FNGs in 3rd Platoon just stared silently at Woodruff and Lafley. The Marine statistics on life expectancy in combat told the whole story. If a "newby" (new Marine) could make it past his first month in the field without getting his young ass blown away, his chances of living through the remainder of his tour increased to around 90 percent. Personally, I think his chances of getting hit (wounded in combat action) were about 90 to 100 percent for the rest of his year in country. Captain Doherty of the original Hotel Company had stated after Tuscaloosa that Hotel had taken around 120 percent casualties in combat. In other words, on average, every Marine in Hotel Company had been wounded at least once, and a fifth twice. I had been wounded superficially on Operation Tuscaloosa by gunfire and fragments but did not claim a Purple Heart. This was the case with many Marines on Tuscaloosa, including Hamilton, Sergeant Ybarra, and Woodruff.

The gunny's commanding voice cut through the morning air. "Lafley, get on point, you and Culbertson get this herd headed for An Hoa. We got wounded troopers, but we'll march home like men. We never had any of them fucking helicopters at the Chosin Reservoir. By God, it was cold enough to freeze metal where it would snap in two. You boots don't know about that, do you? Move 'em out, Cowboy!"

The platoon of thirty Marines filed across the dikes into the foothills surrounding the river. Even footing was gained as Lafley guided Hotel onto the river trails that sped our return to An Hoa. The regularly traveled trails did not, however, guarantee safe travel. Lafley and I, as the point scouts, stopped the column periodically as we crossed terrain that looked suspicious or likely to harbor hidden mines or booby traps. The morning passed quickly and without incident. John Lafley and I had picked up the pace of the march, and probably were too focused on reaching An Hoa instead of watching the trail itself. Even so, stepping onto a patch of sandy soil that ran for about twenty meters along the trail, I stopped to observe the flat-lying fields on our flank running for miles into the Arizona. Turning back to the front, I resumed my normal stride. A knifelike agony thrust deeply into my shin, sending fiery jolts of pain up my lower leg into my knee. As I crumpled to the ground with a scream of pain and fear, I shocked Lafley, to my front, who spun around to see what was wrong. Woodruff and Burns had raced to where I was writhing in the sandy patch atop a shallow rise in the trail.

Woodruff and Lafley, Burns, and some others turned me upright where I lay on my side. Lafley yelled down the column for the gunny. "Corpsman up, Culbertson's hit a punji trap! The stake's all the way through his shin, Gunny. Burns, you and Woody grab him under the arms and we'll pull him off this sucker. Okay, pull steady now!" The eighteen-inch-long shaft of two-inch-thick bamboo had been cut to form a spear, the white bamboo inside the shaft blending perfectly with the sandy ground. The bamboo slid out of the ragged, bloody hole and returned to its slanted position in the ground surrounded by hundreds of similar stakes.

"Jesus, Gunny, look at this sandy ground! We're all standing in this patch of punji stakes. Don't nobody move! All hands step to their flank, off this trail. Step gingerlike now. These sons of bitches will kill you with all the piss and shit the gooks rub on these stakes." Of course, I felt real good when he said that.

The gunny had taken the radio handset from Tom Jiminez and had called in a medevac chopper from An Hoa. The gunny gazed across the fields that ran off our platoon's flanks to the paddies that lay in the rice valley below us. "Lafley, you and Woodruff get a gun up here on this high ground and spread the rest of the riflemen out in a firing line down the trail. This little knoll is the perfect spot for Charlie to ambush us. We got a medevac H-34 en route from An Hoa. Get the corpsman to tag Culbertson. Doc, you got that leg wound closed off? That punji stake poison can kill a man if we don't get it treated."

Burns yelled out from his position down the column. "Gunny, the chopper is coming into the sun. Permission to throw a smoke grenade?"

The gunny got on the radio frequency directly to the chopper to identify his position and tell the chopper pilot to identify his smoke. "Okay, Burns, one of you throw a red smoke in that flat area off the trail to the east." The gunny then told the chopper to set down near his red smoke.

The big H-34 flared into the hasty LZ below the Marines of 3rd Platoon. Lafley, Burns, Woodruff, and Jessmore carried me into the medevac's cargo bay. The chopper door gunner helped me seat myself against the aluminum bulkhead in the rear of the bay. Then the chopper's engine throttled up, and the pilot leaned the aircraft forward as we skimmed the paddies to our east and gained speed for the short hop to BAS (battalion aid station) in 2/5's combat home at An Hoa. I lay in the rear of the chopper, wincing in pain as the bandages the medic had wrapped around my leg soaked up my blood. It seemed an eternity until the chopper flared out and settled onto the PSP (perforated steel plates) of An Hoa's runway.

The chopper was met by a corpsman and orderlies who held my arms as I hopped off, throbbing in pain. We finally entered the BAS, and a corpsman cut off the filthy, bloody bandages that had been applied in the field. The deep puncture wound was swabbed out with hydrogen peroxide and left open to drain. My temperature was taken every two hours, and the corpsman gave me a shot of penicillin, and God knows what else, every four hours. After a fitful night's sleep, I awoke to blurred vision, covered in sweat-stained, powder-blue navy pj's. My temperature had reached 104 degrees, and I was on fire! I remembered the words of my favorite drill instructor, Sgt. John Faircloth, during boot camp at MCRD (Marine Corps Recruit Depot) San Diego to the effect that if any of us had any brains whatever, we would have no doubt joined the navy, because Marine boot camp under Sergeant Faircloth would prove to be so sadistic and brutal that no recruit with any sense would want to experience it. That gave me a short chuckle. Even if my temperature hit 105 degrees, it wouldn't affect my mind, because I was a fucking Marine!

CHAPTER EIGHT

The Battalion
Aid Station

I remained a patient at the BAS at An Hoa for four days
and nights. The navy physician looked in on me regularly.
My temperature hovered about 104 degrees for two days,
then broke in a cauldron of rapid sweat that drenched my
bedclothes. I was allowed to remain the fourth day to re-
claim my strength, then dismissed from the battalion hospital as a member of the "walking wounded," meaning
that I had five days light duty with no field exposure. The
navy doctor stopped in to see me as I finished getting back
into my jungle utilities and worn jungle boots. My 782
gear was slung over my shoulder, and I held my helmet in
one hand. My trusty M-14 rifle rode high on my right
shoulder at sling arms.

"Well, Private First Class Culbertson, I'm pleased you
healed so quickly. Many Marines are ill enough from
punji stake wounds to require several weeks' recuperation. I admit that I'm not overjoyed to see you returned to
duty. Your medical records indicate this is your second
wound requiring over forty-eight hours hospitalization.
You should be transferred to a support unit or finish your
overseas tour out of Vietnam. I have notified your commanding officer about your status and the navy regula-

tions regarding twice-wounded Marines that are hospitalized. Unfortunately, your company officers can countermand my recommendations. I am very dejected over the numbers of young Marine casualties that your regiment has accumulated in this senseless war. Evidently, there are powers that want the Vietnam War to continue forever."

A commotion behind the doctor drew our attention to a pair of ARVN soldiers who sauntered in with a balled-up Vietnamese in a fishing net suspended from a bamboo pole resting across their shoulders. The two ARVN exchanged a guttural Vietnamese command and acknowledgment, and unceremoniously dumped the Vietnamese man onto the ground at the surprised physician's feet. I looked the Vietnamese over. He was young and appeared in good physical shape, but he moaned and flopped onto his other side, exposing his left arm. A great wound had channeled through the flesh where his left shoulder should have been, and his left arm dangled by sinewy threads of muscle and tendon in his armpit. He writhed in pain and stared helplessly toward the doctor through tear-clouded eyes.

The physician called for an orderly, who immediately appeared at the flap entrance to the medical tent. "Corpsman, bring me two bottles of hydrogen peroxide, some gauze, and a large pair of scissors." One of the ARVN soldiers who delivered the Vietnamese in the net spoke quietly to the doctor. The physician nodded and stared unkindly at the groaning man with the gaping shoulder wound. "Our ARVN friends say this Viet Cong guerrilla was hit by a bullet from one of their M-1 rifles as he ran away from their patrol. He was planting a mine in the trail when these soldiers surprised him." The doctor turned as the corpsman delivered the supplies requested. "Private, let me show you how I treat these Communist soldiers who have killed and wounded so many of my Marine patients. Watch closely!"

The doctor bent over the Vietnamese, who still twisted in the dirt. Grasping the Viet Cong's wounded shoulder, he began deftly snipping away at the little tissue holding his arm in place. After half a dozen snips, the doctor ripped the remaining flesh from the shoulder of the VC, and holding the severed limb aloft, exclaimed, "This son of a bitch won't ever hurt one of my boys again!" The doctor then hurled the bloody limb down the dirt road leading to the ARVN compound. I could almost feel the wave of hatred course through the physician. As sweat poured down my face over my neck, I glanced toward the ARVN compound. The severed arm was already bouncing down the dusty trail as a wild pack of dogs converged on it, chewing tendrils of human flesh and crushing the bones in slavering jaws.

The doctor ignored the frenzied yelping of the dog pack, unscrewed the cap from the bottle of hydrogen peroxide, and poured the contents over the VC's wounded shoulder. The peroxide raised a cascade of frothy blood, and the now alert Vietnamese screamed for mercy. I turned my back on the brutal scene and threaded my way back to the hootches on Hotel Company's main street.

CHAPTER NINE

Home Again at
An Hoa Combat Base

I had returned to 3rd Platoon's hootches north of the airstrip. After four days in the BAS hospital, I missed greeting the returning Marines of 3rd Platoon. They had stumbled in a mud-splashed disarray through the barbed-wire defenses along the runway and crossed the line of bunkers into the company billeting area. As I picked a bunk in my old hut and hung my rifle on the nails in the rafter, I realized that about a third of the bunks were empty. These were the losses from Operation Tuscaloosa that had not been replaced. It was early March 1967, and Hotel was running seven- and eight-man rifle squads with platoon strength around thirty. The company troop levels, including weapons platoon, numbered around 140 Marines. Casualties during Operation Tuscaloosa had reduced company combat personnel by around fifty Marines, plus another ten who had rotated home after their thirteen-month tours came to an end.

After stowing all my gear under my bunk, I grabbed my M-14 and headed to the chow hall. As I joined the chow line, I found the faces of some Hotel Marines, but it appeared 3rd Platoon had either gone back to the field or was standing lines at the airstrip in my absence. After finishing my hot meal, I strolled back to my hootch and lit a Camel. It was nice to sit quietly and watch the smoke drift lazily into the cool breeze. The hot season would arrive in another month, and I knew the battalion would increase the activity level of patrols and combat operations into the Arizona. Tired after my fever, I entered my hootch and lay down on my cot awaiting the return of my buddies. The rays of the afternoon sun broke into thousands of fiery lances as they filtered through the mesh screen along the sides of our hut. The warmth of the golden beams spread across my body, and I quickly dropped off into a deep sleep.

I was startled out of my dreams by loud voices and the thumps of boot heels on the wooden deck of the hootch. I opened my eyes to greet the rest of my squad returning from guard duty along the lines running down the landing strip. Momentarily, I was alert and asked Lafley what had gone on since I was medevacked from the field.

"Well, man, we been standing lines during the day for three days. We heard you were sick as hell. Woodruff and me went down to the ARVN camp yesterday to get haircuts. Foxtrot ran a night ambush up the trail to Liberty Bridge two nights ago. They opened fire on some Viet Cong digging holes for mines in the roadbed. Guess what they got when they inspected the dead gooks? You guessed it! The fucking camp barber was lying there dead as a mackerel. Barber and friend to the Leathernecks by day, but Viet Cong sapper and booby-trapper deluxe by night. I told you, Culbertson, you just can't trust none of these slippery fuckers. Just kill 'em all, let God sort their sorry asses out!"

"Hey, Culbertson, did you hear Gunny Jones ain't platoon leader no more? Gunny Jones is taking over weapons platoon. Gunny Gutierrez is going home, and we're gettin' a brand new lieutenant! Name's Pindel, and he used to be a corporal. Hell, he might work out all right. At least the man will know that spit-and-polish bullshit ain't no use around here." Burns smiled and held his M-14 out in front of him in the "on guard" position for bayonet drill. "This here steel is what old Charlie understands! Ain't that so, Culbertson?"

I just smiled and nodded my head at Burns and at the rest of my squad's faces framed in the halo of light from the hootch's single, naked lightbulb. When Burns and the others started discussing combat and the devious and brutal ways they would employ to kill Charlie, it was a foregone conclusion that any sober opinion would be shouted down as cowardly or sissified. Looking at the wild faces of the young Marines, it was obvious how callous and bloodthirsty we had all become. The average age of Hotel's troopers wasn't much over twenty, but the collective combat experiences and amount of death and destruction witnessed by each man was overwhelming.

Tom Jiminez entered the hootch and announced that the new lieutenant wanted all the squad leaders and platoon sergeants up to his hut for a mission-planning session and the dissemination of the "five part order"; the lieutenant would explain in detail the forthcoming operation and "who, what, where, when, and why" the 3rd Platoon would be taking the field to accomplish a specific mission. Jiminez said the platoon was to hump to the Song Thu Bon and cross by amphibious tractor. There we would consolidate with a weapons platoon and cross the Arizona Territory into the dreaded Antenna Valley northwest of Nong

Son firebase. Jiminez said it would be Lieutenant Pindel's first operation, but that he had enlisted infantry experience and knew what he was doing. We all said a short prayer that that was so! An overaggressive young platoon commander could easily compromise the troops if he didn't pay attention. After all, the Viet Cong regulars and NVA advisers had decades of combat experience, and the Arizona and Antenna Valley were their backyard.

I hoped my leg would heal in time. Jiminez said we weren't going out right away because we were picking up some new recruits. I closed my eyes and drifted off to visions of the Arizona Territory and the horrors that awaited our next operation.

CHAPTER TEN

Patrol to My Loc 2—
The Well

It had rained steadily during my recuperation at An Hoa. Hotel's 3rd Platoon had enjoyed slack duty standing lines and resting from the month we had spent in the field under the command of Gunny Jones. All the troops had heard about the new lieutenant who was to be our new platoon commander. Before Lieutenant Pindel arrived, however, the platoon would make a short, two-day patrol through the hamlets along the river off Phu Loc 6. I would try out my injured leg and find out if I could stay up with the squad as we ran the paddy dikes looking for signs of Charlie.

First Squad saddled up, and Luther Hamilton had us carry extra hand grenades, and two Marines from a 3.5-inch rocket launcher team joined us on the company street. Weapons, ammunition, and the condition of the individual rifleman's gear was checked out by the platoon sergeant and squad leaders. Two C-ration meals were handed out to each man, with the understanding that we would be resupplied in the field. An engineer team joined the platoon, and the word was passed that we would be checking several local villages for contraband weapons caches and rice supplies hidden to provision the Viet Cong.

Third Platoon numbered thirty-eight Marines with the addition of the rocket team and the engineers. We filed down the red, mud-caked path along the airstrip, past the bunkered Marines on lines. Lafley and Woodruff were on point as 3rd Platoon filed through the barbed wire marking An Hoa's outer perimeter, then strode purposefully onto the trail leading north up Highway One into the Arizona.

The road was still muddy, so our jungle boots slid and slipped up the short inclines toward Phu Loc 6. Corporal Kirby was the squad leader in 1st Squad, which had taken the point of the platoon's split column as it trod along both edges of the road, and Kirby ordered Gary Woodruff into the point scout's slot at the head of the file. Woodruff marched ahead with his M-14 in a jungle sling, cradling the rifle at waist level, from where a burst of fire could be immediately delivered if the enemy was sighted. Woodruff was short, but powerfully built and would not hesitate to engage if we encountered any trouble ahead.

After another hour's march, Phu Loc 6 came into view up a shallow incline a quarter mile ahead. The sandbag defenses were clearly visible, clustered in a thicket of drenched bush and grass. Kirby yelled at Woody to lead the column off on our port flank where the river trails branched off to the Song Thu Bon. Another klick of humping brought the tired and thirsty column within sight of My Loc 2. The two 105-millimeter howitzers used for support in Foxtrot's flanking assault on Operation Tuscaloosa had been positioned on the low-lying, flat knob of My Loc 2. My Loc was well known to the Marines and Charlie as the most prominent terrain feature facing this heavily traveled artery of the Thu Bon River. The Thu Bon River was the only navigable river in the Arizona that flowed from near the Ho Chi Minh trail in Laos unimpeded to the South China Sea, so it served the Viet Cong as a main link in their supply line, bringing weapons, ammunition, medical supplies, and new recruits to replacc their dead and wounded as they terrorized South Vietnam.

As Woodruff rounded a shallow bend where the trail descended toward the river, a stone well came into view five hundred meters up the trail, where a village path led through a thicket of bamboo into a small knot of huts. Corporal Kirby passed Woodruff as he strode toward the well. Three other Marines collected canteens from their buddies and followed Kirby and Woodruff. Anxious to slake their thirst after four hours' slow march along muddy roads, the Marines did not scan the surrounding village and its protective tree lines with much concern. The rest of the platoon fell out on either side of the trail in a loose perimeter and lit the smoking lamp.

As Woodruff approached the well, he glimpsed the fleeting form of a Vietnamese woman supporting a water vessel on her head. She turned away from the well and scurried toward the first group of huts another eighty feet up the path. The young woman turned and looked at the platoon of Marines bullshitting along the trail, then stepped quickly from the path and disappeared into the clutch of tall bamboo sheltering the hootches. Woody took note of the woman's stare and felt a twinge of uneasiness creep along his neck. However, the promise of fresh well water to tired and thirsty Marines was nearly overpowering.

Woody dropped to a knee and began sinking the plastic canteens into the clear water. So immersed were he and Corporal Kirby in their resupply mission that neither Marine noticed when four Viet Cong slithered out of the bamboo stand at the village's edge. The VC aimed their rifles at the water boys leaning into the well.

The soft stone around the well disintegrated, as the Viet Cong fired their first volley toward Kirby and Woodruff. The three Marines who had accompanied Kirby had carried armfuls of canteen bottles and had left their rifles with their squad back along the trail.

These three unlucky Joes huddled in fright behind the well structure between Kirby and Woodruff. They had fumbled their armloads of canteens when the next shots sang through the air over their heads. Canteens lay everywhere, scattered like marbles, as all hands squatted low to avoid the next flight of Viet Cong bullets. Dropping his canteens into the well, Woodruff executed a belly-flopping dive behind the stone parapet. VC rifle shots whined and sang as ricochets tore flakes off the stone wall of the community well. As shards of stone and lead cascaded around his helmet, Woodruff yelled, "Kirby, where are the gooks firing from? Man, I got my head down and can't see shit!"

Tim Kirby was a true mountain man from Tennessee and was as tough as the iron skillet his ma used to fry his breakfast. Kirby had hunted the hills and "hollers" near Knoxville, Tennessee, since early childhood, and he never humped a hill that got the best of him. However, unknown to Gary Woodruff, Kirby now found himself in a world of shit. One of the Viet Cong bullets had clipped his right arm. Corporal Kirby then fell back from the well, behind a small ledge of earth. The problem with Kirby's evasive action was that in his haste to get behind some solid cover, he had left his rifle leaning against the well. Kirby wanted that rifle, but the Viet Cong riflemen were having none of it! They were firing their weapons point-blank into the stone structure that harbored five Marines who had not even gotten a first glimpse of their enemy.

The rest of the platoon was far to the rear and directly in the line of fire, so any return fire from the platoon would endanger Kirby, Woodruff, and the three stooges who lay behind the well pissing in their utility trousers. At that moment, for God only knows what reason, Gary Woodruff snapped the safety off his M-14, twisted the selector switch to full automatic, rose to his knees with a rebel yell, and began firing low bursts into the bamboo thicket from which the Viet Cong's first gunfire had emanated. Emptying the first magazine, Woodruff fished a second full mag from his cartridge belt and snapped the twenty rounds of 7.62-millimeter ball ammunition into his rifle. Rising to his feet, Woody hugged the blazing, full auto M-14 to his hip and fired low, grazing bursts into the VC positions. Finally, some Marines from the platoon back down the trail reached the well and fired over Woodruff's head into the tree line as Woody hugged the earth, his left arm tucked protectively over his head. No further shots came from the silenced Viet Cong position. The Leathernecks stared at each other and smiled, sharing that uncomfortable mood in which you are at once uneasy yet damn glad to be alive.

Getting to their feet, the troops looked around, trying to put the reason for their trouble back into perspective. The need for water had all but been forgotten, when several *thumping* sounds reached the ears of the Marines gathered loosely around the well retrieving their scattered canteens. The first VC rifle grenade was lobbed into a pool of mud at the foot of the cluster of men. The explosion was muffled and chunks of slick clay spun into the air and fell, covering the Marines, who had instinctively gone to ground. Then three more grenades slapped into the general area where everyone huddled, saturating the men with muddy clods, grass, and plants. The Viet Cong were long gone, as the water detachment rose to its feet in utter dishevelment.

Woodruff looked petrified! He had lain low under the rifle fire of his own troops. Then, when it had seemed safe to get up, the rifle grenades had poured onto the Marines. Burns got his massive body out of a ditch full of mud and God knows what else. Looking at Lafley and me, as we dusted our uniforms back into a semblance of order, Burns smiled. "You know, Lafley, the hospitality is so fucking bad in Nam, the locals won't even let you have a drink of their sorry-ass water!" That broke the rest of us up. After getting shot at every time we went out on patrol, death had become our companion, and our humor had become a little morbid. The smile on Burns's face also meant that Charlie would pay for chickenshit ambushes like this. If Burns, Lafley, and Woodruff had their way, Charlie would pay in full. And soon.

After finally getting to replenish our water supplies, we formed up in column and began our circuit of villages bordering along the meanders of the Song Thu Bon.

CHAPTER ELEVEN

Searching for Weapons and Rice

Our column struck out through the tree line where the Viet Cong had opened fire on Woodruff and Kirby. I took the point with Lafley at my shoulder and cut across the shallow ditch into the bamboo thickets ringing the village. As I trod carefully on top of the berms, I was especially watchful for trip wires or freshly dug holes that could contain booby traps or mines. A careful inspection of the ambush area turned up scattered brass in 7.62-millimeter-short Russian caliber. At eighty feet, the SKS bullet will tear into a Marine's body just like our 7.62-millimeter NATO bullet. We all had an abiding respect for the enemy's SKS rifle and AK-47 assault rifle. Up close and personal, the Communist rifles were an even match for ours. But the marksmanship of some VC was not up to Marine standards. Thank God!

I peered into the grasses that lay on top of the ditch partially concealing the Viet Cong position. Fresh bloodstains spotted the green blades, and along one patch of mud was a dark cloth that had recently sopped up a large quantity of blood. Lafley said, "Kirby, take a look at this rag here! The son of a bitch is covered with fresh blood. Looks like a chest hit to me, man! This gook is probably a goner already. Good shooting, Woody! That was some genuine John Wayne bullshit back there at the well. I just wish Mexico was here to see this shit!"

Kirby knelt down by the VC blood trails, then said, "Woodruff, man, take a look at my arm. I don't think it's deep, but it burns like crazy." Kirby had rolled up his utility jacket, exposing the bullet wound just under his shoulder along the side of his biceps. The bullet had burned rather than cut Corporal Kirby's arm, barely penetrating the flesh. Woodruff looked the wound over carefully and put his first-aid dressing back in his belt pouch. "Jeez Louise, Kirby, the wound ain't even bleeding. Man, it looks like somebody branded you instead of shot your ass! Are you sure you want a Purple Heart for that, man?"

Pausing briefly to examine the bullet wound in mock horror, other members of the squad filtered by Kirby. Lafley and Burns looked at each other and started laughing. "Hey, Burns, that wound looks like the hit Mexico took in the ass back on Phu Loc 6!" Burns always tried to top Lafley when they teamed up to give someone shit over anything amusing. "Yeah, Lafley, that is a badass bullet hole. Remember when I caught the clap in Dogpatch last year? Hell, I pissed more blood than Kirby lost, and I didn't get no Purple Heart for it. It was the fucking they gave me for the fucking that I got!"

Everyone laughed aloud at that remark, no disrespect to Corporal Kirby intended. Kirby was one of the toughest Marines in Hotel Company. It was just that nothing was sacred when it came time to dish out a little shit. Every Marine took his share of harassment, like it or not. The fact was, Vietnam was a debilitating war for everyone, and the men who fought in that war became emotionally detached, or the war tore apart their souls. Some people just got sloppy and soft and let the war kill them. As for myself, I was growing very thick skin, and I had a reckless and ruthless look. Nothing would stand in my way when living became critical. I didn't come to Vietnam to die; like all good Marines, I came to kill!

Corporal Kirby radioed to battalion command center at An Hoa that Hotel's 3rd Platoon had engaged enemy soldiers near My Loc 2. One Marine was wounded by gunshot—noncritical—and several large blood trails were found in the enemy bunker. Battalion came back on the net, ordering 3rd Platoon to continue a search-and-clear of the throng of small hamlets bordering the river. Supplies or foodstuffs discovered should be reported to 2/5 command immediately.

"Lafley and Woodruff, get the column back on the river trail. We've lost almost two hours screwing around at this water hole. Make time for the first group of hamlets. We'll split the platoon into squad-size search teams when we reach the first villages." Kirby wanted to make up some lost time on our approach march. He knew we would need all day to conduct a thorough examination of each village's huts, bunkers, and the surrounding small fields and gardens.

Lafley and Woodruff picked up the march cadence and, stepping lightly over tree roots and small ditches and holes, wove their way ever closer to the sleepy villages along the river's bends. After half an hour of uninterrupted humping, the wispy smoke from a cooking fire was spotted twisting through the tall trees along the bank. Lafley and Woodruff took separate paths, approaching the village from the riverside and from the tree line in the rear of the huts. This enveloping movement would prevent peasants from escaping the cordon of Marines that was about to descend on their village.

As I strode onto the main street, I was greeted by a flock of chickens that rose with frantically flapping wings, darting and squawking, as though the tall Americans were the incarnation of terror. The few peasants who ran after their prized livestock looked at us in fear. I knew that entering strangers' homes and callously handling their property was not going to be a pleasant experience. However, in the Marines, even more than in every other army, orders were orders, and we had been told specifically to search every nook and cranny in the vicinity.

Teams of three and four Marines entered each hut and removed the large pieces of furniture, mostly small tables, chairs, trunks, and an occasional chest of drawers. Pots and pans and agricultural implements were stacked in the corners of the interior rooms. Once the floor areas were cleared, Marines dropped to their knees to probe the earthen floors for hiding holes or false surfaces that could be slid back to reveal dugouts or tunnels. Each Vietnamese hootch was unique and had to be diligently gone over by the teams as they probed for weapons and rice. Finally, one of Woodruff's group found a small tunnel behind a log that led back into a shallow mound of earth. Jessmore was at the entrance, gauging the size of the cavity, before Kirby got the word that a bunker had been discovered.

"Jessmore, be careful, man. There may be booby traps or punji stakes in there. Something about these people just ain't right. I think Charlie's been through here, and not long ago. What do you think, Burns?" Kirby was careful, and his attitude reflected the fact that he had under sixty days to serve with 2/5. Even Marines became cautious and reluctant to take the normal risks our missions required when they became short-timers in Vietnam.

Burns ran his eyes along the row of thatch-and-wood huts that constituted the village proper. He rested his M-14's buttstock against his jungle boot. "I say Charlie has been in this shithole in the last forty-eight hours. These people panicked when we walked in here. There's rice and ammo buried here, and I'll bet my fuckin' life on that. Hell, Kirby, let's burn this dump and get on down the road!"

Kirby considered Burns's opinion. He was probably right about contraband being hidden somewhere in the village. But where? Kirby decided to let Jessmore dredge up some evidence before any irrevocable actions were initiated. "Jessmore, get in that hole and be careful. Man, all we want to find is evidence. Then we can blow this whole son of a bitch to smithereens. Okay, go, man! Lafley can back you up if you get stuck."

Jessmore, who was probably the most experienced tunnel rat in the 5th Marine Regiment, slipped off his utility jacket and took a crooked neck flashlight from his pack. He held a cocked and locked .45 pistol in his right hand. Several Marines had taken out entrenching tools and widened the entrance to the tunnel. Jessmore stuck his head into the dark cavity then pushed his body inside. The soil in the tunnel mouth was moist and pungent from the end of the spring rainy season. Large chunks of mud gave way as Jessmore churned his legs—thrusting his mud-spattered torso deeper into the ground.

Something pricked his arm as Jessmore turned back toward the dim light at the tunnel entrance. He twisted and shined his flashlight along the corridor's wall. The bones of a decayed body were touching his flesh, and he recoiled in horror from the twisted skeleton. Jessmore had all the courage anyone ever expected a Marine to exhibit in combat, but that situation was different. Jessmore let out a scream that would have made his DI shit his pants. Scuttling like a sand crab, sideways out the tunnel, Jessmore reappeared, covered in mud, but his face was ash white. When he caught his breath, he faced the crowd of Marines and told his tale.

"Jeez, man, an old gook is dead up in there. Hardly nothing left but bones and tatters of his clothing. When I turned to look back out the hole, the dead man's fingers grabbed me. Man, I'm not shitting you, it was scary down there! I didn't see no weapons or equipment. I'll bet that dude was wounded bad and crawled in there to escape a patrol or something. He probably died inside, and no one ever knew he was in there."

From the rear of the squad, Burns said, "Well, tunnel rat, we'll never know what the hell happened to old Luke the Gook unless you get your bellyaching ass back down there and ask him." Burns chuckled as everyone waited for Jessmore's response.

"I ain't going down in that hole, Burns, 'cause I've already been, and there ain't nothin' there but that dead gook. Maybe you can fit your wide ass into that tunnel and check the situation out your damn self!" Everyone was looking at Burns and laughing as the freckles on Burns's face blended into the red mask that colored his anger.

Kirby stepped into the middle of the melee. "Nobody's going down any tunnel. The engineers are going to blow it as it lies. Let's get these other hootches checked. We got beaucoup work left to do today."

After forty minutes of probing and digging, nothing of any note had been found. The Marines of 3rd Platoon saddled up to move into the next village, less than a quarter mile down the trail. Lafley and I took the point and marched ahead, looking into the jungle for signs of ambush. Finally, we entered the curving path of a small, nameless hamlet that looked little different from the one we just passed through. We broke the platoon into search teams and rifled through the peasants' belongings as though they had no rights of their own. I was starting to let down my guard and feel sorry for the local villagers and their heartrending misery, when a shout went up from the rear of one of the huts. PFC Conard Brown from North Carolina had dug under a trough of cut stone honed out to hold chicken feed. Under the heavy stone base, there was a wooden trapdoor that opened into a large bin holding sacks of rice stacked one on top of another.

"We got us some rice over here. Somebody get Kirby! Man, I think this rice bin goes all the way under the hootch." Brown was excited. It was always a rush to discover that Charlie was up to his old tricks, especially when everyone had sweated all day and had come up empty-handed. Corporal Kirby and Luther Hamilton gathered on top of the wooden hatch that opened into the larger dugout below. A discussion was undertaken as to the best way to dispose of the rice. Kirby radioed battalion and was ordered to blow the bunker in place. After holes were dug into the top of the rice bin, engineers went about setting the charges. We estimated that there was approximately one thousand cubic meters of rice in the hole. The bin itself was lined with wooden slats. Even so, no doubt rain had seeped into the cache of rice, and we all assumed rats or snakes were curled into the jumble of sacks.

The engineers placed shaped charges into the rear of the cache. Once detonated, the charge would tear through rice, wood, and earth, and scatter the contraband into the river that ran in front of the hootches, not twenty meters distant. C-4 was placed in deep holes in front of the hootches to destroy the riverbank while the simultaneous blast from the shaped charges blew the rice out the cavity into the river. The charges were wired into the detonation control boxes, and the engineers herded the Marines back up the steep riverbank a hundred meters from the river. All hands in 3rd Platoon hunkered down in ditches and holes in the tree line facing the village. Corporal Kirby and Luther Hamilton took a head count of their men and got down in defilade positions. The engineers had run electric detonation wires into the tree line and had set up two control boxes to initiate the blast in the rice bin with the C-4 ignition in front of the huts. The head engineer sergeant yelled "Fire in the hole," and the two plungers were depressed, sending current simultaneously to the two locations of buried explosives.

The ground heaved, and the explosion filled the air with smoke, chunks of earth, and shards of fractured wood. The explosion was so pronounced that the primary blast of C-4 was at first cloaked by the spiraling cloud of dust and smoke over the rice cache. The shock wave slammed into the prone Marines and jolted them off the deck. Leaves and small branches cascaded down over the platoon from the tree line to their rear. The hut itself was gone as the smoke and pieces of burning thatch dispersed over the village common. Shortly, the Marines were able to see into the village and assess the devastation done to the trail where it ran along the riverbank in front of the destroyed huts.

The jaws of most of 3rd Platoon were agape, as we saw that the entire bank was blown away, replaced by a cavity the size of a pair of locomotives. The rice bin itself had thrown up its contents into the river. The riverbank looked as if a gigantic steam shovel had gouged the earth, cutting a box-shaped trench forty feet wide and eighty feet long to a depth over ten feet. The river was covered with flakes of rice. Rice and pieces of sacking covered the village itself, and a stunned group of peasants hopelessly looked about as they reentered their homes.

It wasn't the mindset of the average Marine to punish the peasants. We knew they were forced to smuggle rice and weapons for the Viet Cong. We also knew that their villages were used to hide rice stores for the Communists, yet the villagers themselves had no say in that activity. That is, they had no say if they wanted to live. No matter how hard the Marines could be on the local population, the Viet Cong were a hell of a lot harder. The poor bastards! The people of South Vietnam really had nowhere to turn and no one to turn to. I felt sorry for the simple folk of that village, who stood crying in the smoke-laced street of their destroyed home. Their only crime was that they owned the rice that the Viet Cong needed to fuel their war machine.

Corporal Kirby had radioed battalion headquarters and reported the engineers' destruction of the rice cache. The engineers would provide a more technical briefing on the demolition upon their return to An Hoa. We were ordered back on the trail and to continue our search of the hamlets along the Song Thu Bon until nightfall.

Lafley and I led the troops through the burned-out village and along a narrow jungle trail that climbed halfway into the tree line overlooking the river. It was around 1500 hours, and the pace was fast. In Vietnam, some missions were clean, and the results were understandable, but there was always the dirty job you were ordered to do that left everyone heartsick. Everyone except Burns, who lit a cigarette as we patrolled the shadow-blanketed trail. Burns hoped we would run into another Viet Cong patrol or ambush. He relished the thought of getting another dink in his rifle sights and making an easy kill.

Corporal Kirby stopped the column and gazed at the next group of thatch hootches that had come into sight ahead. "Everybody take ten minutes and get some chow in ya. The next village is in sight, and there is to be no smokin'. Burns, that means you, too! Put that fucking butt out and fieldstrip it. Those pint-size assholes can smell cigarette smoke a quarter mile away!" Burns took a last pull on his fag and, knocking the fire off with his thumb, crumbled up the rest of the paper and tobacco into a wad.

"Lafley, you and Woodruff take Culbertson here down to the village. Go in the back side and make sure the villagers are home. If that place is empty, the VC may be waiting for us up ahead. Teach Culbertson how to snoop and poop in that built-up area. Burns, take Jiminez and Jessmore on top of the village. Sit in the tree line and give Lafley covering fire if the shit hits the fan. Everybody get their gear. Let's move out." Kirby had entered plenty of villages up on the DMZ with Hamilton, Lafley, and Woodruff. He knew how to cover his ass if Charlie was waiting in ambush. Burns wouldn't let Viet Cong open fire on Lafley's team when he held the high ground and could observe the village and everything in it.

Lafley and Woody led me down the steep bank from our sheltered position in the tree line to the back of the village. Nothing stirred in the hamlet or on the street. A few chickens ruffled their feathers and flew out of our way, but the huts themselves appeared empty. John Lafley was first to enter the main street. He knelt down and peered ahead into the late afternoon mist that rose off the river. No villagers presented themselves, nor did any activity signal its existence. Woodruff and I knelt down at Lafley's side and raised our weapons across our chests, ready to fire. Lafley looked back toward Kirby and shook his head. Nothing!

Kirby could see Burns and his team had taken a commanding position with good visibility and fields of fire into the village. The remainder of the platoon rose and, spreading out into a skirmish line, moved rapidly down the slope into the village. Lafley had risen, and our group moved through the village, scouting the farther reaches of the dwellings. Quickly, Marines were strung out along the main street and moving through the hootches completely devoid of life.

As we cleared the village, Burns came down from his hillside lookout and joined the column. Just as we passed the last group of huts, several guerrillas pushed the cover off camouflaged spider holes, and a loud explosion detonated at the front of our column. As the Viet Cong opened fire with SKS carbines and Moishin Nagant rifles, the hidden Chicom mine ripped into the group of engineers, knocking three men to their knees. The rifle shots cut through the Marine column and gouged out chunks of mud in the trail as the shocked platoon dived for cover. Blocker was hit in the side, but the bullet sliced through his flak jacket and only grazed his ribs. Gedzyk felt a round graze the side of his helmet, tearing a jagged hole in the camo cover but failing to penetrate the steel shell. He was knocked down and momentarily stunned, as he tried to locate the source of the enemy fire. The engineers were not dead, but one had bad shrapnel wounds in his leg that were pumping arterial blood. He required a tourniquet, but the others had less serious wounds to their arms and faces. The corpsman covered the worst wounds with battle dressings to stop the bleeding, then checked and drew the tourniquet stick tighter on the serious bleeder.

Burns wheeled about and dropped prone, looking for the muzzle flashes that had sent the first volley of bullets into the platoon after the charge exploded at the head of the formation. He saw something move along the ground forty meters behind the platoon and he stared hard, trying to make out a form. The shape grew larger until Gerald Burns was certain that a Charlie was sticking his head out of a spider hole looking for another target. Burns threw his M-14 into his shoulder and clicked off the safety. He held his breath and took aim in the center of the shadowy mass emerging slowly from the ground. *Blam! Blam!* The grass-covered lid blew off the hole as the Viet Cong reared up inside the spider trap. Burns leveled his rifle and squeezed off another pair of shots.

The flesh across the Viet Cong's forehead exploded into a shower of bone and brains, laced with the smoking tendrils of his jet-black hair. Burns rose to his feet and walked toward the dead VC. At that instant another gook, who had seen Burns's rifle fire cut down his comrade, leaped from his fighting hole to run back toward the smoking village, away from the now alerted Marine platoon. Burns had been joined by Woodruff and myself as soon as he fired the first shots into the VC bunker. So as the frantic Viet Cong ran from us, we leveled our rifles and fired together into his churning legs, his back, and the back of his head. The bullets tore away great pieces of flesh and bone, and the Cong was dead before he hit the ground. But Burns kept walking toward the fractured body, firing slowly with each step. Pieces of the dead VC flew into the air and crimson pieces of flesh splattered the ground. When the last round in his magazine discharged and the empty case ejected out of the M-14's receiver, Burns lowered his rifle to port arms while Woodruff and I stared in fascination. Burns had stopped just a yard behind the dead man and hovered over the bloody corpse. He smiled. "That was for my big brother, you godless cocksucker! Remember him! My work with you Commie bastards is a long way from done. Let's go finish the rest of these punks! Watch me close, Culbertson, I'll show you how it's done."

Woodruff looked at me and said, "Don't worry about Burns. Since his brother got killed, he's not been right. He's a hell of a combat Marine though, and it's nice to have him on your side when the fighting gets rough."

We had reached the rest of the platoon, where the men were formed in a tight perimeter awaiting a medevac chopper for the three engineers. The chopper swung in over the river, and the prop wash covered us in dust. The engineers were hustled into the cargo bay, where they were attended to by a corpsman. Then the H-34 throttled up and, changing the rotor pitch, lifted off down toward An Hoa.

Third Platoon had experienced an eventful patrol. We had destroyed a thousand cubic meters of rice and burned a village to the ground with our explosives. Then we had killed two Viet Cong guerrillas and shot the next village to pieces. Kirby told us to saddle up, Lafley and I to take point back to base. If we couldn't march all the way to An Hoa from our position along the river, the platoon would stop for the night at Phu Loc 6.

The sky was showing the first tinges of purple as the sun faded over the river. Lafley and I stepped out fast, knowing that every Viet Cong in the area knew where we were. The enraged VC could easily be waiting for us in ambush along the trails we had crossed earlier in the day.

CHAPTER TWELVE

Third Platoon
Returns to Phu Loc 6

Lafley and I wove our route carefully back along the trail network that had brought us to the river. It was a standard procedure never to return by the same route that a patrol had taken to arrive at an objective, but when a river or a hillside channeled movement, a patrol was sometimes unavoidably restricted to doubling back along an approach. We stayed alert, but we saw nothing of note. It was growing dark when we broke out of the river basin and humped the trail to higher ground running southeast toward our firebase at Phu Loc 6.

Our water supplies had been rapidly depleted during the long, nonstop march. A new Marine, Private First Class Hall, had failed to listen to Hamilton's instruction about carrying at least two full canteens. A stout young man of twenty with wavy blond hair and blue eyes, Hall had spent the majority of his childhood hunting for good waves to surf in his hometown along the beaches of sunny southern California. Hall was the only Marine from California left in the platoon, since Holloway had been medevacked and Gunnery Sergeant Gutierrez, the hero of Operation Tuscaloosa, had rotated home. Most of the lean, hard Marines in Hotel were from the southern United States, guys like

Kirby, Jessmore, and Gunny Jones. Luther Hamilton and I were Okies, but we were Rebels at heart.

Holding his throat, Private First Class Hall looked at Burns with pleading eyes and rasped, "Can you spare a bit of water, Burns? I've used up all I had in my canteen."

Burns glared at the new recruit. He didn't move a muscle or even break stride, as Hall drifted back down the column to shuffle along at Burns's side. The cooler night air was little consolation when Lafley stopped the column for a short break along a grove of bamboo in a shallow bend in the trail. I heard the young Marine ask for a drink from one of the four canteens that Burns fastened to the belt of his 782 gear and his haversack blanket-roll straps. Burns stood and faced Hall, who by then had gone down on one knee and was staring at the ground. "How many canteens was you told to hump, surfer boy? My job description is not to nursemaid you rookies. Private Burns don't drink nobody's water. You'll learn quick that your sorry life depends on water out here. One reason you'll learn quick is that I ain't givin' you none!"

Private First Class Hall was the same clean-cut kid that had raced at my shoulder down the jungle trail on a patrol weeks before Operation Tuscaloosa. Hall had been with me, covering my back, when I fired into the Viet Cong waiting in ambush for our squad. I had wounded three of the VC seriously, and Hall had laid in covering fire as we withdrew under bursts of AK-47 fire. I probably owed Hall my life for rescuing me from my impulsivity. I had a reputation in Hotel Company as a daring rifleman, and I was most likely found at the point putting out suppressive fire anytime 3rd Platoon got hit.

I removed one of the full canteens from my cartridge

belt and tossed it toward Hall, who remained kneeling. He was ashamed to look at the platoon members. Burns looked up at me and just shook his head. I stared back at him and spoke in a soft voice. "Dammit, Burns, he's one of us! Don't you care anymore? He's one of us!" Burns took out a smoke and, lighting it up, blew a torrent of smoke into the air above his upturned helmet. I turned to John Lafley and whispered. "God, Cowboy, Burns is starting to worry me. I think he's starting to go Asiatic. Did you see the way he followed that wounded gook in the second village this afternoon? Must have shot a dozen holes in the VC's back, and most of the shots were after the dude had already bled out. I'll tell you straight, Lafley, I'm halfway scared of Burns myself!"

Lafley had taken a good-size plug of tobacco, and chewing slowly, he lowered his head with his eyes still on me and spit brown juice into the dirt. "Culbertson, you ain't got nothin' to be afraid of with Burns! He's just gone crazy is all. Since the gooks killed his big brother, he's gotten meaner than a cobra. The fucker gets worse every week, but he's a Hong Kong killing machine when the shit gets started. I'll talk to the new lieutenant when we get back to An Hoa."

Kirby yelled up the column. "Saddle up, men. It's 2130 hours already. We still got five klicks to Phu Loc 6. I already radioed ahead that 3rd Platoon would be marching in the backside before midnight. Lafley, move out and stay off the trail as much as possible. Let's move, Marines."

The night had grown inky black while we took the short break. The troops instinctively closed the interval to five meters, but noise discipline was reinforced by the veteran Marines, as we were still vulnerable to an ambush by any

Viet Cong unit that was patrolling in our sector. After an hour's march, the troops halted and knelt down to savor some water. Hall drank deeply from my canteen and nodded in my direction. I smiled back. Hidden under my socks and ammunition, I carried an extra full canteen in my haversack.

Suddenly, a distant report carried over the light night breeze toward our position, three klicks northwest of Phu Loc 6. The shell was fired from An Hoa and burst high over the sandbagged lines at Phu Loc 6. The illumination round popped and descended from its parachute high over the Marine firebase, splashing the firebase and its emplacements with twenty thousand candlepower of brilliant light. As the flare swung gently back and forth, the fields rising toward Phu Loc 6 were momentarily revealed. Shadows were cast among the clumps of trees and tall stands of grass that were left standing or had grown after Phu Loc 6 was first manned by 2/5.

A minute later, after the illumination round was extinguished, an M-60 barked and spit a red splash of tracers across the fields stretching toward the Song Thu Bon, perpendicular to our line of march. Then the 4.2-inch mortar section went into action and fired several rounds a thousand meters toward the river across our front. Corporal Kirby and Luther Hamilton had huddled with the radio operator and dialed in the frequency of Phu Loc 6's command post.

"Phu Loc Command, this is Hotel Riverman. Over." Corporal Kirby didn't know the call sign for the platoon that manned Phu Loc 6, but he was certain they would know Hotel had a patrol returning from the river. He had radioed the platoon's sitrep earlier that afternoon.

"Hotel Riverman, this is Golf Guardian Command.

Over." That transmission answered the question of which platoon stood watch on the Firebase.

"Golf Guardian, this is Hotel Riverman. Approaching your northern perimeter at 2300 hours. Are you under attack? Over." Kirby needed an explanation for the fireworks coming from the Marine positions.

"Hotel Riverman, this is Golf Guardian Command Actual. Our position took probing AW (automatic weapons) fire this P.M. My troops have fired H & I* as warning. Bring your patrol within one thousand meters my perimeter. I will give a compass heading to guide you into our back gate. Identify my azimuth with smoke that I will designate at that time. Over."

"Golf Guardian Actual, this is Hotel Riverman. Will halt one thousand meters from perimeter. Will comply with smoke as ordered when azimuth instructions received. Hotel Riverman on approach march. Out." Kirby knew the drill blindfolded. Third Platoon would approach within sight of the Marine firebase. Once halted, the platoon would ring up Golf Company and get a compass heading to line up their column into the base. Once the platoon was within a hundred meters, Lafley or Woodruff would throw out a colored smoke grenade. The color would correspond to the Golf platoon commander's request so that no mistake would be made as to whose platoon was entering the backside of the firebase.

For the next forty-five minutes, 3rd Platoon picked its way slowly through the rolling fields and occasional paddies toward Phu Loc 6. Finally the dark silhouette of the

---

*Harassment and Interdiction: artillery fire directed at random intervals at trail intersections, likely avenues of approach, suspected or possible enemy marshaling points, etc.

firebase loomed in the distance, two thousand meters to Hotel's front. Lafley called back to Kirby that the firebase was in sight, then continued the march. By that time, everyone was keyed up and aware that since enemy troops had fired into the firebase, they could be waiting in ambush as we closed the distance to the shallow hill. At about one thousand meters, Lafley held his hand up beside his head. The column stopped dead in the road, and all troops knelt down silently.

Corporal Kirby took the handset and called Golf Guardian for the approach azimuth. The Golf platoon commander told Hotel to take azimuth 320 degrees, or "three-two-zero," and to pop a red smoke grenade when they reached the bottom of Phu Loc 6's hill. Kirby repeated the instructions verbatim.

Lafley rose and assumed the point of the weary column as the heading three-two-zero was followed. Lafley steered for the middle of the hillside defenses, while Kirby held the compass and gave arm signals to steer the point. Lafley and I really did not take the situation very seriously until another cannon shot resounded across the rice fields from An Hoa. Another illumination round burst over Phu Loc 6, and the platoon was bathed in a silvery glow that silhouetted our bodies for as far as a man could see. Lafley knelt slowly like a robot until he had flattened himself on the trail, then the rest of the grunts down the column also melted into the ground. In five seconds, no one was visible, and an enemy soldier might just think he'd been seeing things if he had been observing in our direction. Then again, a veteran Viet Cong patrol might be crawling toward our motionless group, waiting for us to get to our feet.

My heart was stuck in my chest, and I could barely

breathe until suddenly the illumination charge fell to earth and went out. Lafley got to his feet, and 3rd Platoon fell into a quick-time march until the base of the Marine fortifications was broached. Woodruff threw out the designated red smoke grenade, and we ascended the trail into the firebase, six miles north of An Hoa. We passed the Golf Company sentries on guard and barely acknowledged their presence. The Golf Company gunnery sergeant arrived shortly and led us off to a bunkered area on top of the hill, where all hands hit the sack, still dressed in rotting jungle utilities and boots.

CHAPTER THIRTEEN

Sergeant Wadley
Comes Aboard

Morning broke just before 0600, and 3rd Platoon stirred alive after fifteen klicks of brutal abuse along the river. The men were filthy and showed several days' beard under bloodshot eyes and tousled heads. Their uniforms were splattered with dried clay and burn holes where blowing chars of thatch had landed on the olive drab jungle utilities. Boots were drying, but still caked with rice-flecked mud. Weapons were clogged with burnt powder and silt from the river. Hands were crusted with soil and filth. Fingernails were blackened from the fires, and chipped. In a word, Hotel's 3rd Platoon looked like shit.

I rolled from the haversack that served through the short night as my pillow and stood stiff-legged and aching as the sun rose, promising an early end to the rainy season. An older Marine with a tin mug of joe steaming in his fist was standing nearby, looking our squad over. He was trim and well muscled and had that confident air of an old salt who has campaigned enough to win his spurs. The Marine eyed me, and I nodded. Surely he wasn't our new platoon commander, Lieutenant Pindel? This Marine was definitely enlisted and commanded our attention with his casual demeanor.

Gunny Jones sauntered over to the platoon, where we were trying to rub off the layer of filth that covered us. He brought the stranger with him. "Men, this is a new member of Hotel that has come to our aid, as we are short of NCOs, as you are aware. Sergeant Harold Wadley served in Korea fifteen years ago with the 5th Marine Regiment. Harold fought in the same unit as Gunnery Sergeant Gutierrez in the campaign called the Nevada Hills. On Outpost Vegas, Sergeant Wadley won the Bronze Star Medal with combat V for leading wounded Marines back to the Marine lines after an attack on a North Korean hill called Ungok (Hill 31-A). Sergeant Wadley led his platoon through an enemy mortar barrage after his commanding officer had been killed. The Marines under Sergeant Wadley's command carried their wounded comrades across a frozen creek, under fire, with dead and wounded Marines tied to their cartridge belts with comm wire. Sergeant Wadley's platoon, along with that of Sergeant Roberto Gutierrez, continued to hold Vegas ridge for ten days under siege by a Chinese division making human wave assaults during the night. The Chinese would blow their bugles and storm across the snow and ice up the Marine hill. The Communist first wave would be well clothed and armed. The second wave would be clothed but only partially armed. The third wave would be armed with spears and sticks and often attack without shoes or headgear. Sergeant Wadley's platoon would fire into the massed attackers until the barrels of their automatic weapons glowed in the dark.

"The next morning, the defending Marines would gaze out of their frozen foxholes at a mound of corpses. That night the Chinese leaders would mass their troops and hit the Marine outpost again. Sergeant Wadley is a true combat leader and will add some maturity to this platoon. Listen to his advice closely. He knows of what he speaks."

Sergeant Wadley took a couple of steps closer to our group. He looked us over again and smiled. "Get your gear together, and we'll get on the road back down to An Hoa." That was it!

Burns looked in my direction and said, "I already like this new sergeant. Killed a lot of Commies in Korea. This Marine is going to be just what old Private Burns was hoping for!"

Everyone tugged on their packs, grabbed their rifles, and assumed marching order, with Sergeant Wadley following along behind Corporal Kirby, who ordered us out the Phu Loc 6 perimeter and down the trail joining Highway 1 and a six-mile hump to An Hoa.

CHAPTER FOURTEEN

Back Home with Hotel Company

Our platoon dragged along the muddy bends in Highway 1 for two hours before the escarpment leading up the shallow hill to An Hoa became visible. The red clay banks of earth along the airstrip bulged with olive drab sandbagged bunkers guarding the outer perimeter of the combat base. It was late morning, and the sentries on lines would not be relieved until 1600 hours. It was spring in Vietnam, and the air was warm, the sky hazy.

As 3rd Platoon rounded the northern edge of the strip, a C-130 transport from Da Nang landed at the far end of the runway and reversed its engines, braking to stop. The four-engine plane had air force markings and taxied in front of the huts of the supply section lining the strip. In minutes, a file of Marine replacements disembarked the aircraft and headed into the receiving and transit NCO shack. I thought of the rainy day in December nearly four months earlier when I had arrived at An Hoa. I had come to Vietnam with fervent expectations about America's prosecution of this war, and I had come to doubt America's resolve in finishing it. I wondered what preconceived ideas and naive notions the new Marines would bring with them as they waddled with their heavy seabags across the mud-crusted PSP of the airstrip.

Corporal Kirby called out as the platoon filed through the double apron of barbed wire. "Clear your weapons, men! Check your gear into 3rd Platoon's hootches and clean your weapons for inspection by your squad leader. After rifle inspection, you can hit the showers, and then the platoon will go to chow together. Platoon halt. Dismissed." After that informality, we meandered through the rows of hootches until we found our squad's billet. We cleaned our weapons while dressed in our filthy utilities. Our hands were soaked in kerosene and oil as we fitted our spotless rifles back together. Then we filed onto the company street to stand in loose formation as the squad leaders moved down the ranks and inspected the weapons. After that most serious of Marine duties was fulfilled, we stripped off our grungy jungles, wrapping clean white towels around us, and plodded in flopping rubber thongs to the showers.

The showers consisted of a wooden set of stalls lined with corrugated tin sheets to deflect the water. The water supply itself came from two huge metal cylinders that served as tanks. The propulsion system was strictly gravity-fed, and the water temperature was freezing, in distinct contrast to the air temperature. There was no lack of soap, however, and each Marine slid into freshly washed jungles. Clean socks were a true luxury, and were laced up in a fresh pair of jungle boots kept under our racks. It felt so good to be clean again that many of us eyed our buddies, disbelieving the platoon's good fortune.

We fell out into the street into a loose formation to march to early chow. It felt wonderful to still be alive!

However, it is difficult to appreciate the beauty and value of life until a man has seen it snatched mercilessly away. Death was still roaming the Arizona Territory looking for souls, but the Reaper had spared us for the time being. We had clean clothes, sunshine, and a hot meal to look forward to; the Marines of 3rd Platoon would revel in their good luck.

Inside the chow hall, we piled the food onto stainless steel trays and joined our friends at long, picnic-size tables. Everyone was hovering over the chow like a pack of jealous bulldogs, when I heard someone call my name and turned to see Gunny Jones standing behind me. "Culbertson, report to the duty hut after you finish chow. You have orders to Da Nang for TAD (temporary assigned duty). I'll fill you in when you report." Nodding my head, mouth stuffed with food, I did not rise as the gunny turned and strode out the chow hall door. Wondering what the hell I was getting into, I washed the last bit of food down with a cold glass of fresh milk.

I rose from the table, took my tray to the steaming GI cans of soapy and hot water, and scrubbed out the tray. Adding the shiny tray to the clean stack, I pushed open the screened doors and walked into the main street, heading toward Hotel Company headquarters. At the hootch, I knocked on the wooden door and announced my presence. A voice spoke out, "Enter, Culbertson. Have a chair. The new lieutenant is in with Gunny Jones, and he will see you in a moment." Sgt. Lacey Smith had been the head administration clerk under the command of Capt. J. J. Doherty (Hotel's commanding officer during Operation Tuscaloosa). Sergeant Smith had written all the correspondence for Hotel Company's killed in action, and I remember Captain Doherty's remarking that

Lacey Smith was one of the hardest working admin heads in the battalion. All the record books were correctly filled with combat operations, wounds received, promotions, award presentations, and, lastly, courts-martial. Sgt. Lacey Smith was a perfectionist.

Gunny Jones's voice boomed from the office where our new platoon commander was seated behind his desk. I entered the office and, snapping to attention, saluted, and announced that Private First Class Culbertson was reporting as ordered. Gunny Jones said, "Culbertson, this is our new platoon commander, Lt. J. P. Pindel, Jr. Second Lieutenant Pindel is not new to our beloved Corps, Culbertson. He has served on the East Coast as an NCO and has four years enlisted experience."

I nodded my head and said that I was pleased to welcome the lieutenant to 3rd Platoon. I waited without speaking to learn the reason for my presence. Lieutenant Pindel looked me over through thick Marine Corps–issue eyeglasses and began. "I have just today joined Hotel Company. We have received a requirement from 1st Marine Division headquarters in Da Nang to provide a team of two Marines to attend division Scout-Sniper School at the Happy Valley Rifle Range near the Seabees camp in Da Nang. Gunny Jones has recommended you, along with Lance Corporal Bolton, to represent Hotel Company. Four other Marines from the other companies in the battalion will fill out the team. There will be eighteen shooters in the school drawn from the entire 1st Marine Division. You were picked because of your aggressiveness in the field, your GCT scores in boot camp, and the fact that you are an expert rifleman. Gunnery Sergeant Jones thinks you have the personality to be a sniper. Personally, I think all the troops are infantrymen first, and all this fancy sniper business is secondary. However, when the division HQ calls, we listen! Gunny, do you have anything else?"

Gunny Jones picked up a sheet of paper stamped with the Marine Corps emblem and United States Marine Corps written across the middle. "You are now a lance corporal in the United States Marine Corps, Culbertson. I noticed you have been a PFC for over a year, and I suppose—like myself—you are a better field Marine than garrison boot polisher. Get your gear packed for sniper school. You need two weeks' jungle utilities, and green T-shirts, etc. You know the drill by now. Be ready to embark at the landing strip at 0800 hours. You will draw a new match rifle from the battalion armorer later this afternoon. Sergeant Smith will give you trip manifest vouchers for you and Corporal Bolton from Hotel Company. Remember, the best shots in the division will be at this school. A Marine who does not shoot superbly is no Marine at all. Do not embarrass the lieutenant or myself by fucking off. Is that clear, son? Carry on."

I saluted the new lieutenant and, smiling at the gunny, did an about-face and reported to Sgt. Lacey Smith. Sergeant Smith handed me the flight manifest vouchers and wished me a sincere success. I strode off toward the armorer's hut, not believing my good luck. Since my childhood, I had shot rifles and shotguns under the supervision of my father. My dad was a clay pigeon champion and had once recorded a score of 175 straight in skeet. I knew I could shoot well and was getting better each patrol, mostly because it was important to me to be a Marine marksman. Marines were legendary in skill at arms, and I wanted desperately to be part of this magnificent breed of riflemen. No matter what other shortcomings the Marine Corps had in combat, their strong suit was their riflemen. Outstanding combat proficiency in weapons had assured the Marines of a worldwide reputation as the finest light infantry on earth. I joined the Marines to exercise my love of hunting and shooting. Soon I would get a chance to shoot with the very best. I wouldn't have traded that opportunity for a scholarship to Stanford.

Entering the armorer's shack, I eyed stacks of M-14s along the floor in racks. Vises on steel-clad benches held barrels and receivers. They were surrounded by clusters of screws, pins, bushings, and screwdrivers. A thin film of oil hung in the air, and smudges of grease and oil covered the worktables. The armorer wore a black plastic apron covered with grease. The apron had a pocket on the breast that was filled with pens, pencils, and small metal gauges.

"My name is Culbertson," I said. "I'm flying to Da Nang tomorrow to attend 1st Marine Division Sniper School. Gunny Jones from Hotel Company told me to see you about drawing a weapon." The armorer turned and pulled an M-14 with a light-color stock off the wall. It looked new, and mounted a matte black rifle scope held in a military mount with large-headed, slotted screws.

The armorer held the rifle toward me and, admiring the weapon, said, "Culbertson, this M-14 has a glass-bedded match barrel. The receiver and bolt have been deburred and polished inside. The stock is walnut and the scope is a Redfield 3 × 9 power variable. I have adjusted and honed every inch of this rifle, and it should shoot inside ten inches at one thousand meters. The scope graduates in quarter-minute clicks. One click will move the bullet strike one-quarter inch per one hundred meters of range.

The trigger is a crisp two pounds with no creep or over-travel. Son, if you can't kill the gooks with this rifle, you better join the fucking navy. Good luck! I want a full report when you get back from division."

I thanked the armorer. The reputation of Marine Corps armorers has always been outstanding. It was clearly understood in the Marine Corps that the really fine armorers gave a big advantage to the troops, as all company weapons were completely inspected and brought into milspec before seeing action.

I had to get my gear packed and get some sleep; 0800 would come early, and I hadn't even met Lance Corporal Bolton from Hotel Company yet. Hell, I was wound up and certain I could make those Marines at 1st Division pay attention to how well this skinny Oklahoma boy could shoot.

CHAPTER FIFTEEN

First Marine Division HQ Base—Da Nang

I arrived at the An Hoa airstrip's transit duty shack at 0720 but nothing was happening except small gusts of wind lifting red dust into a haze that covered the fuselages of the two ancient Sikorsky H-34 medevac choppers resting on the helipad in front of the battalion aid station.

Ten minutes later, a young Marine sauntered down the edge of the strip. He was tall and had broad shoulders. His baby face was capped by a soft green utility cover. He carried his M-14 rifle at sling arms, and a half-filled seabag hung across his back. He stopped when he reached where my pile of seabag, pack, and rifle was stacked at my feet. Extending his hand, he said, "I'm Buddy Bolton, and I guess you must be Dr. Livingston?" We both chuckled. I replied that no one was on duty, and the air force C-130 was late. As I finished berating the air force's tardiness, Bolton and I heard the high-pitched throbbing of turboprop engines; the C-130 in question was banking over the Que Son Plateau. Then it turned into the final approach to An Hoa. The giant transport touched down gracefully and threw its powerful engines into reverse. Using all the runway An Hoa offered, the Hercules slowed, then it turned and taxied back toward the transit facility.

More Marine and navy personnel had joined our group as we stared at the growing bulk of the approaching plane. Several moments passed before the transport braked to a stop. Then the rear loading ramp lowered, and Bolton and I entered the cargo hold, giving our manifest vouchers to the air force crew chief. Several wounded Marines were carried into the hold by corpsmen. One corpsman attended the men during the flight to Da Nang. We eased back in nylon-web fold-down seats along the sides of the C-130. The plane taxied to the end of the strip and, turning, throttled its engines into a high-pitched whine and went speeding down the runway. As the plane climbed free of An Hoa, I glanced out the porthole at the tiny hootches, sandbag bunkers, and Marines fading away as green rice paddies below blotted out the view.

In twenty minutes, we banked into the hazy valley leading to Da Nang Air Base. The Hercules turned into its final approach and touched down on the long tarmac. We taxied forever, passing military jets of every description, and braked in front of a line of metal sheds. Bolton and I waited for the wounded men to be off-loaded into waiting ambulances, then shouldered our gear and stumbled down the cargo ramp into the glaring noonday heat of Da Nang.

A six-by-six USMC truck picked us up, and we slung our gear aboard for the short trip to Happy Valley. Four other Marines were aboard the truck, and we assumed they were going to be shooting with us at Sniper School. We passed miles of corrugated huts, warehouses, and motor pools lined with transport trucks and an occasional tank. Thousands of airmen, Marines, and sailors moved about, performing duties supplying the 1st Marine Division's troops in the field. I looked at Bolton, who gazed dumbfounded at the abundance of men and materiel stockpiled at the Da Nang supply depots.

"Jesus, Culbertson, I've never seen so much equipment and buildings full of maintenance crews and support personnel. How in hell could the United States fail to kick Charlie's ass with all this stuff?" Buddy Bolton held his hands wide with his palms up in silent disbelief. I was also having trouble understanding how our country could defeat Japan and Germany simultaneously, yet be totally inept in pursuing a winning strategy against a third-rate power like North Vietnam. Perhaps our failure had more to do with a lack of national resolve and unity of purpose than the pure functionality of our military machine. Bolton and I might not count for much among that grandiose display of endless hardware, but we weren't in Vietnam because we had to be there. We were there because we wanted to kill every Commie in the country. Hell, that was the American way!

Our truck had joined another in a small convoy that wound out of the airbase into the countryside. We passed open fields worked by peasants just like in the Arizona. We wound along dirt roads and passed through a large Seabee camp, near a rock quarry not far from Hill 55. The trucks climbed a shallow hill where a half dozen large green canvas tents stood starkly silhouetted against the sky. Our convoy halted in a swirl of dust and engine noise. As we bounded off the trucks, we were met by a Marine sergeant who led us to the tent that would serve as home for the next few weeks of Sniper School. We had the rest of the day to unpack our gear and inspect the camp and the rifle range that stretched far away to the west. Classes would not begin until 0800 the following day. We all took time to get acquainted and discuss the operations and duties in our respective battalions. We were all Marines and, friendly competition aside, we were brothers.

Several of the sniper candidates had come from the 1st Marine Regiment, based north, near Phu Bai. A team of shooters was from a battalion in the 7th Marines that provided security for Da Nang Air Base itself. Our team of six Marines from the 5th Marine Regiment rounded out the eighteen members of the Sniper School class.

We talked into the early evening and turned in at 2200 hours. Curling up in just our utilities, without wearing our jungle boots, was a luxury compared to our usual foxhole procedures. In moments, the row of Marines on the canvas cots fell silent.

CHAPTER SIXTEEN

First Marine Division Sniper School— Happy Valley

We were awakened at 0630 by the sergeant who had shown us to our tent. He gave us fifteen minutes to shit, shave, and shower before presenting ourselves at the mess tent for chow. After a breakfast of dry cereals, fruit, and milk, we reported to a large tent that would serve as the classroom during our stay at Happy Valley.

A young sergeant walked into the tent and passed between the two sections of folding chairs that held the eighteen Marines of our class. We were desperately eager to learn the skills of professional marksmen. Sgt. Douglas M. DeHass of Orange City, Iowa, introduced himself as assistant NCOIC of 1st Marine Division Sniper School.

"Two-man teams have been selected from throughout the 1st Division to report here at Happy Valley Range for a formal two-week course. A new refresher course has also been designed to allow previously graduated snipers to polish their skills while getting their weapons checked out by division armorers. We will conduct classes in the principles of map reading, the effects of wind and weather, and the study of ballistics. Finally, we will discuss the principles of live firing, target acquisition, cover and concealment, position, and camouflage. In the past, this school has been such a success that the Marine marksmen gathered here will be joined later in the course by U.S. Army Rangers, U.S. Air Force Security Guards, and Korean Marine troops from the 2nd Korean Marine Brigade based at Hoi An. U.S. Navy SEALs from the IV Corps area will also take part in the live fire segment of this training. I expect the Marines in this room to be ambassadors for the other services that will attend our school. No one is to degrade or jeer any shooter from the army, navy, or the air force. The Koreans will kill you if you give them any shit, so I won't even get into that!"

We all cracked up, but we had all heard how tough Korean Marines were in the field. Hell, I was looking forward to meeting the ROK Marines. They were called the "Blue Dragons." I liked that, too. During the Korean War, the U.S. Marines had fought so hard and sacrificed so much— and so many—for their country that the Marines were still heros in the eyes of the Korean armed forces. I felt closer to them than I did the air force and navy SEALs. The navy SEALs were another case altogether; we heard they were a bunch of underwater psychos who would rather use knives than guns anyway. I hoped the ROK Marines and the SEALs got along, or it would be a long two weeks!

Sergeant DeHass's opening address continued, but the eighteen of us would rather have been on the range busting caps than listening to a lecture. "We are very fortunate in acquiring the services of our NCOIC, who will head up the training at this school. Gunnery Sergeant V. D. Mitchell is from Chula Vista, California. Gunny Mitchell is a veteran of World War II and the Korean War. Gunny Mitchell began his competitive shooting career at MCRD San Diego in 1952. He shot continuously on Marine Corps rifle teams, and in 1965 he won the National Individual Rifle Championships at Camp Perry, Ohio. In 1958, Gunny Mitchell won the National Service Rifle Championship and shot a rapid-fire record in the Coast Guard Match with fifteen of his twenty bull's-eyes in the smaller V-ring. At the commandant's request, Gunny Mitchell has come out of retirement to train you men to be the finest snipers on earth. There is no finer marksman or instructor in the Marine Corps than Gunnery Sergeant Mitchell.

"If you youngsters give Gunny Mitchell your undivided attention for the next two weeks, I am certain that you will return to your rifle battalions and give your commanders a long-range rifle threat that the Viet Cong will greatly fear. Without any more discussion, I give you a Marine legend, Gunnery Sergeant V. D. Mitchell."

A middle-size Marine in his midforties strode to the podium. Gunny Mitchell was a bit overweight and had a kind face that was nondescript except for shining, dark eyes that seemed to take in the whole room at a glance. There was a seriousness about him, but it lacked the excessive hardness of the drill field. Gunny Mitchell was low-key yet emphatic as he began. "I've had a lot of shooters come to me for instruction over the years. The best marksmen are the ones who are able to shoulder their weapons while blotting everything else out. A good shot can see his sights and the target. He can squeeze the trigger properly and hold his position. The great shots can do all that and still visualize the bullet streaking toward the target and hitting where they intended it to hit. Mind over matter! You've got to become part of your weapon and think like a hunter. You cannot become angry or fearful. A great marksman gives his rifle permission to kill. When he squeezes the trigger, the rifle begins a sequence that will result in a kill. The shooter is only part of that process, and I must help you Marines understand your part in the act. Today, Sergeant DeHass will give a weapons familiarization and technical function and ballistic analysis for your Remington Model 700 sniper rifle. Pay attention, and I'll see you back here in the morning." The gunny nodded and walked out of the tent, leaving the dry subject matter of nomenclature and bullet performance with Sergeant DeHass.

Sergeant DeHass took the podium and talked about our primary rifle training in boot camp. He concluded that since we were all taught to shoot by Marine Corps PMIs (primary marksmanship instructors), we should all know and utilize the same basic principles of firing. He handed out sheets of blank notepaper and had us write from memory the correct methods of live firing. Sergeant DeHass emphasized that the principles taught in the school would be learned as the culmination of almost two hundred years of practical combat experience earned by Marine riflemen on the battlefields of the world.

After collecting the papers from the class, Sergeant DeHass read a statement from an old notebook that he produced from under the notes on the lectern. It read:

COMBAT MARKSMANSHIP
Principles of Rifle Marksmanship

In combat marksmanship the main objective is to seek out and locate the targeted enemy. Then correctly utilize established principles of rifle marksmanship to engage and destroy the enemy by focusing controlled and accurate fires on the target. The reason the words "focusing controlled and accurate fires" are used is to emphasize a major tenet of marksmanship. Specifically, the fundamentally sound rifleman must employ and rely upon his mental powers of concentration and control as he delivers an accurate shot on target. He must not let the mechanics affect his Position, Sight Alignment, Breathing, Trigger Squeeze, or Follow-through. The concept to understand is that the marksman is in complete control of the weapon and by rigid implementation of proper technique cannot fail to squeeze off an aimed shot regardless of the external distractions or disturbances. Proper technique is the natural sequence of operations that are mentally rehearsed until the shooter performs the necessary steps of taking a "balanced position" utilizing available cover and concealment. Next, the marksman must shoulder his weapon establishing the correct "spot weld" with his cheek against the stock. The stock must be pointed naturally at the target and butted straight into the shoulder without twisting or "canting" the rifle. The shooter's eyes must fall naturally onto the "sight plane" and visualize the front sight post in the aperture of the rear sight. The blade of the front sight must be centered on the target, normally at a 6 o'clock hold while maintaining the correct sight alignment with the front post centered in the rear sight aperture. The shooter then draws a breath, exhaling half his air while holding the remainder as he steadies his aim and begins to squeeze the trigger. The "trigger squeeze" must be even and methodical until the rifle discharges. Perfect trigger squeeze should not be anticipated by the shooter, which eliminates any tendency to pull or flinch, throwing the shot off target. "Follow-through" simply requires the marksman to hold his sight picture on target until the shot is discharged and reaches the target before taking his weapon down off the shoulder.

Sergeant DeHass placed the booklet on the table next to the lectern. Looking over the eighteen shooters under his instruction, he knew he had made his point clear: good marksmanship is a combination of several simple tasks. Any one of those functions can be taught, but the problem is in mastering all of them and utilizing them in concert to produce accurate shots even in the midst of battle. The true combat marksman is a rare individual who is able to shut out interferences while going about the serious business of taking another man's life. There wasn't anything personal about the killing we were training to perform. Firing at ranges up to one thousand meters, the sniper would rarely see the target's face. From the perspective of the enemy soldiers who were targeted and cut down at long range, the Marine sniper was an invisible terror on the battlefield, one that struck without warning. We were so used to being ambushed by Charlie that I was happy that I would have a chance to turn the tables and fuck up his parade.

Our class ended with a short discussion of the 168-grain 7.62-millimeter NATO match ammunition we would fire in our Remington "bolt" guns. The match ammo was slower than regular ball due to their heavier boattail bullets. But 2,550 feet per second was plenty fast, and out to one thousand meters, Charlie would be ours. The scopes we would use to pick the Viet Cong out of their jungle were Redfield variable 3 × 9 power tubes mounted on integral steel bases. The Redfield rifle scope had a high light-magnification and was sealed against moisture and shock. The equipment we would be issued was technically superior to anything the Marine Corps had ever fielded in past conflicts.

CHAPTER SEVENTEEN

Principles of Sniper Marksmanship

Promptly at 0800, we reported to class for a continuation of Sergeant DeHass's training lecture in shooting principles, which any young Marine sniper would have to master before successfully engaging the enemy at extended range.

Sergeant DeHass began his presentation while Gunny Mitchell sat in a contemplative mood nearby. The first subject introduced was shooting position. Gunny Mitchell pulled down a chart illustrating Marines in various poses firing their rifles. DeHass said that the shooter must find the most stable position dictated by the surrounding terrain. Prone is best for maximizing the number of body areas in direct contact with the ground. Prone is also the best position to create a low silhouette providing some degree of concealment. However, if the sniper must fire over a hedgerow or the top of a small paddy dike, the prone position will not provide enough visibility. When firing from the offhand (standing) position because of an obstacle, Sergeant DeHass instructed us to always use a fixed rest. Sniping was about performance, not about attempting tricky or fancy shots. Performance would be measured in VC KIAs, and the distance to the kill wouldn't make

Charlie any more dead. Each one of us was expected to be an expert in utilizing prone, sitting, kneeling, and offhand positions efficiently. We were reminded to use our slings at all times to steady our aim. A hasty sling twisted inside the shooter's left arm worked best for snap shots.

We covered the action of butting the rifle without canting (twisting) the piece. Spot welds must be integral to the rifle stock where the rifleman's cheek embraces the wood, and identically placed for each shot. The firing hand had to grasp the small of the stock in the same place for each shot. The trigger finger must clear the wood of the pistol grip, allowing independent movement rearward during trigger squeeze without friction against the stock ("dragging wood"). The trigger finger, which should be the index finger, should touch the long end of the trigger in the center of the finger's first joint, opposite the nail. DeHass warned us that the pressure exerted on the trigger must be constant until the shot is fired. In a weapon with a standard military trigger, the slack in the first stage of the trigger mechanism should be taken up, allowing a smooth final-stage squeeze until discharge.

Sergeant DeHass demonstrated how to align our sights with the front sight post centered in the rear sight aperture when using iron sights. Once the sights were aligned with the target held at 6 o'clock, or wherever the shooter wished to place the shot, proper "sight alignment on target" must be maintained through discharge and held momentarily as "follow-through," to assure that the shooter doesn't flinch. DeHass stopped and asked how many of us remembered buddies in boot camp who failed to qualify on the rifle range? He said they often have perfect sight alignment on some other asshole's target. So, sight alignment must be oriented at the target the shooter wishes to hit. He said, "That sounds routine, but there are instances of Marines hitting friendlies in the heat of battle." Concentration and single-mindedness are the keys to being a Marine sniper. Sergeant DeHass reminded us that we were part of an elite fraternity which performed all military tasks with pride. The single job that Marines do best is their marksmanship; Marines are generally respected as the finest combat riflemen in the world.

Gunny Mitchell told us a story about a beleaguered army platoon that had been pinned down by a tenacious North Korean machine gun team. The army troops had taken several casualties trying to take out the North Koreans, but could not approach within range without coming under deadly fire. The soldiers' lieutenant called to the rear for help. Then, minutes later a muddy GI jeep turned into their position, and two Marines with M-1D sniper rifles dismounted and eyed the North Korean position. After the army lieutenant told the two Marines his problem, the senior Marine sergeant asked the army lieutenant to have one of his men stand up and fire a few shots at the Koreans.

The army officer said his man would be gunned down. The two Marines just smiled at him and loosened the slings on their match-grade Garand rifles. Taking up sitting positions facing the Korean bunker, the Marines chambered match .30-06 boattailed bullets and waited. As the army trooper stood and fired, the Koreans manning the machine gun sat up in firing position. One Marine fired his rifle, and then the second. Two Korean skulls split into shards of bone, and blood sprayed over their comrades. The army lieutenant's jaw was slack as the remaining Koreans scuttled up the hill over six hundred yards away.

The two Marine snipers climbed back into their jeep and turned down the bills of their campaign hats. The older Marine leaned back and yelled to the army officer that all he needed to do was call if they had any more problems! Then the jeep bounced along the muddy craters in the road back to 1st Marine Division headquarters.

Gunny smiled in his casual way. "Now, you boys don't go spreadin' any rumors, but you all are some of the few that know old Gunny Mitchell always uses the sitting position at six hundred meters."

Sergeant DeHass said, "You men have a legacy to carry on! Only through the application of lessons learned in this school can you continue as the best shooters on the battlefield. Never underestimate the enemy, but always believe in yourself."

DeHass talked to us about sighting through the Redfield variable scopes on our Remington bolt guns. He emphasized the placement of the shooter's eye at the proper distance from the scope's eyepiece. The "proper eye relief" should be 3 to 3½ inches. If the correct spot weld is maintained and the rifle points naturally, the target should come into clear focus without cutting out any illumination. The field of view should be full, and the reticule (crosshairs) should bisect the sight picture horizontally and vertically without canting. He stressed that when the shooter aims his rifle with proper position, spot weld, eye relief, and reticule placement, that the bullet should hit the target in exactly the same place each shot. The problem in achieving that level of accuracy lies in the difficulty of duplicating each and every shot. Shooting well, methodically, requires lots of practice, and DeHass made us feel better by saying that few Marines are natural shots.

Gunny Mitchell gave us a break for lunch, and told us to be back in class for a talk on the effects of weather on marksmanship. By way of introduction to the subject, he said moisture, temperature, wind, and light all play a role in how snipers target their enemy. Gunny Mitchell made no bones about his serious intentions in making us effective in our job, which was simply to engage and kill the enemy before he killed us.

We filed out of the classroom into bright sunlight, squinting and shielding our eyes. The introductory discussion about the effects of weather made me aware that I sure as hell didn't know all I needed to stay alive. I joined Bolton and several others strolling over to the mess tent. A light lunch would enable me to stay alert during Gunny Mitchell's afternoon talk. Our classroom wasn't back at Culver Military Academy, where I could take the lecture again with a different class if I dozed off. The information being presented to us was crucial to staying alive and helping my teammates survive a confusing war, one in which it seemed like no one was on our side except our parents back in the World and our best buddies. All we had there in Vietnam was our fellow grunts, and our closest friends were our rifles. I decided to use my rifle more effectively after I finished the school. I didn't give a shit how long Charlie had been fighting the Chinese, the Japs, the French, and the Americans. Charlie wasn't going to kill my young ass because I failed to wake up and pay attention!

After we finished chow and took our seats in the classroom, Gunny Mitchell rose and, facing the class, noticed some men nodding off after eating too much food. He pulled up the flap at the rear of the tent and let the brisk afternoon wind gust in, covering us with dirt and grass. Covers were knocked off heads, and most Marines leaned sideways to protect their eyes from the sudden blast. Then the gunny let the tent flap fall, shutting out the breeze.

Gunny Mitchell smiled broadly at our disconcerted group. He said there are no certainties in combat! There are no guarantees of mild weather or absence of rain or flood. To be combat-ready, we must be ready to adapt to all circumstances. Our enemy lives off the land and is not pampered by comforts such as we have become accustomed to. Charlie is hard as the ground he sleeps on! The Viet Cong will attack in the tumult of a monsoon storm or in a steaming jungle. He is comfortable in his environment. We are not so well adapted. We must be better prepared by understanding how to fight in a climate that is unfriendly and unforgiving. He asked how many of us could have fought off an attack with dust and grass blowing in our eyes. Would we have survived? There are no "do-overs" in combat. You live or you die!

Gunny Mitchell said the lessons were going to help us stay alive and be effective snipers by teaching us the important weather factors and how to read them. He reached back and propped up a chart with graphs, then he continued. "First, the wind poses the greatest threat to the ability of the marksman to place his shots accurately. The more directly wind crosses the flight of the bullet, the greater the round's deflection. By tossing dirt or grass into the air in front of you, you can estimate the wind's speed and direction. Another estimating method is noting the effect wind has on grass, which will bend in a three-to-four-miles-per-hour breeze. At five to eight miles per hour, leaves will rustle in trees and bushes. At eight to ten miles per hour, small trees and large plants will bend. Twelve to fifteen miles per hour is enough wind force to sway large tree limbs and violently disturb small trees and bushes. If a flagstaff is visible, the angle between the bottom edge of the flag and the pole divided by four will approximate the wind's velocity at that point."

Gunny Mitchell reminded us that wind velocity is not constant for the entire length of a field or woods. Gusts and eddies may change a wind current's speed or direction along the bullet's path. The longer the distance the sniper fires, the greater effect the wind will have on bullet placement. The professional sniper must take these variables into consideration before engaging. The gunny's personal advice was always to work closer to the target before taking the first shot. After the first shot is fired and the bullet's strike noted, the marksman will be able to adjust his sights or "hold off," which is commonly called "Kentucky windage." If a sniper fires at an enemy at five hundred meters and hits the target, then he knows the dope (range) he has on his sights is correct. When a second target appears at six hundred meters, he may not have time to adjust for elevation. He can hold off by aiming two feet over the target with his five-hundred-meter dope still on his sights. The additional hold off will increase the range to six hundred meters and a kill should result. Always employ hold off relative to the center mass of the target, and you should get a kill. The gunny chuckled, saying no VC had ever walked away from a chest wound.

Gunny Mitchell smiled broadly when he cracked a joke. Still, it was hard for me to make light of the task at hand, knowing if I fucked up that might cost my life. We went outside for a short smoke break. The classes were long, but the message was vital, and nobody bullshitted themselves about the future value of what Gunny Mitchell had to say.

Gunny Mitchell apologized for keeping us off the range. He said he knew we had come there to shoot, not to sit in class. However, like the first piece of ass each of us had gotten not much earlier in our young lives, it was important to know what hole to put it in. Gunny Mitchell felt shooting was a lot like fucking: anyone could do it, but not everyone could do it well! There is something wonderful about the Marine Corps, and every old salt will tell you that of all sergeants, gunnery sergeants are the most beloved by the common troopers. This stems from the fact that gunnies are not so burdened with work that they have no time to teach the troops. Secondly, gunnies have enough rank that few people screw with them, and they do not have to be an asshole like the first shirt (sergeant) to get the job done. Every man in the classroom had been won over by Gunnery Sergeant Mitchell's personality and earthy cleverness. Now Gunny Mitchell had our attention, and he could get his points about life and death through to us. There is an art to teaching, and rapport with the students was Gunny Mitchell's long suit.

"I want to make a few short observations about weather and how it impacts our shooting." Gunny Mitchell sat on the edge of the table in the front of the classroom. "A drop in temperature causes the air to become denser and more moist. A drop of twenty degrees at night necessitates an elevation adjustment of plus one MOA (minute of angle) for each hundred meters of range. A temperature increase of twenty degrees from morning to afternoon requires a corresponding decrease in elevation on the shooter's sights."

Gunny then discussed live firing: In engaging moving targets, the shooter must quickly estimate the velocity of the target; the angle of the deflection from straight ahead; range to target; and wind direction and velocity. He said the sniper must lead the target by swinging his rifle through the shot and be prepared to note the bullet strike and hold off for the second shot, immediately engaging the target before it is out of view or range. If you shoot from a prepared camouflaged position or "hide," it is wise to learn the exact ranges of the significant terrain features near the impact zone. Then, by comparison, a target moving into the kill zone can be "range-estimated" using a known terrain feature. This type of sniping is an ambushing technique that dates from the medieval period, when archers knew the range of their arrow's flight and approximately what terrain feature they could reach— such as a point on a hill. If the enemy was allowed to approach to the foot of the targeted hill, then the archers could be assured of hitting the enemy in a "beaten zone" much like our machine gunners use. The advantage to the modern rifleman is that there are few targets he cannot reach if he can analyze the distance and conditions correctly.

"Tracking" can be defined as following the enemy with the rifle sight, maintaining a moving aim point on the target. "Trapping" is waiting until the enemy walks into the "kill zone" at a previously known range before engaging him. The gunny told us, "After you have tracked enough enemies and made enough kills, you will sense the best way to take Charlie out. The tiger cannot tell us how he stalks and kills, but he does both with energy and grace. So will you, Marines! Remember, a sniper is always patient, awaiting the enemy to fall under his sights." Gunny Mitchell said he would see us early the next morning for the last day of classroom instruction.

CHAPTER EIGHTEEN

Last Class Before Taking the Range

Gunny Mitchell looked chipper for our last day of class. Leaning back in my canvas chair, I felt as if I had spent a lifetime learning the traditional principles of rifle marksmanship all over again. The Marines on either side of me were eager to get the final lecture over with and get on the rifle range.

Gunny Mitchell told us he would be brief about the handful of subjects that he was responsible for covering. He told us a story about how he began his shooting career, about always wanting to spend his time on the firing line even when he didn't know nearly all there was to know about the art of shooting. He admonished us to memorize the most important aspects of shouldering, aiming, firing, and understanding weather effects on our efforts to shoot accurately and deadly. Finally, he handed out a small booklet on technical training and employment of the USMC Scout Sniper in combat. The gunny held the little blue booklet in the air and made it clear the facts therein would save our lives if committed to memory.

Walking to the side of the tent, Gunny Mitchell flipped a large chalkboard upside down. It revealed the increasingly smaller circles of hills and the increasingly smaller Vs of draws pinched between the slopes of two adjacent hills. He wiped the slate clean and drew valleys and saddles, narrow passes and cliffs. Listening to the master sniper describe the type of terrain needed for certain vantage points taught us how a professional reads a map. The contour lines become shapes in a Marine's mind. The more we familiarized ourselves with different topographical features on maps of different areas, the more easily the terrain features the gunny had drawn for us stood out. Gunny Mitchell assured us that in time we could start a visual journey at one corner of a map, and trace our path through the myriad of terrain obstacles as though we were walking the land. He pointed out that the reason good reconnaissance units were so skilled in map reading was their continual reliance on a map to aid in escape and evasion if surprised by an enemy and to pinpoint targets for supporting arms. We figured a sniper team might get surprised also if they were waiting for Charlie too long in their camouflaged hide.

Now, I was getting the message loud and clear. The techniques involved in becoming an effective sniper had as much to do with external knowledge like weather and range estimation and map reading as they did with the theory of rifle marksmanship. I knew I was focused in the jungle, and I could sense a dangerous area where we could encounter booby traps and mines. I had learned how to look for signs of spooked water buffalo or flights of wild birds tearing aloft. The smells in a deserted village, or enemy food containers or cartridge cases found on the trail made my senses come alive. In the bush, I was learning to think more like Charlie, and my responses were becoming instinctive, requiring little forethought. I was becoming an animal that could sense other animals and track them over long distances. When the moment came, I knew killing was merely the natural consequence of the hunt. Killing was not a personal thing to me. Killing was my way of proving to Charlie that I had won and he had lost. No debate about that!

Gunny Mitchell ended the classroom segment of Sniper School with a short discussion of camouflage. He emphasized the use of natural vegetation and dirt, mud, and contrasting colors and textures to break up any hard outlines that would be visible to an enemy at a distance. Taking the class outside, he asked us to visually scour the slopes of our hillside class and pick out the hidden sniper. All of us shielded our eyes and, holding our soft covers over our brows like card dealers, looked in vain for the camouflaged man. After a few minutes of our fruitless searching, the gunny raised his arm and waved from side to side. A hundred meters off the hill right in front of us, two men stood and waved back to Gunny Mitchell.

"Come on up, fellows," the gunny yelled. He waved the short soldiers toward our motionless herd, and as they approached, it was clear to us that they were not Americans at all! The two grinning soldiers jogged up the hill in sandals, khaki pants, and shirts with green streaks, from a soft vegetable dye, that blended excellently with the surrounding grasses. Their soft hats were completely concealed by green grass like the short plants that grew in patches on the hillside. Their faces were dulled with dirt and a black tar-like substance. The shoots of green grasses protruded from every fold of their clothing. They held wood-stock SKS rifles in front of their chests, and the rifles were tightly wound with a green-and-brown gauze. Each Marine looked embarrassed, and for ten thousand dollars, there wasn't one of us who could even remember what part of the slope they had risen from.

Gunny Mitchell turned with a wide grin and, placing his hand along the larger Vietnamese's shoulder, chuckled. "Marines, this is Sergeant Liang and Corporal Nguyen Lao of the People's Army of Vietnam. They have recently seen the light and come over on *Chieu Hoi* programs to serve your units in the capacity of Kit Carson scouts. In all the world, there are no finer light infantrymen fighting today than these gentlemen. Their use of camouflage, noise discipline, tunneling, and escape and evasion frankly makes me ashamed of Marine Corps training. You will learn much from watching our new friends. They are here to perform demonstrations like this for your education. But now it's lunchtime, and I'm sure you gentlemen are hungry from working your eyeballs this hard. We'll meet on the rifle range at 1300 hours. This exercise concludes the classroom portion of Sniper School. See you at 1300."

We just stood in a bunch, looking Liang and Nguyen Lao up one side and down another. It was just amazing that every time I felt like I was getting pretty salty, someone like Sergeant Liang or Nguyen Lao would show up and make me look dumb! Well, at least I could understand why Hotel Company got ambushed all the time walking through the middle of rice paddies like a bunch of amateurs instead of finding the enemy and cutting him down. Sergeant Liang and his little friend would make pretty short work of any Americans in the dense forests of I Corps. Any American unit that bragged about ambushing the NVA and tearing their asses up on a consistent basis was just a bunch of fucking liars. I thought a lot of them got the words "guerrilla" and "North Vietnamese Army" confused. The fact that Nguyen

Lao and Liang were both over thirty years old seemed to indicate that they had not spent too much of their field time on the losing side of any ambushes.

Some Americans, particularly the World War II veterans, falsely believed the Marines were in Southeast Asia fighting savages who were not professionally led or equipped. It was interesting to note that these North Viets had been the only soldiers in history to whip the living shit out of France's finest fighting unit, the French Foreign Legion. It bothered me that the papers in the States lamented our efforts in the war, as though the ice-cream-bloated civilians back home could have an inkling of what the hell was really going on over here. I pushed Sergeant Liang and Cpl. Nguyen Lao from my conscious mind for the time being and strode with new humility into that most American arena of excess—the mess tent.

CHAPTER NINETEEN

The Rifle Range at Happy Valley

At 1300 hours, eighteen shooters were eagerly gathered at the top of a flattened knob a hundred meters north of our classroom tent. As we stood gazing downrange at a single black target six hundred meters distant, a lone Marine sat shouldering his rifle in an open-legged sitting position. His shoulders were bent over the rifle, his cheek folded along the linseed-oil finish of the stock. An old PMI's campaign hat was tucked low on his forehead, but the bill was turned up, allowing clear vision along the rifle's sight plane. The rifle barked, and the shooter rode the recoil, settling back into his original position. He fired shot after shot until we heard a loud ping as the black stamped metal en bloc clip flew from the rifle's receiver and landed next to him.

Gunny Mitchell got slowly to his feet and faced the throng of surprised Marines. He asked someone to fetch the target that hung motionless downrange. Gunny loosened the leather sling that pinched his left bicep at the top of the muscle, and bent over, allowing the tight loop of leather to fall from his arm. Standing, he held out the burnished rifle, which looked something like an M-14, as we huddled behind him. "Men, this is the old war-horse of the Marine Corps. The Garand M-1 rifle in U.S. caliber .30 will outshoot any military rifle ever made if it is properly tuned and maintained. This rifle has killed more enemies of the United States than any other."

The Marine who had gone to collect the gunny's target came up the shallow hill from the butt. He handed the target to the gunny, who—without even looking at the results—passed it to the nearest Marine.

The black bull's-eye was the standard USMC "A" target, with a twelve-inch-diameter circle. Inside the circle was an eight-shot group that measured five inches across at the widest point. Gunny Mitchell had fired one clip of eight rounds from a sitting position at a twelve-inch bull at six hundred meters and put all his shots inside five inches. He hadn't used a fancy state-of-the-art weapon like our Remington 700s with their high-power scopes. He had cut the heart out of the target in a rapid-fire string without taking thirty seconds to deliver all the shots. The humility monster took hold of our group with a vengeance. We would-be snipers looked from man to man with disbelief as the target was passed around.

Gunny spoke up from the firing line, where two Marines could lay prone or stand and shoot side by side. "Let's get our weapons and be back here in five minutes to snap in and get some dope on our sights before the sun glare gets too harsh." We ran to our tents and returned with bolt-action Remingtons and match-grade M-14s.

The gunny started our exercises by having two-man teams assume the prone position, muzzles downrange, to demonstrate the proper use of the sling and elbows to steady the rifle. He hovered over each shooter as he sought to improve the student's position in order to achieve a natural balance that reduced excess tension. Sergeant DeHass had joined the group by that time and was busily adjusting Marines' arms and legs to straighten out the natural pointability of our rifles. As Sergeant DeHass emphasized, once we fell into position, we should not have to twist or adjust our torso or legs to sight the target. The proper position should indicate a straight line to the target once we took it up. We were made to practice falling into the correct prone position for an hour, until it was becoming second nature.

One stocky red-haired Marine from some bastion of southern hospitality and manners had bent his knees and leaned forward, thrusting his rifle butt into the deck preparatory to falling into the prone position. As he leaned into his crouch, he farted loud and terrible, choking the closest Marines into defensive postures as though mortar shells were raining down. The perpetrator turned his head and volunteered a squeaky, "Excuse me, fellas." He then assumed a perfect prone position.

Gunny Mitchell held his hand to his chin, rubbing the stubble of his beard. "Well, youngster, you southern boys do have some impeccable manners, but Charlie will definitely take advantage of your problem with noise discipline." A faint rose-colored tinge crossed the shooter's face as he lay prone on the deck, no doubt trying to stifle the next announcement from his bloated intestines.

We got back to the firing line and worked our trigger

squeeze, trying to surprise ourselves each time the firing pin clicked home. It felt good to smell the gun oil and linseed odors that impregnated our stocks. Shooting is an action that brings a man closer to his roots as a hunter and provider for the family. In the modern world, the men who wielded the rifles had their images tarnished by a society that did its hunting at the local Safeway. The killing was done by machines and butchers in blood-splattered smocks who presented too grisly a picture for the average housewife to consider it real.

I was proud of being a rifleman and a hunter. The most exciting part of our operations against the Viet Cong was locating the enemy and driving him against an obstacle which prevented his escape or evasion. Most often, the Marine Corps trapped the Viet Cong and created a battle by fielding more troops and sacrificing some of them to initiate the contact. Artillery and air support were hardly used by the Marines until the battle had been joined. The USMC simply did not have the artillery and close air support resources to waste unless the situation had grown critical enough to necessitate extra firepower in order to extricate the troops under fire. In Operation Tuscaloosa, the Marine commanders had waited too long to engage the heavy artillery. Whether by accident or design, the result had been the wounding or death by gunshot of practically every member of Hotel's 2nd Platoon. I supposed the Marine Corps, in its infinite wisdom, had undertaken a program where snipers would masquerade as individual artillery pieces until events warranted using the real thing. There was no doubt that a Marine platoon or rifle company with its M-60 machine guns, 60-Mike-Mike mortars, and

M-79 grenade launchers could deliver devastating fire upon an enemy target. But the facts of jungle warfare were such that the crafty Viet Cong never took us under fire unless they did so from a prepared, fortified position. If the Marines, after being attacked, gained fire superiority, then it was an easy task for the VC to break off the fight and head for their escape tunnels. The main problem for the gunslingers of the 5th Marines was forcing the enemy to stick it out in a battle long enough to allow the Marines to do their thing. The thing the Marines always did was charge savagely out of their holes and trenches. Firing small arms from the hip as they advanced like the lost battalions of World War I, the sea soldiers of every battalion in the Corps were taught to take the fight to the enemy. Charging blindly ahead with fixed bayonets and rebel yells, the troops that were not cut down by enemy fire would leap into the enemy's trenches and kill him. I really *hated* that type of attack, because success was inevitably paid for with the lives of slaughtered youngsters.

Firepower was the way to crush a bunkered enemy. Artillery, and even snipers, played a role in keeping the enemy's head down until an enveloping force could reach the objective. I thought we should use our machine guns to fire overhead as we assaulted, but the Marine Corps always made its machine gunners assault *with* the riflemen so they would not be without the guns when the assault snagged or hesitated. It is tough duty to ask the machine gun teams to set up their weapons on an exposed field under fire, but from as far back as twelve hundred meters, a machine gun could reach any target under assault. So could a Marine sniper team. I though it was sensible to set up the support weapons early, in protected sites, so they could fire into probable enemy strongpoints along unimpeded firing lanes while still maintaining a margin of safety for the crew.

Suffice it to say that the Marine Corps wasn't about to change any tactics that had worked on Iwo Jima unless they had to, and no one ever questioned the tactical effectiveness of the Marines on Iwo. Except me, and on Operation Tuscaloosa, my comment about firing artillery prep across the river onto the enemy bank had been correct. Captain Graham, acting as officer in charge, had cut me some slack by diplomatically telling me to get my butt in the river instead of shooting me. However, I continued to wonder if the sad lessons of Operation Tuscaloosa would cause any Marine officers to rethink their tactical errors.

I snapped myself out of my daydream and heard my name called out. Shouldering my M-14, I walked up to the small mound that served as a firing line. I assumed a prone position with six-hundred-meter dope on my sights, and the crosshairs came into focus, sharply bisecting the dull black bull's-eye that appeared downrange. I flicked off my safety and drew up the slack from the trigger. Suddenly, the rifle bucked as the round discharged. The Marine armorer back at An Hoa wasn't bullshitting when he said the trigger was smooth, without creep or overtravel. I fired another four shots in slow-fire cadence into the target. The gunny called out, "Cease-fire," and I rose and walked to the butts. In a few minutes, I was back on the T-shaped firing line and handed Gunny Mitchell my target. All the rounds in the five-shot group were inside four inches. The gunny looked me over and said with a quick smile, "Culbertson, I forgot to tell you that I fail any young Marines that try to outshoot their instructor. That means outshoot *me*! By God, now this here is a group a sniper can hang on the wall. Give Culbertson one of those Remington bolt guns, and let's see how well he handles things at one thousand meters."

Grasping the Remington, I stroked its wooden Monte Carlo cheekpiece and tall Redfield scope with what looked like a baseball-size objective lens. The trigger was a two-pound Canjar match setup that you could blow on and set off. The sling was olive-drab military web, hung slack under the fat bull barrel manufactured by Douglas. The barrel was a result of their revolutionary air testing, which resulted in assured accuracy.

I squatted and touched the butt to the ground, leaning into a prone position. I spread my legs wide and reached up with my right hand to cinch the sling down on my left arm. Tucking the toe of the butt into my shoulder, I rotated the weapon until the sight came up in front of my right eye. I slid my cheek back a hair on the stock and the field of view leaped full into the eyepiece. I twisted the adjustment slightly and the reticule came into clear focus, cutting across the small target far in the distance. The sight was on nine power, and my hold was solid and balanced. Taking a breath, I let the air slip out between my lips and held a half breath. My finger pressed evenly against the bottom of the trigger. It discharged and sent the 7.62-millimeter boattail match bullet downrange. I heard the characteristic slap of the round piercing the paper target. I fired three more rounds in that fashion, then rose and walked down the dirt path along the firing lane toward the butts. Retrieving my target, I trotted back to the line and the group of shooters looking my way.

Gunny Mitchell took the target from me and held it up against the skyline. Holding the bull's-eye out for the snipers to see, he asked how many rounds I had fired. When I answered a certain four rounds, the Gunny asked how many hits were on the target. Someone next to Gunny Mitchell remarked that there were three bull's-eyes and a miss. I could feel their eyes on me, knowing I'd fucked up and bucked a shot off the paper. This was not a good thing at our level of shooting expertise. The gunny held the target aloft and stuck a live round through the hole that pierced the exact middle of the target. A space appeared to the side of the bullet hole like a small moon in eclipse. Gunny Mitchell looked at me with another of his smiles. "Culbertson has outdone Robin Hood with his shot. Look close, Marines, there are two bullet holes here—one on top of the other! I thought I'd seen everything by now, Culbertson. This here is nigh on impossible to perform. You weren't just playin' with old Gunny Mitchell, were you, son?"

Clearly, I'd won over Gunny Mitchell with the luckiest group of shots I had ever fired in my life. "No, sir, I wouldn't mess with my rifle instructor, and I would greatly appreciate not having to fire that bolt rifle again today!" Gunny Mitchell looked at our group and just shook his head. "Let's get some chow and be on the range bright and early at 0800 tomorrow. Culbertson just might give us a repeat performance then! If Culbertson got his nerves this calmed down dreamin' William

Tell stories last night, then I guess you boys better hit the rack early."

We all gave that remark a good laugh as we climbed the slope from the rifle range to the mess tent atop our hill.

CHAPTER TWENTY

Korean Marines Invade Happy Valley

At 0800 the next morning, we met Gunny Mitchell and Sergeant DeHass on the rifle range. Benches and folding chairs had been set up in a semicircle around the firing line. Gunny Mitchell began his morning lecture on live firing. He discussed the effects of shooting over ravines or gullies, where the target would appear closer than it actually was due to the void space between the shooter and the enemy. It was another problem to shoot in the dying light of late afternoon because the target looked farther away than it would appear in bright light. Smoke and rain could also distort the width of shapes targeted at a distance. A seasoned professional had to await patiently the right moment to fire, or he would risk compromising his position without inflicting any damage on the enemy. The gunny stressed that those extraordinary situations were just some of the difficulties snipers would face in the field. Each shot was unique, and experience was paid for in blood. Hopefully not ours!

A loud growl of diesel engines interrupted our morning's ritual pep talk. Two olive-drab USMC six-by-six trucks churned up the dust as they ground to a halt next to our billeting area. A shrill command emanated from the lead truck and a dozen stocky troopers in blue fatigues and steel helmets jumped from the truck bed. The soldiers formed two ranks and stood at a braced attention as their leader exited the six-by's cab. The leader marched stiffly toward his men and gave a facing command, pointing their column directly toward us. The troopers snapped their rifles to port arms and, on command, marched up the slight incline to the firing line, then halted before Gunny Sergeant Mitchell. We eyed the compact soldiers and their officer. He was taller than his men and held a leather swagger stick under his left arm. The men in formation did not move, scratch, or appear to breathe. Their eyes were locked to the front and their left hands held the upper handguard of well-worn U.S. World War II–era M-1 rifles. We could scarcely believe our eyes.

With a sharp movement, the officer faced Gunny Mitchell and snapped a salute. He stated—in passable English—that he was the commanding officer of the detachment of Korean Marines from the 2nd Korean Marine Brigade based at Hoi An, south of Da Nang. Gunny Mitchell returned the Korean's salute and identified himself. The Korean captain announced himself as one Captain Lee. He told the gunny he had graduated from college in America at UCLA. He then said that all the Koreans were excited to meet such a famous Marine as Gunny Mitchell. Lee said that the U.S. Marines were still admired by the educated Koreans, and respected as saviors in their country's struggle against the Communists. Captain Lee said that while he was quite young at the time of the Korean War, he nonetheless had read with great interest the feats of bravery performed by the U.S. Marines in combat against overwhelming North Korean and Chinese Communist invaders. Captain Lee said his father had fought with the Marines who were trapped inside the Pusan perimeter.

The eleven Korean Marines were still immobile as Captain Lee waved his swagger stick across the Korean ranks. He told Gunny Mitchell that they were his finest troopers—he added that he didn't actually have any bad ones! Captain Lee said the first enlistment for the ROK (Republic of Korea) Marines was eight long years, and that the Korean Marine Corps was quite small, but it was patterned after the USMC, and its troopers were the finest light infantry in Asia. Captain Lee asked that the U.S. Marines treat his men like fellow soldiers and not become uneasy if his men referred to all U.S. Marines as "Sir." He continued to explain that his men had heard so many tales of U.S. Marine bravery in Korea that the ROKs looked on Americans with awe.

Gunny Mitchell welcomed Captain Lee and said that, for our part, we were honored to have such a disciplined unit at our school. The gunny also mentioned, in a voice loud enough for us to hear, that the combat reports he had seen placed the Korean Marines far above their U.S. counterparts in terms of combat effectiveness measured by kill ratios. Facing our group, which stood in sloppy repose in contrast to the still bracing Koreans, Gunny said the Korean Marines had a kill ratio that approximated thirty-three enemy kills for every ROK lost. Hell, I could scarcely believe that. On Tuscaloosa, the 5th Marines had traded casualties with the Viet Cong one to three by body count, only marginally in our favor. Those ROK Marines had to be supermen. Glancing at their starched fatigues, polished boots, and dead-cold eyes, I knew for sure that those guys weren't there to screw around. None of us knew what they were thinking, but we sure as shit didn't want to piss any of 'em off!

The gunny offered to show the Koreans their quarters, but Captain Lee said his men had come to learn shooting from the U.S. Marines and that they could sleep on the range if there was insufficient tent space. The gunny managed to convince Captain Lee that we had proper billets for his men. Then Captain Lee issued two sharp commands, and his Marines immediately broke formation, stacked their rifles, and, removing their packs, set them down in a neat row in front of their M-1s. Captain Lee spoke harshly again, and the ROKs formed a single rank facing the gunny. This time the Koreans assumed the position of parade rest and did not move or look aside. At that point, we U.S. Marines started pulling our covers straight on our heads and squaring away our utilities. Glancing down, I noticed the toes of our boots were a roughened white leather where the mud in the rice fields had worn off the polish. God, we looked like shit compared to the ROKs, and I started thinking maybe military presence had its place, even in Vietnam.

The gunny continued our discussion, and evidently all the Koreans understood English. We took turns shooting the Remington bolt guns in teams of two. The U.S. Marines worked with the ROKs in snapping them in with our weapons. The ROKs shot well, but they were a long way from being in our league; all the U.S. shooters got their spirits back to a degree. In all, the ROKs were good men and learned fast. They sure as hell didn't talk much, and Captain Lee had his eyes on his troopers every minute. We finished shooting for the day, and the gunny had us gather 'round for a general evaluation of the training. The Koreans were starting to relax a bit, and Captain Lee said his men were honored to shoot with their new American brother Marines. Lee seemed sincere and extremely intelligent. Then all the Koreans rose, faced our group, and bowed. Returning to formation, they marched to the billeting area.

Gunny Mitchell turned to us and in a whisper pointed toward the Korean column cresting the hill. "Now, you have met our Korean friends. They are excellent fighters and loyal comrades. *Never* ask them for anything and *never* criticize them. Those men are killing machines, and one word from their captain will set them off. All those troopers are career Marines. All are black belts in Tae Kwon Do, which is the Korean martial art of kicking your ass! When these guys fuck up and present a dirty rifle, their officers take the weapon and beat their damn brains out with it. The hardships of the Korean War have made these men the toughest bastards on earth. I hope and pray some smart-ass SEAL doesn't lip off to one of those ROKs and get himself killed. Oh, well, you can only teach the navy so much! Get your uniforms straightened out for tomorrow. That's all."

CHAPTER TWENTY-ONE

The SEALs Arrive
at the Range

The following day was midweek through our second phase of Sniper School. The first week had involved technical classroom instruction for the Marine shooters only. We had been joined early in the second week by the Korean Marines, who had proved themselves to be good shots, extremely disciplined and tough. I had befriended a staff sergeant named Kim who had become my shooting partner. Sergeant Kim was also one of the Korean Tae Kwon Do master instructors, who led their Marines in the morning ritual of calisthenics and martial arts. I had sat at the edge of their practice area for two mornings watching them train.

Each morning, Sergeant Kim had the ROKs form two ranks and begin after ceremonial bows and fifteen minutes of stretching exercises. The Korean troopers would perform windmills, bend and reach, and scissors splits with their foreheads touching the knee of their outstretched legs. At the end of their preliminary warm-up, the Koreans partnered up and did split-leg stretches, forcing each other's legs completely to the sides from the seated position. I couldn't understand their excessive focus on limbering up until they began their punching and kicking drills. From wide-legged horseback stances, the ROKs punched straight ahead in perfect rhythm with such blinding speed that I had difficulty telling a right-handed punch from a left. Their kicking was equally mind-boggling. Front snap kicks were followed by round kicks and turning back kicks that would easily knock a standing opponent senseless. The Koreans then mixed their assorted kicks and punches into a kind of rhythmic dance that I had never seen before. All eleven Koreans moved as one, throwing kicks, punches, and yells with such methodical fury and precision that they looked like a maddened centipede slashing and turning on its prey, all the time emitting terrible howls. No wonder every army in Asia was afraid of the stocky warriors from the Land of Morning Calm. The Koreans would be, in a word, terrifying as opponents.

Kim noticed my wide eyes watching their formal practice, called *hyungs*. He completed the final *hyung* and, approaching, told me to stick around and he would teach me some Tae Kwon Do. The bare-chested ROKs faced their teacher *Sabum Nim* and, bowing formally, broke formation and returned to their tents. Sergeant Kim took me behind one side of a tent and began to show me the stretches, punches, and kicks of his martial system. He told me the practice of Tae Kwon Do was over two thousand years old, and although he could only show me a few basic moves, that I would be wise to continue training in the United States upon my return. He said many former ROK instructors taught Tae Kwon Do the world over, and if I could suffer the harsh training of a master that I would become strong, like the Korean tiger. But my arms and legs felt leaden even from the short bout of exercise as Sergeant Kim faced me and bowed solemnly. As I turned toward my tent to ready myself for class, a hint of a smile formed on Sergeant Kim's face. At that moment, I knew some day I would be a Tae Kwon Do master no matter how tough the training was reputed to be in the United States. The Korean Marines had inspired me by their example, always the most effective form of military leadership. If I hadn't been six feet tall, at the moment, I would have considered putting on a blue set of Korean fatigues for good.

A loud churning of trucks coughing up the road to our camp sent another cloud of dust our way. The trucks squealed to a halt and the most motley band of soldiers I had ever seen jumped from the staked cargo beds. Men hit the ground in small groups, looking around like a scout group at the zoo. They were clad in tiger-striped utilities, some wearing fatigue caps and others with bandanas wrapped tightly on their heads. They wore every sort of beard and mustache. Some just looked unshaven! Knives dangled at their hips—tied down at the leg. One man wore a bright red scarf at his throat, and I couldn't tell if he was their leader or was merely affecting the Gen. George Custer look. Most of the troops had rifles slung on their shoulders with the muzzles pointing toward the deck. Some had lit cigarettes thrusting from their teeth, and one chomped on the unlit butt of a fat cigar. Those dudes looked like pirates, not soldiers, and any second, I expected to hear French commands come from the guy who looked like Jean Laffite but was probably their commander.

Bolton walked up beside me and said that the SEALs had landed at last. He thought our Marines had looked like a clusterfuck before those assholes had arrived, but he stood corrected. Looking toward the Koreans' tents, I said that the Koreans were hard-core and wouldn't take any shit from anyone, much less the navy yahoos. Meanwhile, the SEALs grabbed their duffels and headed for a tent atop the hill, one that was segregated from the row of tents in the main billeting area.

We were all on the range by 0830, and split up into shooting teams with one Marine manning the sixty-power Bushnell spotting scope while his partner fired the Remington bolt gun downrange at one thousand meters. After ten slow-fire rounds, the marksmen would switch positions, and the spotters would get to fire the weapon. Sergeant DeHass had taken the newly arrived SEALs to another range on the other side of the hill, but he called Bolton and me to coach the navy shooters, who had missed the first part of the week's training. We brought our spotting scopes along, but left the Remington rifles with our new Korean buddies. Sergeant DeHass spent thirty minutes discussing position, sight alignment, trigger squeeze, and common mistakes like flinching, dragging wood, and improper sighting intervals. The SEALs acted as though they had never received any kind of preliminary marksmanship instruction. We had heard that they trained in scuba, submarines, and rubber boats. The SEALs also had U.S. Army Airborne parachute training at Fort Benning, Georgia. All that was well and good, but now these rogues of the sea were at a Marine Corps school where every sniper candidate was handpicked from among the twenty thousand proven riflemen in the 1st Marine Division. Sergeant DeHass had seen how the Marine snipers could shoot, and it was said that we were the best in the world. It remained to be seen just how proficient these muscular frogmen were at the business end of a bolt rifle.

Sergeant DeHass formed the SEALs into two-man teams that shot together at three-hundred-meter targets placed halfway down the six-hundred-meter range. Buddy Bolton and I hovered over the SEALs and adjusted positions, slings, spot welds, and eye relief. The SEALs began banging away at the targets without taking calming breaths or pausing during trigger squeeze. It was obvious that those dudes didn't know shit about marksmanship. When the targets were fetched, a loose pattern of hits spattered across the paper with little or no grouping. One SEAL swore under his breath that the CAR-15s and Stoner rifles that they had been issued were used primarily on full-automatic fire. He said they never trained to shoot slow-fire rifles at a distance because their area of operations was mangrove swamps and river estuaries with visibility rarely exceeding seventy-five to a hundred meters—usually through reeds, grasses, and thick clumps of bamboo. Sergeant DeHass said that he would give the SEALs a modified basic rifle course like the instruction taught to Marines in boot camp. The SEALs groaned! I bent over my three charges and told them that if they paid attention, we would snap them in at least to the point where they could develop long-range shooting skills without leftover bad habits.

The morning progressed with highly pissed-off SEALs learning to shoot the correct way for the first time in their training. The SEALs were intelligent and learned quickly, and by late afternoon my trainees were squeezing their shots and following through after each round smacked through the paper target. The three shooters with Buddy Bolton also showed improvement, bringing back targets with the bull's-eyes shot through with eight-inch groups at three hundred meters. Sergeant DeHass stopped the firing every half hour or so, and went over the principles of firing again. No doubt the SEALs thought Marine Corps training was boring and redundant, but when one SEAL came back from the butts with his target showing a five-inch group, he was all smiles. Sergeant DeHass held the target up for the rest of the navy shooters to see and told them they were starting to make progress.

Class concluded for the day, and the SEALs shuffled back to their tents with wounded pride. Frankly, I thought they shot well considering how poorly they had been trained. No soldier or sailor can train in all the disciplines the SEALs were supposed to learn and be worth a shit at any of them right out of school. But I was impressed with their efforts, and Bolton and I promised them we would work hard with them the next day.

CHAPTER TWENTY-TWO

The Koreans Give a Demonstration

Buddy Bolton and I met Sergeant DeHass at the six-hundred-meter range promptly the next morning. The SEALs had not arrived, and DeHass spoke to us again about the need to practice the basic fundamentals: position, sight alignment, trigger squeeze, and follow-through redundantly until it sunk in permanently. DeHass explained that we didn't have time to spend on each area of rifle basics to give the SEALs a Marine Corps shooting course like each of us had gone through. He did feel that the navy shooters had the natural ability to continue to train themselves after they left Happy Valley if they abandoned their bad habits and misunderstanding about correct shooting principles. Bolton and I assured DeHass that we were making progress and the SEALs were shaping up quickly.

Eventually the SEALs ambled onto the firing line in twos and threes. I thought that those sailors weren't much for discipline as I reflected on the Koreans moving fluidly through their morning Tae Kwon Do practice. Maybe the SEALs were stressed about their relatively poor performance at the range the past few days. Even so, I didn't care much for excuses. If those navy shooters would listen to Bolton and me, they would fit the pieces together just like the rest of us. For my part, I knew if I could get their positions squared away each and every shot, and get them to line up their sights and squeeze the trigger, then they had a chance to hit the target. Practice makes for confidence, and confidence makes for proficiency, and proficiency creates a marksman's destiny. My goal was to see those wild-looking, brown-water warriors make it home alive. But it was hard to stay alive in the bush if a soldier or Marine couldn't shoot straight. In I Corps, our rifles were our lives, and on Operation Tuscaloosa, the 5th Marines had laid low a seasoned enemy battalion with deadly accurate small-arms fire.

We took our teams of two navy shooters in relays and had them fire five shots slow-fire, then reload, firing five more. Then, after the ten shots were expended, targets were collected and the shot groups analyzed by Sergeant DeHass. A group which drifted to the left and off the target indicated pulling the left hand as the rifle fired. A group that tapered right indicated dragging wood or flinching. Closing the eyes at the moment of discharge usually pushed the shooter's shoulder into the stock, forcing the muzzle down and causing the bullets to strike under the aiming point. Failure to align the sights would send rounds right and left of target.

One of the SEALs grimaced after bucking a shot off target. He said the rifle was so damn sensitive that he didn't think he'd ever learn to shoot well. Sergeant DeHass asked if any of the shooters had ever heard a novice warm up on a violin, then said, "Nothing done well comes easy! If proper marksmanship training was a snap to master, every Viet Cong in the jungle would be a dinger, and a lot of you boys would be dead."

We got back with the program: shoulder the weapon, adjust position, align sights on target, breathe and hold, squeeze trigger, and fire! Over and over until the SEALs began to appreciate that strict discipline and repetition were the strong points of Marine training.

We had the shooters place their rifles in their hard cases, and taking a last glance at the defiant targets downrange, broke for a brief hour, and headed for the mess tent. The chow was cold cuts with potato salad and plenty of iced tea or lemonade. The SEALs glanced disdainfully at our meager luncheon fare. All the Marine snipers had served as riflemen in grunt outfits before their selection to Sniper School. In the field, the Marine diet consisted of C rations almost exclusively. Hot rations had occasionally been choppered out to line companies during prolonged engagements or after fierce battles like Operation Tuscaloosa. We had heard that the navy made every effort to insure that the SEALs were pampered not only with the finest and newest weaponry but also with the better quality long-range rations (dehydrated) and special K rations that field Marines could only dream about. None of us understood the fuss about the SEALs.

We were certain that they were dedicated and probably tough as nails, but Marine infantry units saw more combat action than troops from any of the other branches of the service with the exception of the army's 101st Airborne Division, that had taken on the NVA directly to our north in the A Shau, I Corps' valley of death. The SEALs had an arrogance about them that did not lend itself to patient, controlled shooting. All the Marines felt the SEALs were "profiling" their assumed toughness to impress us. I thought those squids had good potential, but none of us were deceived by their Hollywood bad-boy routine. We had endured fights to the death against crack enemy troops, so there wasn't a hell of a lot these guys could claim to have done that would get our attention.

After finishing chow, we smoked a quick cigarette before returning to the range. Gunny Mitchell and Sergeant DeHass had already berated us for smoking during the first classroom day of the school. The gunny talked about nicotine's deleterious effects on pulse rate and breathing, not to mention that the enemy could smell cigarette smoke in the jungle a half mile distant. Smoking at night could compromise a concealed hide and get a sniper team killed. I looked at the stub of my Camel and sucked a last puff. It was hard as hell to quit when the war constantly tore at our nerves, but fieldstripping the butt, I promised myself to quit "soon," then hustled toward the group of shooters gathered at the firing line.

The gunny announced that the Koreans would demonstrate their version of fire and maneuver. He reminded us that much of the fighting in the Korean War had taken place in cities and built-up areas that afforded the enemy good protective cover. So the Koreans had devised techniques not unlike those used in World War II by the Marines to assault Japanese pillboxes and gun emplacements. The key factors in the Korean assault system were continual suppressive fires aimed at the enemy position while the ROK maneuvering teams leapfrogged ahead, advancing to extremely close range.

The Koreans had set up a Korean War–vintage Browning machine gun with an ammo crate full of belted .30-caliber gun ammo coiled inside. Captain Lee divided his Marines into two fire teams on either side of the gun. Facing the target area three hundred meters downrange, the Koreans assumed prone positions, keeping their silhouettes as low as possible. As Captain Lee blew his whistle, the machine-gun team cranked off bursts of three to five rounds, striking the target. The starboard (right) ROK fire team jumped off and dashed at a forty-five-degree angle toward the enemy position. After covering fifteen meters, they hit the deck and, rolling, took up firing positions and commenced slow fire on the target with their M-1 rifles. The machine gun ceased fire, and the port (left) fire team advanced at a forty-five-degree angle away from the first team. The two teams had now spread into a wide V and poured rifle fire on the target while the gun team waited.

Another shrill whistle broke the air and the left team advanced straight ahead while the right team continued to fire. When the left team went to ground, those ROKs rolled and assumed firing positions and peppered the target area again. Then the machine-gun crew opened fire, and the right team leaped ahead. The two fire teams angled toward the enemy position with one team always maintaining fire on the target as the other team jumped off. The machine gun began firing a wide band across the enemy as both teams went down into low crawls and approached within thirty meters of the objective. Then the machine-gun team fired tracers overhead as the Koreans closed on the target and formed a squad firing line under the raking bullets from their gunners. Instantly, the gun ceased firing, signaling a team of the ROKs to run to the side of the bunker as the other team rose to a knee and threw live grenades into the enemy position. When the grenades detonated, the first team leaped into the enemy bunker with bayonets flashing. Making their kill, the Koreans split on either side of the objective and withdrew as the machine-gun team blasted away to cover the retreat.

Mouths hung open and nobody spoke as the barely winded ROK Marines formed up halfway down the range and marched toward us. Their assault had lasted barely five minutes, and at no time during the Koreans' advance had the deadly suppressive fire slacked off. No enemy would have been able to concentrate fire on either maneuvering fire team, as the Koreans cut across the battlefield in diamond-shaped advances. The SEALs looked pale, and it was a fact that none of us had ever seen a squad assault run that smoothly and deadly. It was no wonder every Communist in Vietnam was scared shitless about going up against the Koreans. Personally, I bowed when the ROKs rejoined our class group. These troopers had really done their homework, and the Korean War had served as the classroom. Glancing down at the machine gunner's ammo box, all we saw was a pile of steel links and one unfired belt left dangling from the Browning's receiver. The Tiger Division and the White Horse were the Koreans' best infantry units. But with the Korean Marine Blue Dragons' just completed demonstration, we all felt that we had witnessed the zenith in infantry tactics. Although, bless their hearts, some old 5th Marines of Guadalcanal and Pelelieu fame might justifiably argue with that.

We finished the day polishing our skills at one thousand meters and had become very comfortable with the bolt rifles, but after shooting the semiautomatic M-14, most of us felt spoiled not needing to open the bolt to extract the spent cartridges. The Remington rifles with their bull barrels and light-gathering Redfield scopes were decidedly more accurate for one shot. That was all it was supposed to take, although in the field, I often took two shots to get on target at ranges that were initially unknown. Getting a second shot off before the sound of the first report reached the target was my speciality. A bit of Kentucky windage had enabled me to make several long kills by adjusting the second shot to the strike of the first bullet. Rifle range shooting was important, but the real thing required the added ingredient of calm nerves and courage. In my own case, I wanted the kill so much that every other thought was forced from my mind as I took up the trigger slack and burned the sight picture into my enemy. Sometimes, I could feel the steel bullet speeding toward the target and slamming through flesh and bone, completing its mission. Gunny Mitchell taught us that, critical to being a good shooter, the sniper must absorb himself in the final act of killing his opponent.

Sniper School ended officially at 1200 hours the next day. We assembled by units and were presented with certificates by Gunnery Sergeant Mitchell and Sergeant DeHass. My assessment of the school was that the instructors were probably the most talented marksmanship teachers in the Corps. The course had covered a lot of material—map reading, camouflage, weather conditions, firing principles, and tactics employed by the sniper. All the shooters, even the SEALs, had learned how to shoot effectively in a variety of conditions. Confidence is an important factor in accurate shooting, and Gunny Mitchell and Sergeant DeHass, by their example and explanation, had motivated us to shoot with greater confidence. Just meeting Gunny Mitchell and Sergeant DeHass was a privilege. These salty old riflemen had become legends in the Corps and anywhere professional marksmen gathered to talk shooting.

Personally, I also would always remember the kindness shown me by Sergeant Kim and his Korean friends. The ROKs had impressed me with one thought. No army ever got to be as salty as the Korean Marines without working their asses off. U.S. Marine Corps training was tough as hell and all the troops bitched about it, but if hard training kept us alive in battle, I was all for it; the thought of ever having to fight a hard-core outfit like the Korean Marines was intimidating.

We said good-bye to our new friends and wished them luck in battle. We six Marines from the 5th Regiment stored our gear and, preparatory to returning to An Hoa, planned a little outing in Da Nang.

CHAPTER TWENTY-THREE

Liberty in
Dogpatch RVN

We flagged down a Marine Corps six-by-six truck and requisitioned a lift to the bustling Da Nang Airbase. After lurching along rutted clay roads from the Happy Valley range, we passed under the shadow of Marble Mountain and turned south to enter the airbase. There we left behind the blowing dust of the countryside and sped along asphalt highways choked with every sort of military traffic imaginable. Convoys of trucks were followed by jeeps crammed full of officers. Huge trucks towing flatbed trailers churned along in puffs of diesel fumes. Artillery pieces jerked along, yoked to the rear of troop-laden canvas-top trucks. As we stared, we compared the chaotic activity with the relative calm of An Hoa.

As we halted at the sentry gate that blocked the entrance to the airbase proper, I said to Bolton, "You know all this gear's not getting to the rifle companies that are fighting this war. Hell, I already counted a dozen new M-60 tanks along this road, and about all they got back at An Hoa are those old M-48s. Our fucking artillery ain't exactly blue-chip stuff either. The gunners at the 11th Marines told me their 105-Mike-Mike howitzers are damn near shot out. Jesus, Bolton, who the hell is getting all this equipment?"

Bolton stared down at his white jungle boots. "Come on, man! You know the Corps does the toughest fighting in I Corps. We go on hard-core operations with shit borrowed from the army and obsolete Korean War and World War II gear fished out of some forgotten warehouse in the States. It don't matter; Charlie knows we're gonna tear his ass up anyhow."

A pair of air force Phantom jets streaked over our heads, making conversation momentarily impossible. Bolton pointed upward and covered his ears against the roar. Planes in a long column lined up in twos, then blasted down the airstrip, slicing into the clear blue sky at steep angles. Once formed up, the flights of four aircraft closed up into "fighting four" formations and, climbing slowly, disappeared into the west. We wondered if some outfit in 2/5 had gotten into the shit with the Viet Cong or the ever-growing numbers of North Vietnamese infiltrating the Arizona. We knew we had to return to An Hoa and assume our duties, but before we left Da Nang, we promised ourselves a visit to the giant PX (post exchange). We had heard a trooper could purchase almost any luxury at the airbase PX that you could buy Stateside. After the Spartan accommodations that we had been accustomed to at An Hoa, the existence of such luxury in Vietnam was hard to believe.

Thanking the airmen truck jockeys, we asked for directions, then headed for a giant corrugated tin building ahead in the huge cluster of warehouses and garages moving the military hardware from the rear to the front lines.

Crowded with corrugated steel Quonset huts, a side street ran to our flank. The Quonsets were made of gleaming new metal with screened front doors opening onto small porches. Portable air-conditioning units protruded from every window, promising that the inhabitants would have relief from the noonday swelter that radiated through our boot soles. Several airmen strutted by us in starched utilities with spit-shined jungle boots and gold-frame aviator sunglasses. They sported wristwatches and sucked on American cigarettes like there would be no end to the fucking supply.

Bolton and I stared at the airmen with loathing rather than envy. I believe that is the crystal clear moment that I first understood what gave us so much pride in being Marines: we were never given the best equipment; our helicopters were older than some of us; our packs and web gear were from Korea and World War II, but the stuff worked just fine; our officers made us wear our jungle boots even when our toes wore through the leather; we wore flak jackets with bullet holes in them, flak jackets taken from the stiff, cold bodies of our fallen brothers. The whole persona of the Corps was Spartan, and that's the way the Marines had always kept things. Hell, we didn't want to look like a bunch of REMF pukes; we were combat Marines. We looked the part, and we talked the part; we *were* a part of the heritage of Marines—the Devil Dogs of Belleau Wood, and all the others—I was a part of the heritage and reveled in the hard and dirty, no-bullshit image that made Marines the acknowledged ass kickers in Vietnam. The SEALs tried all that camofatigued, two-gunned, tied-down-knife profiling, but everyone knew who the combat badasses were. On Operation Tuscaloosa, 2/5 had fought through more Viet Cong bullets on the sandbar in one morning than most SEALs would experience in their six-month tour of duty.

We strolled into the PX, and our eyes lit up at the shelves of radios, TVs, hardware, lawn chairs, and every conceivable luxury. We walked down aisles stuffed with colorful plastic-wrapped packages from the good old USA. The smell of food drifted over the aisles. We followed the scent like bloodhounds to the quarry. The lunch counter was real Formica with round-top soda fountain stools just like home. Behind the counter, a six-foot grill sizzled with the pop of grease where thick hamburger patties crowded for space. Rows of fresh wheat buns stood in formation, awaiting their garnish of ripe tomatoes, lettuce, and pickles. I could scarcely believe my eyes. We had forgotten completely what kind of life we'd left back home. So many cans of C rations had passed down our starving throats on patrol that I don't think one of us recalled how wonderful an American burger smelled. That afternoon we ate hamburgers until we thought we'd puke.

Finally, Bolton looked hard at the mayonnaise swirls and crumbs covering my empty plate and remarked, "Think that'll hold your ass awhile? I feel like I ate twenty foot of anchor chain—grease and all."

We heaved slowly to our feet and turned to walk out of the PX, but before we'd gone three steps, the short-order cook who had fixed our burgers scratched his head and muttered, "Haven't you boys forgotten something?"

We responded in the negative.

The cook pointed out that all the airmen paid for their lunches in the PX. How about us?

We told him we were combat troops from the 1st Marine Division with an afternoon to kill before heading back to An Hoa for duty.

He laughed, "You Marines don't get any money in the boondocks, do you? This one is on Uncle Sam. Have a good afternoon, fellas! We're all proud of what you Marines are doing on the front lines. Take care of yourselves."

That airman was a nice dude. Evidently, some REMFs felt a glimmer of gratitude for the combat troops who usually ate "ham and motherfuckers" washed down with half a canteen of paddy water. We nodded in appreciation and filed out into the sunlight, heartened by our good luck. We walked the manicured lanes of the airbase as if in a surreal dream, one that temporarily shut out the nightmare of the Arizona Territory.

A navy truck squealed to a halt beside our party, and a couple of swabbies peered out the open cab window at us.

"You guys Marines?" an older sailor inquired. He wore green utilities with short sleeves and an insignia with several upturned chevrons and an eagle on top. I figured he must be a chief petty officer. He asked us if we wanted a lift, but we replied that we were lost and only had the afternoon to kill.

The chief scratched his chin and a mischievous grin spread over his face. "You boys been to Dogpatch yet?" The driver leaned over into the window frame and interjected, "If you only got a few hours, then Dogpatch is the place to get it taken care of. Jump aboard, men, and the USS *Goodtimes* here will take you there."

Bolton and I climbed aboard and just stared out the window wondering what the hell Dogpatch was and why the chief thought everything was so damn funny. Fifteen minutes later the truck bounded along the dirt road outside the base, through nondescript wooden huts and old French buildings. Vietnamese of every description thronged the street. Women carried goods bound in ropes on the end of poles just like back at An Hoa. Bicycles and pedicabs twisted and turned, fighting for clearance on the congested road. Finally, the truck halted at a club that had a hand-painted sign out front, SILVER STAR CLUB. All of us piled out of the truck and filed inside. The club was open, with small round tables bordering a polished wood dance floor. The bar was built of bamboo and had tall chairs pushed up against the front. Mirrors behind the bar were draped in gaudy crepe, and pictures had been taped and nailed around the walls. A crack angled down the mirror and traced through three holes that looked bullet-size.

The music box in the corner of the bar was belting out current American rock-and-roll tunes. A thin haze of smoke filtered through the slowly revolving blades of a pair of ancient ceiling fans. The light was gloomy inside the club and emanated from gaily colored bulbs hung from the ceiling around the dance floor. The chief said that he and his mate would be back to pick us up after they got off duty. He told us to have a good time and that the bar was a safe place to drink.

"Them girls are the cleanest in Dogpatch. Use protection and don't leave alone. I told 'em we'd be back. They won't cheat you 'cause I'm a regular here. We'll catch you in a few hours. Have fun, boys!"

At that signaled departure, the girls lounging around smoking at the other tables drifted over to our group as we huddled over cold Bier 33 and Tiger beers, deciding strategy.

"Hello, Marines, we so happy you come to Silver Star Club. Where you from? You not from Da Nang? How you come here?"

We told the girls we were from An Hoa down Highway 1. They seemed not to know where An Hoa was located but we didn't give a shit, anyway. Our visit to the bar was not about geography.

The girls continued to talk, snuggling down in chairs next to us. They draped lovely arms across our shoulders and smiled into our hard faces. "You Marines want to have good time here? We got nice girls. They love you long time, no shit! You got twenty dollar American? She give you everything—you like around-the-world? Me young girl! Only sixteen year old and got tight pussy. You Marines so handsome!"

Another round of beer arrived in long-neck bottles of brown glass. Flecks of ice ran cold down the sides as we tilted the Tiger beers in a toast to the Marine Corps, and what had that one girl said? Yeah, to the Marine Corps and tight, sixteen-year-old pussy. Hoorah! Our war cries were driven by inebriation, of course. Some of the girls were sitting in our laps hugging us and tossing back their black-locked heads, gaily laughing at our every stupid joke. We called for more beer, or as one Marine called it, Tiger Piss. The stack of empty bottles was growing, and one by one, we grabbed our girls by the wrist and led them to the small private bedrooms that bordered the bar, hidden behind the thatch-covered walls.

I stared at the young Vietnamese girl who sat close to me, attentive to my every move. She tilted back her head and the soft glow of the bar lights caressed her cheek. Her skin was clean and white as ivory. Her long black hair glistened like oiled ebony as it cascaded along her graceful neck. I wanted to shut out the war, the mud, the bullets. Reaching over the table, I clutched her small hand and led her from the table, through the now boisterous dance floor, toward the intimacy of the back rooms.

Inside a thatched cubicle, I lay intoxicated by beauty and drink as she undressed me, kneeled on the edge of the bed, unbuttoned her silk blouse, and let it fall to the floor.

"You like, Marine?" What the hell had I been thinking to get myself into a situation like Nam? When I was out in the field with Hotel Company, girls hardly entered my thoughts. Maybe that was because I was trying desperately not to get killed. The cooks at An Hoa could have put saltpeter in our chow! I tried to tell myself to forget that shit. It didn't matter right now. I was drunk and having all kinds of crazy thoughts. I pictured all the bottles of Tiger beer stacked on the table.

The ceiling spun in the hidden room where I was alone with the beautiful Vietnamese girl. She put her palms on my shoulders and pressed her silken body gently on top of mine, and rocked me to sleep.

I awoke back at the table. The girl was wiping the sweat off my forehead and gently brushing her cheek against mine. Strong arms reached under my shoulders and lifted me through the blur of gaily sparkling lights out into the cool night air. The navy truck chugged back down the road into the base. The soft night breeze was invigorating as I fought off the memory of cigarette smoke and Tiger beer from the raucous atmosphere of the Silver Star Club.

CHAPTER TWENTY-FOUR

Back to the War

Feeling like I'd been run over by a tank, I awoke in our tent at Happy Valley. I got to my feet unsteadily, wove my way to the washbasin, and poured the cool water over my head and down my aching limbs. Shuddering, I struggled into my jungle utilities and boots and staggered into the mess tent. After a bowl of Cheerios and powdered milk, I really felt wonderful, so I ran outside the tent to prove I could still throw up. I could. In fact I was very good at it. Hangovers aren't pleasant for anyone, but in the previous four months, I hadn't drunk more than a few beers a month at An Hoa's clubs. I was one sick puppy!

Bolton came into our tent and said we were manifested out of Da Nang to An Hoa on a 1000 hours mail run. We really had to move our butts to get to the airstrip in time to catch the hop. Bolton and I feverishly crammed our gear into our seabags. We had collected sheaves of notes on map reading, camouflage, and firing principles during the lectures at school, and we stuffed our notebooks into our duffels along with our dirty clothes.

Outside, we hailed a truckload of grunts from regiments up north who were also headed to the airstrip. We said hasty and sincere good-byes to our fellow snipers.

But regardless of the inspirational speeches we'd heard during the two weeks of Sniper School, we knew that the Viet Cong and NVA were not exactly without sniper resources of their own. We all knew the VC and the NVA fielded deadly sniper teams. During Operation Tuscaloosa, four Marines had been killed by VC Main Force snipers armed with antiquated but reliable Moishin Nagant scoped rifles in 7.62 x 54-millimeter Russian caliber. Each of the Marine KIAs had a single bullet wound to the head.

The truck bumped along and finally lurched into the air-base transient-duty-station parking lot. We jumped off the six-by-six truck and formed up, awaiting our flight manifest orders. At 1200 hours, the air force C-130 landed and taxied to the loading ramp. Huge mail bags of orange nylon were hoisted aboard the plane. Two U.S. Navy corpsmen preceded us and strode into the cargo hold for the short hop to An Hoa, then we followed, and the Hercules taxied past a waiting flight of F-4 Phantoms with engines whining, poised to take off. I marveled at the rakish lines of the F-4s and flashed back to a morning on the sandbar when the Phantoms attacked the VC trench line. They had flown in a long column formation and one by one peeled off, diving low over the enemy positions and dropping canisters of napalm that smothered the jungle in balls of fire. Finally, our plane turned, and the engines throttled up to a scream as it flung itself down the runway and lifted smoothly into the sky.

The jumble of buildings, the teeming men and equipment of Da Nang's bustling port facilities came briefly into view, only to be replaced by the soft variants of green as we sped southwest to catch up to the real shooting war outside the bunkers of the little combat base at An Hoa. I had mixed feelings about going back. Da Nang was exciting, and my brief moment of pleasure at the Silver Star reminded me that there was a life out there where people didn't spend every day trying to kill Charlie or the NVA. The Vietnamese in Da Nang had presented a stark contrast to the numbing poverty of the peasantry in the Arizona Territory, where the people's greatest luxury was to get to live another day. Da Nang was a whirlwind of motor scooters, cars, and young women dressed in silk *Ao Dai*s and calmly strolling the streets while spinning gay parasols above their pretty heads. I understood that I had to get the Da Nang pipe dream under control. Soon the Hercules was banking into the final approach.

After touchdown, the hootches and control tower spun into view. The cargo ramp lowered, and a blast of humid air clung to our bodies as we lugged our gear along the dirt road leading back home to Hotel Company. It seemed as if we had never left An Hoa and that Da Nang was nothing but a dream. Bolton and I checked our gear and reported to the company clerk that we had returned from Sniper School and wouldn't mind getting some chow. We were informed that Hotel was manning perimeter lines around the airstrip and that our company commander would like a word with us after lunch.

The food at battalion mess at An Hoa was actually a hell of an improvement over the dried cereals and C rations at Sniper School. The fresh milk tasted great, and Bolton and I stuffed ourselves. A trooper in 2/5 learned quickly that he might just find himself in the field for a month "tomorrow," so if he had hot chow today, he damn well better take advantage of it. That may have been the first time in my life that I truly understood what it meant to live just for the day and be glad as hell I was alive. Tomorrow would speak for itself.

Back at our hootches, we got word that Lieutenant Pindel said the company would be going out in the morning, and I would be head scout for 3rd Platoon. Buddy Bolton would be assigned temporarily to a platoon in Foxtrot and provide scout-sniper services at their discretion. Hotel would go to Phu Loc 6 and relieve the platoon manning the firebase. Bolton would be the first of us to get back into action and test out his newly developed sniper skills against the Viet Cong. Lieutenant Pindel said that Bolton and I could be requisitioned by any company in the battalion to provide a sniper team for an operation. Personally, I felt that Lieutenant Pindel intended to keep us on a short leash. Pindel was smart and had been an NCO in the grunts at Camp Lejeune before Vietnam. He was not about to volunteer his best shooters if he could keep them to himself. I didn't care which unit I patrolled with as long as I got a chance to blow Charlie's ass away. I didn't know exactly why everybody else had come to Vietnam, but I had requested transfer orders to WestPac (Western Pacific) via my congressman. I didn't join the Marines to spit shine boots; like Woody, Luther, Lafley, and Burns, I had joined up to kill the Commies any way I could. After four months of killing the bastards, I knew there were lots of 'em I had overlooked.

Buddy Bolton and I returned to our hootches and attempted to square away the mess of gear and uniforms that we had used at school. When we were done sorting and sifting our stuff, we took our match rifles outside for a thorough cleaning.

CHAPTER TWENTY-FIVE

Incident at Phu Loc 6

Morning came without a trace of the cool breezes that swept An Hoa during the short winter season. Actually, Vietnam had a monsoon or rainy season during the last months of the year that continued through February. March was a transitional period that led directly into the short spring/summer hot season. It was early April 1967, and each new day ushered in a longer period of unrelenting heat that grew more pronounced into the late afternoon. It was also the growing season, and the fallow, rain-drenched rice fields were clogged with stooped-over peasants thrusting sheaves of young rice plants into the rich black soil. The colors of the peasants' smocks moved in a swirl of activity as the conical reed hats on their heads bobbed up and down.

Third Platoon grabbed its gear and formed up for a brief weapons check before leaving the company area. The platoon sergeant gave marching orders, and the point fire team hustled forward to guide the forty Marines down the runway to the wire. The clomp of combat boots vibrated off the road as the men tugged at their packs and cartridge belts to ease the strain of the march. Past the sentries on lines, the platoon spread out into its standard

The author as a lance corporal at An Hoa after Operation Union II, 1967.

(Left) Sgt. Manuel Ybarra, Hotel Company squad leader, on the back side of Nong Son Mountain. Utility pants and boots were typical jungle attire. The boots started life black but under Vietnam's conditions quickly were worn to light brown on the toes and sides. (Right) Sgt. Manuel Ybarra at An Hoa after being wounded, 1967.

L.Cpl. Stephen Gedzyk, 3rd Platoon machine gunner, at An Hoa, 1967.

Luther Hamilton (left) and Silver Star winner Sgt. Guy McDonald, 1967.

USMC scout-sniper team in I Corps, 1967, observes the far side of a large rice paddy. The sniper is using a Remington M-700 rifle with a Redfield 3 X 9 scope.

Kirby, Ybarra, McDonald, and Hamilton at Phu Loc 6 firebase, 1967.

M.Sgt. Vic Ditchkoff as a drill instructor at Parris Island, South Carolina.

Recon Mountain as seen from Nong Son Mountain. Antenna Valley is behind Recon Mountain.

Third Platoon, Hotel Company, on bunkers atop Nong Son Mountain after Operation Tuscaloosa, 1967.

Luther Hamilton (left) and Gerald Burns atop Nong Son Mountain. To the right is the trench line from which Hotel Company would fight off an assault by the NVA.

John Lafley (left) and John Culbertson on Nong Son firebase, summer 1967.

Hotel Company fires a 106mm recoilless rifle off Nong Son Mountain into the Que Son Valley, 1967.

Marine CH-46 helicopter taking off at Da Nang, 1967.

Cpl. John Culbertson receives his third Purple Heart from Col. Nat M. Pace, CO, Marine Barracks, Subic Bay, Philippines, 1967.

marching interval, with ten meters between troopers. The whips of the two radiomen with Lieutenant Pindel and Sergeant Wadley stabbed the air in the middle of the formation. Once the main road was reached, the point scouts stepped up the pace, and the groans and bitching that always accompanied a new patrol passed up and down the column.

Two hours later, Phu Loc 6 came into view as the bright sun glinted off the weapons thrusting out from the sandbagged perimeter. Hotel entered the wire from the main road and relieved the platoon from Echo Company that had already saddled up in anticipation of their return to the mess hall at An Hoa. The Echo troops were giving our Marines a line of bullshit about giant rats that had gnawed through the bags into the machine-gun bunker. They said their gun team had opened fire on the rats, but the bullets had bounced off the beasts. They had teeth like punji stakes and claws like tigers. The Echo dudes laughed and pointed at us with derision.

"Now, you boys get some rest up here and remember, if them rats get hungry, don't throw no ham and motherfuckers at 'em. It just pisses 'em off worse than before. Hell, them rats are so big and mean that Corporal Johnson found two of 'em sharin' a grenade for dinner. Have fun in this shithole, boys! See ya later on."

The Echo platoon knew they had pissed us off, and their taunts continued all the way down the main road toward An Hoa. We just sucked it up! A month at Phu Loc 6 would pass quickly. Most of our time would be spent patrolling along the river anyway. Phu Loc 6 wasn't such bad duty. Looking around at the piles of empty C rations and spent brass, we knew it really wasn't that bad. It was fucking awful!

Third Herd divided the fighting holes up by squads. Each of the three rifle squads took a group of dugouts facing off the firebase, ringing the hill around the perimeter just inside the wire and protective minefield. We checked the wire for breaches and, as usual, hung a couple more C-ration cans on the coils of concertina to jingle if Charlie tried to infiltrate. Automatic weapons were emplaced and aiming stakes were thrust into the deck in front of the guns to define fields of fire, while the gunners traversed their weapons, sighting them in. Grenades and flares were stacked on the firing ledges of the bunkers. Supporting three or four layers of sandbags, steel angle iron ran over the heads of Marines to give some protection from a mortar attack. The riflemen hunkered into their sections of the wide holes and sighted their weapons down on the main road and the mass of jungle foliage that had not been cleared from the bald knob of the firebase. Standard two-hundred-meter battle dope would send a bullet into any attacking troops without enough drop to require changing elevation. Extra magazines of ball and tracer ammunition were placed in olive-drab pouches along the firing ledges of the parapets. Some squad leaders and the platoon sergeant had binoculars and scanned the approaches to the hill carefully, looking for disturbed soil that could lead to a tunnel or bunker. M-79 grenadiers stacked 40-Mike-Mike grenades in their positions and divided up and recounted their high explosive (HE) and white phosphorous (WP) rounds.

Up the hill, the thick tubes of the 4.2-inch mortar section raked their muzzles into the sky over the Thu Bon

River's estuaries a couple of miles to the west. Third Platoon also had its 60-Mike-Mike mortars set up in a sandbagged revetment to fire over the lines of 1st Squad to our east, opposite the 4.2-inch battery. Lieutenant Pindel had the platoon command post set up in the thickly sandbagged bunker. From the grunts' bunkers on the perimeter, it looked like a giant beetle. Phu Loc 6 had been probed by the enemy on many occasions, always at night, but the firebase had never been overrun. Except maybe by the giant killer rats that Echo Company warned us about!

The sun was setting in a rich red glow, casting shadows over the Song Thu Bon and the Arizona, where Charlie was waiting for our patrols to come and play "find the booby trap." Small fires cast blue flames from crimped cans holding heat tablets under homemade recipes for C-ration delicacies like beans and franks and the ever-popular jelly and ham loaf. Luther Hamilton carried bottles of Trappey's Cajun Hotsauce with him everywhere. It wasn't a bad idea, and Luther could really amaze us with his variations, like ham and motherfuckers with a hint of cheese sauce and onion.

I thought about the Viet Cong in their tunnels full of spiders and snakes. The VC ate rice with vegetables and rice without vegetables, depending on the availability of fresh vegetables. The Marines really had it made in comparison to the Communists. Then again, the gooks probably didn't know any better.

I thought of the World War I song, "How Do You Keep Them Down on the Farm After They've Seen Paree?" After Da Nang, I needed to get reacclimated to the harsh realities of combat and field living. If you want to kill Charlie, the old-time veteran Marines used to say, you got to live like Charlie and think like Charlie. Charlie is a tough little soldier. Never underestimate the enemy!

Third Platoon stood two-hour watches with four Marines from each fire team splitting up the duty. This was easy unless you caught the two-to-four watch, which broke up your sleep. We watched our front, and periodically the big guns at An Hoa would shoot harassment and interdiction (H & I) fire missions into the Arizona. The muzzle blasts of the big 155-millimeter howitzers and the 8-inch self-propelled guns would flash blinding tongues of fire into the black expanse of sky over An Hoa. Then, as quickly as the guns had flared, they grew silent, until the next mission was shot.

I don't know how much money was spent on those nighttime fire missions, but I was sure glad it wasn't coming out of my pocket! By mid 1967, the Vietnam War was costing the American taxpayer over twenty-one million dollars a day. A bullet from my match grade M-14 sniper rifle cost less than twenty-five cents. It seemed only fair that the Marine snipers should do their part in cutting costs per Viet Cong killed. In Vietnam, the Marine Corps sniper program averaged around one and a half bullets for each Communist killed—or about thirty-seven and a half cents per dink killed, which is a real bargain when you consider that artillery shells cost upward of two hundred dollars each, and bombs, even the inexpensive "dumb" bombs, can cost over a thousand dollars. Maybe that was the way Congress tabulated the effectiveness of the combat effort. Personally, I felt the Marine Corps could attack Hanoi from the sea and link up with the army's 101st Airborne Division attacking from inland and crush the Communist forces in about a month or less. Of course, that would have cost the munitions and military equipment industry in America billions of dollars in lost profits. We all figured that the Marines could stomp the shit out of Charlie whenever we got orders to march, but the fact was that chasing Charlie all over the Arizona would never kill all of them. The war would go on while American corporations grew richer than Midas and our buddies got shot down or blown up keeping the doormat out and the porch light on.

Sleeping in the earthen foxholes on the perimeter of Phu Loc 6 was never comfortable. The cold air and the sounds of the nighttime jungle kept every Marine tossing fitfully, usually with one eye open. We rose from our holes the next morning, fully dressed, and stood stretching out the kinks and cramps. Our uniforms looked like jungle foliage, and unlike the painted profilers from the reconnaissance outfits that passed through our firebase, we required no face paint or camouflage to blend into our surroundings. It is a fact that we also smelled like the jungle—or the latrine—but field Marines got used to that pleasure and adjusted accordingly. Mostly by staying upwind of their squadmates if at all possible.

After a breakfast of C-ration eggs with crackers and a canteen cup of steaming joe, we huddled in our squads to receive orders from the squad leaders. The first day, 1st Squad would patrol the villages along the river to the northwest until sundown, then return to the firebase. The other two rifle squads would stand perimeter watch in our bunkers and be prepared to provide a ready reaction force to go to the assistance of the patrolling element if it got into the shit. I went to the ammo bunker and replenished my load of rifle ammunition and grenades. I also stuck three boxes of tracers into my pack. I would later load the tracers every other round into two specially marked magazines that I kept handy to mark targets for tanks or machine guns. I always kept my K-bar knife razor-sharp at my side, and two extra C-ration meals in my haversack in case we moved off the hill in a hurry.

By lunchtime, the sun glared mercilessly on our tiny hilltop. All the grunts refilled their canteens at the hanging canvas bladders next to the command bunker. I strolled over by the hull of an M-48 tank that was dug into a revetment in the lines facing the eastern approaches to our fortifications. The 90-millimeter main cannon pointed menacingly over the double apron of the barbed wire, and the tankers sat around the machine in folding aluminum chairs. I stopped and talked to the crew chief about the cannon's effectiveness with beehive rounds in the event Phu Loc 6 were ever attacked en masse. Suddenly, the tanker sergeant cupped his hands over his brow and stared hard off the hill.

"Culbertson, look into that grove of trees about five hundred meters straightaway and tell me what you see." The sergeant's arm pointed to a copse of small trees that stretched out of a small ravine off the flank of our hill.

I gazed through the leafy branches of the trees along the sandy, rock-strewn ground that rose up from the tributary of the Thu Bon River flowing south off Phu Loc 6 under Liberty Bridge. Small, dark shapes were walking in a column perpendicular to our position. I counted three figures strung out with a ten-meter interval between them. I couldn't see any weapons, but the men in the file moved adroitly and picked their way through the clump of trees.

As the first man broke out of the cover into the open, the tank commander came up to our position with his binoculars focused on the procession below. He gave an order, and the ninety-millimeter cannon traversed and followed the movement of the three-man squad moving into line about six hundred meters directly to our eastern flank. The crew chief spoke to the lieutenant who commanded the M-48, and the tank officer looked in my direction.

"Sergeant Williams says you just finished Sniper School up at 1st Division in Da Nang. Son, those men down there are not Americans. They are Viet Cong. Where is your rifle?"

I looked at the lieutenant and stuttered that I always kept my weapon with me. I retrieved the M-14 quickly from its resting place against the rear of the tank's battle hull. Snapping a magazine of ball and tracers into my rifle, I pulled back the operating handle and chambered a live round.

Taking my instructions from the tanker's commander, I asked, "What does the lieutenant want me to do now, sir!"

The lieutenant looked at me like I had gone nuts or something. "Since you can't piss that far, I want you to shoulder that rifle and kill those three assholes strutting along like they own this fucking valley."

Immediately, I responded by climbing aboard the M-48 and taking up a tight crossed leg sitting position on the top of the tank's steel fender. I looped my sling into a hasty rig and ran my free arm through the webbing, twisting the loop tightly across my wrist. The M-14's muzzle fell naturally onto the lead dink, and I tucked my cheek into a good spot weld along the stock and gazed into the reticule. I had three-hundred-meter target dope on the sights from shooting at the school range. I judged the target distance at a good six hundred meters moving away from me at a forty-five-degree angle. The men in the file were clearly Vietnamese and wearing uniforms, but looked unarmed.

I requested permission to fire from the tank commander. "Sir, I have the formation targeted. The Vietnamese are uniformed but appear without weapons. Do I have permission to fire, sir?"

The lieutenant was evidently used to a looser brand of discipline in 1st Tanks than existed in the line companies. He yelled at me, "Dammit, Marine, I already said to kill those VC malingerers. Now, are you going to shoot them, or do I have to waste ammo and cut loose with this blasted ninety?"

Aiming a foot in front of the lead VC, I held off a yard high over his head, figuring for the bullet drop at six hundred meters. The trigger took up evenly and the rifle discharged, sending a flaming tracer off the hill in a shallow arc. The 168-grain match boattail broke just under the VC's chin and passed twenty meters past the target, making a noticeable puff of sand and rocks where it impacted. I held tighter to his head and added just a titch of elevation and broke the second shot. The boattail broke along the same path but held a higher trajectory and caught the lead gook across his forehead. The Viet Cong spun off his feet and collapsed in a tangle in the sandy soil on his side. His buddies looked around as I fired my third round at the middle soldier in the file. The bullet dropped below the first two shots and took the Charlie in the thigh. I had rushed my second and third shots, trying to get them off before the Viet Cong could figure out where the firing had come from. The second man clutched his leg and writhed in the sand, while the third VC hit the deck on his belly and lay dog. I had taken up the trigger slack and held a tight bead on the wounded man's head. I hated to see him continue to thrash around in such obvious discomfort.

At that moment a band of tracers flung themselves over our position. Several more men had moved up behind the prostrate Charlies and were madly waving their arms in our direction. I peered through my rifle scope into the faces of angry Marines. Holy shit, what had I done now! The radio in the tank came to life, and an angry voice screamed, "Cease-fire, cease-fire! Marine patrol from Golf Company has taken enemy prisoners. Marine shooters on Phu Loc 6, cease-fire immediately. We are bringing captured hostiles into your position. This is Golf Bulldog Leader. Over."

My guts turned over and my mouth was dryer than the Arizona in August. Could a court-martial be out of the question? As worry lines flooded across my forehead, the tank officer put a huge hand on my shoulder. "Son, you are a hell of a shot! Those boys down the hill from Golf Company will get over this bullshit sooner or later. They ought to be glad I didn't cut loose with our 90-Mike-Mike cannon. Hell, they still got one and a half live gooks to interrogate back at An Hoa."

The tanker had my deepest thanks for coming to my rescue. If I had shot the dinks without permission from a staff NCO or an officer, the commander of the Golf Company patrol would have had me for dinner. As it stood now, I was off the hook because I had obeyed a lawful order. Shit, accidents like that happened all the time in Vietnam. At least my bullets had torn into Viet Cong prisoners and not live Marines. That would have been hell to pay for! The more I thought about the incident, the more certain I was that Gunnery Sergeant Mitchell would have been proud of two hits out of three at over six hundred meters shooting off a hill in a crosswind. Too bad about the Viet Cong, especially if they had been *Chieu Hoi*s and surrendered willingly to the boys from Golf Company.

I cleared my weapon and jumped down from the tank. I thanked the tankers for covering my ass, and they suggested that I make myself scarce. The tank commander would handle the Golf patrol leader personally. The tankers were cool as cucumbers and didn't seem unnerved at all by the event. Hell, I guess it didn't amount to much when the tankers had no doubt wiped out entire friendly villages with short rounds and missiles.

Back at my bunker, I stowed my rifle and joined a card game with Lafley and Burns. They looked sleepy in the afternoon heat, and asked me what the firing up the hill was about. I said some maniacal tankers had opened fire on a Marine patrol that had prisoners stuck out on the point. Burns and Lafley yawned. It was no big deal to them, and the last thing anyone said about it was Burns's standard question.

"Did they kill any of the little bastards, Culbertson?"

I said two of the three prisoners were shot, but I didn't know if they were dead or alive. Burns volunteered that he really didn't give a shit, and we got our attention back on our cards.

CHAPTER TWENTY-SIX

A Sniper's Death
Along the River

The next day, thanks to the lieutenant from 1st Tanks, the huff over shooting the VC prisoners had blown over. I tried my best to go about my business as if nothing had happened. Third Herd still stood watch over the flatlands and paddies stretching to the river in the west. The troops cleaned and oiled their weapons and bitched about being confined to Phu Loc 6 for a month. Once a young Marine had been in the field for a spell, the excitement of engaging Charlie put an edge of anticipation on his every activity. Even dull and boring jobs became bearable because in the back of every trooper's mind, he was only a heartbeat away from a firefight. Within seconds, a long, hot afternoon could flash into chaotic action. Once the bullets had stopped flying and the bombs exploding, the troops fell into a more passive state of mind. But the mental lull was more like an anticlimax, one where men sought release from the paralyzing fear that comes from facing death too closely or too often. The adrenaline rush that forces the body's senses into a high level of alertness eventually becomes a drug that denatures the mundane and stimulates the weary.

Combat addiction had become the motivator for many

troopers in Hotel Company. When orders came to send a patrol into the Arizona, a surge of energy would course through Lafley, Hamilton, Burns, and the rest of the veterans who salivated like starving men over the promise of a meal. I had caught the addiction as well, and always had my gear stacked in an easily accessible pile, ready to suit up for action.

Harold Wadley, the new platoon sergeant, came running down to our fighting holes just as we finished lunch. We had just lit up the smoking lamp and were busy trotting out our best bullshit stories when the Korean War veteran yelled for Hamilton's squad to saddle up. The platoon sergeant was in full combat gear and carried a Remington pump shotgun. Lance Corporals Gedzyk and Jessmore brought their M-60 machine guns and were wound tight with gun belts. Sergeant Wadley instructed us to grab two hand grenades each. Loaded down with four M-72 LAW (light antitank weapon) rockets, a team of two Marines stood casually behind Sergeant Wadley. Blocker carried a PRC-25 radio and followed the platoon sergeant like his shadow.

Sergeant Wadley gave us a brief sitrep: a Marine sniper team had been dug into a hide before first light. A sniper from our unit had shot several VC coming out from a tree line across a large paddy, but that target had turned out to be the point element for a rifle company of at least one hundred Viet Cong. The sniper team had a Marine fire team with them for security, but the gooks split their force and surrounded the Marines in a double-pronged envelopment and caught them in a cross fire. The last radio message had just come in from the team in the paddies south of the river near Le Nam 3.

A pair of H-34 choppers set down on the top of Phu

Loc 6. Sergeant Wadley placed the first fire team in the chopper with the machine-gun team. The second chopper accommodated the second fire team, Sergeant Wadley, his radioman Blocker, and the two LAW men. The choppers spiraled aloft, slicing down off the hill and gaining speed toward the river valley where Le Nam floated in a sea of rice fields. The paddies flashed under the fuselage of the Sikorsky. The rectangles of rice shoots were almost flooded that time of year and promised heavy going when we disembarked to approach Le Nam 3 on foot. The choppers skidded into a hasty, unprotected landing zone, and we jumped out the cargo door into the wet fields.

Forming up on Sergeant Wadley, Lafley and I took the point, followed by Burns, Woodruff, Gedzyk, Jessmore, then Sergeant Wadley, Blocker, and Hamilton. The LAW rocket men and the second fire team followed at ten-meter intervals as the reinforced squad found sure footing on a dike path and jogged ahead to the river. In ten minutes, we heard the rush of the river and struck out to the west along the banks. We passed burnt-out villages that we had torched on earlier patrols, destroying the rice supplies hidden to provision the enemy. The destruction that our platoon had wrought had not been repaired, and the small clusters of huts stood deserted.

Burns muttered behind me, "God, that was a sight when we blew that village into the river. Serves the bastards right, too! Culbertson, I brought four blocks of C-4 in my pack. Maybe we'll get another shot at old Charlie's ass up ahead. I'd have made a damn fine engineer, myself!" Burns chuckled to himself. The old saying, "Call the Marines when it must be destroyed overnight!" was probably a tribute to Burns's hostile and devious mind.

When it came to getting even with Charlie, Burns was in a class by himself.

Lafley turned to our flank and entered a thick grove of trees with underlying vines and brush. After fighting through that mess, we saw the light green of the open paddies filtering through the leaves. A few nearby rifle shots echoed across the rice valley. Sergeant Wadley drew us together and gave us the approach march orders before we entered the paddy. "Lafley and Culbertson will file along this tree line until the sniper position comes into view. Wait there while we set the gun team and rockets into position to provide supporting fire. Lafley, take your team in as close as you can, staying in cover behind the trees. The second fire team will be seventy-five meters behind, ready to put down suppressive fire. When the gun team opens fire, you and Culbertson head for the snipers' hole and radio back what you find. Listen closely for the M-60 to open up before you rush into the open paddy."

This deal made sense to me, and it didn't bother Lafley or me to creep into the paddy as long as the machine-gun team and rockets backed our play. Sergeant Wadley grabbed the sleeve of Lafley's jungle shirt. "One more thing. If the position is secure, throw a red smoke grenade, and I'll bring in the choppers. Sit in the hole a minute and be damn sure that Charlie has 'died' and ain't waitin' in ambush. Go now, be careful!"

Lafley led me through the tree line, skirting the paddy while the second fire team followed close behind us. Woodruff carried his automatic M-14 with the bipod fixed and a twenty-round magazine of tracers to mark positions for the rocket crew. Gedzyk set up the M-60 on its bipod and, opening the top-loading receiver cover, fed a long belt into the gun. Snapping the stock into his shoulder, Gedzyk sighted in on the far edge of the tree line where it melted into the paddy to our front. The rocket men extended the tubes on two of their weapons and gazed through the clear plastic sight that flipped up into view.

Lafley, Woody, Burns, and I had reached the end of the tree line where the edge of the brush faded around to our left toward Sergeant Wadley's position with the gun team. We checked our weapons, then looked at Woody, who would put out suppressive fire with the automatic rifle (full auto M-14) if we got ambushed. Lafley waved across the two hundred meters that separated our team from the command group. The second fire team had tucked itself into position seventy-five meters to our rear, where it could fire across the paddies into the surrounding tree lines.

At that moment, Gedzyk's machine gun coughed into action and spit short bursts across the paddy into the sections of tree line that would likely oppose us. The tracers arced gracefully into the jungle and made a chopping sound as the bullets tore chunks of trees, plants, and vines into so much tossed salad. Lafley yelled "Go!" and the four of us jumped off and, as fast as the mud would allow, ran along the sparse vegetation into the last clump of jungle before the paddy opened for five hundred meters.

The sniper position was discovered by Burns, who waved and jumped into a tangle of jungle vines and plants on the forward edge of the tree line. Lafley and I turned to our left and slid into the position. Gary Woodruff lunged into a prone position to the side of the bunker and threw his weapon down on its bipod, facing any enemy threat that might come from the far tree line.

Knocking back the vines and grasses, we tried to uncover

the Marines who had taken up positions there in the early morning hours just before first light. Burns came across the radio. Bullet holes pocked the metal frame of the PRC-25. It was still dimly lit inside the bunker, and we had to feel rather than see the men who lay inside. Burns grabbed the flak jacket of one of the riflemen, and lifting him into the light saw the bullet wound through his temple. As we moved the body into the light, the heavy reports of a long rifle echoed across the paddy. A couple of rounds slashed through the cover over our heads, but the shots were high.

We could hear Gedzyk's machine gun stuttering in the distance, then Woody's M-14 started to lay down fire. Woodruff cranked off bursts of three rounds into the tree line across the paddy. The VC had left a sniper team facing the Marine bunker in case help should arrive and present a new target. Woodruff's automatic rifle fire tailed into the VC position in a fiery band of tracers. The LAW men waiting with Sergeant Wadley watched Woodruff's bullets impact and sighted their weapons accordingly. The VC came up for another shot and fired another pair of bullets close by our heads as we turned the bodies over in the bottom of the hole, trying to find signs of life.

The M-72 LAW fired a shaped-charge rocket in a shallow trajectory toward the beaten zone of Gary Woodruff's tracers. The projectile slammed into the tree line and blew the vegetation clear for ten meters on either side of the impact. The Viet Cong sniper team was vaporized. The second LAW man lowered his weapon. One shot had been enough. The Viet Cong usually ambushed from fighting holes with secondary bunkers behind and below the firing line as protection from counterbattery Marine artillery or from air support. But the M-72 LAW provided a powerful response that was so fast that the enemy sniper teams seldom had time to enter a protective shelter. The weapon had replaced the Korean War–era 3.5-inch rocket launcher, which was still preferred by some Marine commanders like Captain Doherty to mark targets with WP (white phosphorus) rounds. Once we had seen the devastation caused by the LAW rocket, we felt more secure and dragged the first body out of the hole.

A Marine rifleman's blood-flecked torso slithered out into the bright afternoon light. He had been shot several times through the chest and once in the head. The blood was still bright red and covered his face and shoulders. We left his helmet in the hole. Four more bodies were pulled out by Burns and some of the second fire team members who had come up to our position when the enemy sniper fire ceased. Finally, the five Marines were laid out on their backs, dead eyes staring into space. Their uniforms were covered with blood that leaked out of bullet holes in their chests and backs; those men had been in a cross fire, and cut to ribbons as they stood to sight their rifles and return fire. Looking over the still bodies of my brother Marines, I couldn't tell if I knew any of them until a black shock of hair was brushed aside, revealing the boyishly handsome face of Buddy Bolton.

Lafley and I searched the bottom of the hole and found piles of spent brass shell casings. The rifles were covered in a thick residue of burnt powder, and I knew that the Marines in this trap had fired most of their ammunition before the Viet Cong could get close enough to use their AK-47s. We guessed that Bolton had killed several VC coming out of the far tree line, not realizing they were the scouts for the much larger unit that followed close behind. The VC had then returned fire and, judging by the volume of Marine return fire, figured there was only one Marine position. The Viet Cong commander had then split up his platoons, one left and one right, hemming in Bolton and his helpless fire team. As the gooks closed on both sides of the Marines, they were cut down by the longer-range rifle fire from the M-14s. But as the Marines depleted their ammunition, their fire slackened, and the Viet Cong knew they were trapped without any possible escape. One by one, the Marines fell dead or wounded, manning their weapons and firing into the VC squads as they crept in closer for the kill. Finally, Lafley and I figured all the Marines were shot up and bleeding to death, and the VC charged in behind the firepower of their AK-47s and butchered our buddies at close range.

As I glanced slowly over the bodies of the dead troopers, my vision rested time and again on Buddy Bolton. I didn't cry or feel anything. Something inside me just tightened up, and I knew I would never be the same again. Looking aside, Burns knelt over the dead Marines and lit a cigarette. He pushed his helmet off his brow and looked at me with his glinting blue eyes under that shock of red hair.

"Well, Culbertson, everyone knows Bolton was your partner. He was a Deadeye Dick with that rifle, too. Just let the anger turn inside you. You and old Private Burns are gonna even this fucking score. No question about that shit! You startin' to understand Private Burns better all the time, ain't you, son?"

Looking at the dead and listening to Burns make his plans for retribution, I realized exactly what I was becoming. One of Uncle Sam's bullet stoppers. Baby-faced killers. We didn't come here to save Charlie from Communism. We came here to kill him and thereby save him from Communism!

Sergeant Wadley had moved his command team forward and had radioed An Hoa for helicopter extraction of the dead fire team. Wadley had lived up to his reputation, had run a tactically clean patrol, and had exhibited calm and control under fire. Now Wadley ordered Burns to toss out the red smoke grenade. The H-34s landed with their usual heavy footprint, and we rushed the bodies of the dead into the cargo door. The five bodies were already getting stiff as we piled them on top of each other for the short hop back to An Hoa. The Marines would be identified and their possessions and personal gear collected for the final trip to Graves Registration in Da Nang.

Our team collected the fire team's rifles and boarded the second chopper. The gun team was last, boarding the chopper with the dead. Finally, both choppers lifted off for An Hoa. The paddies swam under the fuselage and gave us our first clear picture of the battle site. The tree lines harboring the enemy troops and our sniper team were opposing lines in an oblong rectangle. The narrower tree lines were the ones used by Charlie to flank the Marines and attack the two sides of Bolton's hole, catching the Marine riflemen in a cross fire.

Looking over the tree line, I noticed the ground fall away behind the spot where the first VC had been shot by Bolton. The shallow hill had concealed the rest of the Viet Cong company from sight until they had split into their enveloping units and merged on both flanks of the Marine bunker. One thing you had to give Charlie credit for was his absolute mastery of the terrain. When Charlie hit you, it was a fact that he already had all his moves laid out in advance. Bolton and his men never had a chance. Rule number one in guerrilla warfare was never attack until you are certain who you are fighting. Buddy Bolton was a damn fine Marine, but he'd been too eager for his first kill. I planned right then and there to be patient and take what Charlie gave me. I would never let the slick little bastards force my hand into any rash action!

The H-34s deposited our squad on Phu Loc 6. We stared at the single chopper carrying the dead team to An Hoa. When you lost friends in battle, it never really hit hard at first. Our crying over Buddy and his friends would be done later.

Sergeant Wadley gathered us together and congratulated us on being cool under fire. We functioned like one man, and that is necessary in the tough battles, he said. Discipline saves lives and also conserves ammunition. Wadley told us we must always gauge the enemy's strength before we jump off, or risk getting into the same world of shit that Bolton and his team found on the other side of that tree line. The Viet Cong do not have artillery, air support, tanks, or medevac choppers. Sergeant Wadley asked us just what the hell Charlie had that made him so damn hard to kill. "Never forget, this is their country, and they know every inch of it. The Vietnamese peasants are their fathers and mothers, brothers and cousins. They tell the VC everything we do and when. These Viet Cong live off the land like wild animals. They are careful in walking and talking, and disciplined in maneuvering. We are clumsy compared to these soldiers! With many years of experience, they are natural jungle fighters. We are not! The only thing we do is shoot better and have more balls. That is enough to win if we learn something from them. Adapt to their ways. Fight like them. You did a good job today. Tomorrow we will fight better. Dismissed."

Now I knew why Korean War Marines were so valuable in Vietnam. Experience! I looked over at Burns, who just smiled through the cigarette smoke curling over his lip. "Culbertson, I told you I like that Sergeant Wadley. We're gonna kill a lot of gooks with him in charge."

CHAPTER TWENTY-SEVEN

Platoon Sweep
into the Arizona

Our squad leaders called their units together and disseminated the five-part order for our patrol into the Thu Bon River's matrix of streams and hamlets. The 3rd Platoon would be commanded by 2nd Lt. John Pindel. A mortar team of 60-Mike-Mike gunners and loaders would be attached. The platoon would depart Phu Loc 6 at 0900 hours for the Song Thu Bon region in Arizona Territory to our northwest. The mission would be to search out the hamlets along the river for Viet Cong and any contraband weapons or supplies we might find. The purpose of the patrol was to interdict supplies of materiel and soldiers along the river. The timetable for our sweep activities would be flexible and dependent upon our success in the field at outwitting Charlie. Not an easy task!

We gulped the last dregs of joe from our canteen cups and fieldstripped our cigarette butts. Each Marine checked his buddy's gear to make certain everything was strapped in place and shipshape. A quick weapons check was made by squad leaders. Special emphasis was placed on ensuring each man carried ample ammunition supplies in his 782 gear and haversack. The incident along the river where Buddy Bolton and his team had been gunned down had made the rounds. No one wanted to be killed because they ran out of ammo. We knew we could outshoot the VC, and it was damn unlikely that they would charge us with fixed bayonets. That was *our* style! Our concern was that by engaging a superior force of Viet Cong, we would run down our ammunition supplies before being resupplied by chopper. If that ever happened, a Main Force Viet Cong or NVA unit could cut us off from An Hoa and kill us before the cavalry came to the rescue.

Early that morning, Lieutenant Pindel had been in radio contact with the 11th Marines artillery battery back at An Hoa. Pindel had made sure the artillery commander knew where our patrol was headed and would guarantee some of his artillery assets for our support if we stepped in the shit. Artillery targets had been fired on in the Arizona for over six months by the gunners of Echo Battery, who had registered specific coordinates throughout the area so that many targets could be fired on quickly and accurately. Lieutenant Pindel could call in artillery fire missions by AT coordinates and request whatever type of warhead and artillery weapon that suited the situation.

First Squad led the long column along the road and through the barbed wire, then turned west down the slope of Phu Loc 6 toward the river. Lafley steered the patrol through the flat pastures, making sure his steps were careful and that he avoided clumps of vegetation or fresh broken ground that might hide mines or booby traps. Those of us with any time in the bush had seen at least one incident of a Marine tripping a booby trap.

Lafley finally reached the terraced dikes of endless paddies that gradually tumbled like a stack of hotcakes toward the river. By that time, the patrol was within sight of the first villages, and Marines checked their weapons, making certain they had a round chambered and ready to fire. The bolts of two dozen rifles clicked home, up and down the column. The point scouts scanned the trees for villagers and Viet Cong. Of course, the Viet Cong often *were* the villagers who shot at us. If we took any incoming, the point scout would lay down fire and call for a "gun up" to spray the village. The cat-and-mouse game we played was nerve-racking and almost never initiated by the Marines. We had to present ourselves as targets and be prepared to jump down Charlie's throat if he opened fire on us.

A throng of kids was forming up at the bamboo-fenced entrance to the village. It was common for Vietnamese children to queue up for candy or cigarettes from the Marines who patrolled the river. The danger lay in getting caught by a Viet Cong ambush with the kids trapped between the VC and Marines. A lot of youngsters had bought the farm in shoot-outs of that kind over the past year. As we neared the bamboo fence, I noticed the children looking at a junction of the dike we walked along where it met up with another footpath that bordered the moat in front of the village. Lafley looked down, stepping over the crossing trails with a hop. Because of Lafley's experience on point, I never failed to learn from how he moved or when he balked or sidestepped some obstacle in the trail. Lafley was the master point scout. Part Salish Indian and raised in the wilds of Montana, John Lafley had a natural way of moving and observing his surrounds that was born of experience and breeding. I had to work at patrolling, and sometimes I felt clumsy as hell watching Lafley move like an antelope, smoothly and effortlessly with awesome endurance.

As I cleared the crossing in the dike, the column closed ranks, anticipating a halt when the village was reached, a mere fifty meters ahead. Paul Blocker was carrying the 3.5-inch rocket launcher tube and several rockets in his haversack blanket-roll straps, but the weight shifted as Blocker stumbled through the dike's intersection, and his boots caught a transparent fishing line strung bootlace-high across the path. The metallic *twing* of the grenade's spoon shocked the column of tired Marines into furious efforts of self preservation. When some dude hits a booby trap, it's every son of a bitch for himself and too bad for you if your ass is in my way!

Blocker was short, five-seven at best, but he could run like hell. So could everyone else! Marines dove headlong into the paddy. Some looked back as they hustled through the shallow water. Blocker froze for a second, then ran about five meters and hit the deck on his knees with his ass sticking in the air. There was a *kaboom* and shrapnel sliced through the air over everyone's head. The shrapnel cut toward Blocker's head, but found his ass in the air where his head should have been, and shards of the M-26 lanced into Blocker's utility trousers and his buttocks. The impact of the shrapnel started Blocker off on a race around the village like a sprinter reacting to the starter's pistol. He didn't stop running until three Marines tackled him and pinned his flailing arms and kicking legs together, waiting for the corpsman to come to the rescue.

After swabbing Blocker's cheeks with hydrogen peroxide, the doc requested that Lieutenant Pindel radio for medevac. Blocker was a short-timer, and he had gotten a million-dollar wound. He would be transferred to Charlie-Med in Da Nang, then make his way home to the bayou country of Louisiana. The medevac chopper spun down through the bright sunshine, landing near the crowd of Vietnamese children. Several Marines carried Blocker into the chopper, then placed him on his stomach with his butt elevated for the trip to An Hoa. It was ironic that a wound to his rear would send him to the rear. Woodruff turned to Burns and Lafley, who were snickering and trying not to laugh aloud at Blocker's misfortune.

"Have you boys ever heard the rhyme that fits this occasion perfectly?"

Burns was looking thoughtfully at the Vietnamese children. Stepping next to him, I popped him on the arm and said Woody was talking to him. Burns turned toward Woodruff, who said,

> There was a Marine with no class,
> Who had balls made out of brass.
> When his balls smacked asunder
> It sounded like thunder,
> And lightning shot out of his ass!

Burns and Lafley went into hysterics as Woodruff looked on with approval, proud that his little ditty was so well received. I did have to admit that Blocker had run through the village like a man with lightning shooting out his ass. It was strange how stupid situations like that generated the finest comedy in Vietnam. If the grenade had blown Blocker's head off, it wouldn't have been so funny. We all looked at each other with tears in our eyes. The

Vietnamese kids were cracking up, but probably didn't understand a damn thing that had gone down except for Blocker's misfortune. When we got home, it wouldn't do at all to laugh in front of the family or a girlfriend about shit like that. They'd think we'd all gone Asiatic over there.

Lieutenant Pindel had our platoon form up and get busy searching the village, but nothing was found of a suspicious nature. We filled our canteens at the well and had time to burn up a fag before we got back on the trail to the next village and any surprises that awaited us there. Lafley slowed his pace and grew extra cautious even for him. I followed, scanning the flanks and looking for enemy movement.

As the next village came into view, Lafley raised his hand and motioned the platoon to halt and kneel down. Lafley and I went ahead with Burns and Woodruff backing our play. Fifty meters from the edge of the village, two women peered around the corner of a hut and immediately ducked back out of sight. Ahead, to the side of a large gnarled tree, I noticed the grass moving. There was practically no wind where we stood, protected by the tree line that ran along the shallow hill behind the village on the opposite side of the river.

I screamed out to the team, "Snipers! Snipers behind the tree to our front. Spider hole opening. . . ." Bullets tore over our heads as we went to ground. The loud cracks sounded like M-2 carbine fire on full automatic and close. Very close! None of us moved. Then Gary Woodruff, Burns, and I spread out into a firing line, low-crawling to the side where each of us had a lane to shoot down. The platoon behind us had hit the deck and stayed down to let us handle the problem.

Lafley whispered, "Wait till he comes up for another shot. Then we drill his ass together." The clicks of our safeties flicking off were drowned out by the rustling of our gear as we settled into position, our rifles trained and our sights on the base of the large tree. As Lafley had predicted, the cover of the spider trap moved and lifted. Seeking a target, the muzzle of a rifle poked from the hole.

Lafley yelled, "Now!" We each fired a few snap shots into the hole and Woody cut loose with a long burst from the automatic M-14. The grass-covered wooden lid of the spider hole exploded into fragments and lifted into the air. The cover was immediately splattered with a coating of bloody brain tissue and skull fragments.

Woody grasped his rifle by the forearm and pushed himself off the deck. "Culbertson, I ain't even goin' to go look at that sorry bunch of bloody shit." We all stared as Burns rose and walked toward the spider hole. Burns's M-14 blasted away into the hole, as he drew closer to the dead VC. He finally stood spread-legged over the hole and pumped round after round into the dead man. Bloody pieces of flesh and uniform flew into the air, while Burns ran his magazine dry. Turning toward us with a spray of blood covering his face, Burns motioned toward the dead gook.

"You know, Culbertson, you got to make sure they're dead. There might be another one in there! Who knows? Old Private Burns don't never take chances with these fuckers. Been through a lot of shit together, ain't we? Never gonna kill my ass over here." Burns dropped to his knees and started crying, and I knew it was time for him to retire to the BAS (battalion aid station) and see the shrink. I was tired of his shit. Killing the Viet Cong was okay, but I wanted nothing to do with butchery. Burns had finally lost it! Lafley and Woodruff were controlled in combat. So were Hamilton and Jessmore, but Burns had gone psycho since his brother got wasted, and had never really returned from Na-Na land. I still had six months to do in Vietnam, and privately I worried that I'd get crazy as Burns if I lived that long.

Lieutenant Pindel called a chopper for Burns and, much to my relief, Lafley took Burns's rifle away. Burns just sat there smoking a cigarette and rubbing his head. He was a great guy in the rear, but he just went nuts when we started firing up the gooks. I walked over to where Burns was sitting and dropped to one knee at his side.

"Anything you want me to do for you? You may be gone awhile, man." I tried to console him, but he just stared into the distance.

Burns tilted his head up and stared at me long and hard. "Culbertson, there is one thing you can do for me. Finish my work here. Remember what I showed you? The only good gook is a dead gook. Kill all the fuckers! That's what we're here for, brother."

The chopper landed and, after checking him for weapons, we hustled Burns aboard. In my mind's eye, I could see Burns commandeering the helicopter and flashing overhead with the chopper's M-60s blazing, screaming at the top of his lungs that his work wasn't finished yet. I started to chuckle. Perhaps I wouldn't require thirteen months in Vietnam to go crazy. After all, one of Burns's last semisane remarks, made to Lafley, was to the effect that I was coming along just fine in my training. Jesus, that shit really worried me!

Lieutenant Pindel ordered the platoon back into column, and resuming march order, Lafley and I headed toward the next group of villages. I glanced to the rear and saw the H-34 chopper lift off and make a low-level pass across the paddies before climbing to the east toward An Hoa. Silently, I said a short prayer for Burns. I liked the big-chested redhead. He was the funniest man in the platoon when he and John Lafley got on a roll. In Burns's tour in Vietnam to date, he had killed about a platoon of Viet Cong himself. Knowing Burns the way I did and the fact that his work with Charlie wasn't finished yet, I guessed that Burns could have killed at least one more platoon of gooks before he rotated home. Maybe two platoons! The changes I had observed in Burns's combat psychosis since we had served together were profound. He had changed from a well-disciplined Marine infantryman to a cold-blooded killer of startling violence. In a sense, Burns was a barometer for the other grunts of Hotel Company's 3rd Platoon. He demonstrated the acute metamorphosis that each trooper had undergone since being subjected to Vietnam's particular variety of combat madness. That metamorphosis, unfortunately, included me.

For the preceding month, I had become increasingly hardened to others' pain and misfortune. If it wasn't my ass that was shot, then it was all right with me. I planned to get back to the World in one piece, and if that meant that I had to get medieval and brutal in combat, so be it! I still thought of Lafley, Hamilton, Woodruff, and Matarazzi as my brothers. But if I worried about the dumb bastards all day, that might get *me* killed.

Lafley and I rounded a wide bend in the river channel and gazed down a long row of huts facing the river where, at the entrance, four Popular Forces soldiers were burning up some American cigarettes. The PF (Popular Forces) soldiers wore U.S. utilities like Marines wore Stateside, not jungle utilities. Web belts snugged fitted jackets over tailored trousers. The jackets were resplendent with patches that designated units and God only knows what else. They wore bright red scarfs that, except for the color, looked like American Boy Scout scarves. Instead of wearing combat helmets with steel outer shells like ours, the PFs wore only the plastic helmet liners. Lafley said they wore the liners because they were lightweight. Since those PFs certainly had no intention of seeing any combat if they could help it, we figured they probably didn't need the steel helmet for protection anyway. The PFs were holding hands with their buddies or standing with an arm draped across a fellow PF's shoulder. Needless to say, we Marines found the PF's code of field behavior offensive to our conception of manhood.

As we passed abreast the four PFs, Lafley suggested we have a bit of fun with our allies. He and I halted, facing the group of PF soldiers, who were standing easy with cigarette butts in their mouths and M-1 rifles held like fishing poles over their shoulders. We motioned the four PFs to the point of our column, which spread out a hundred meters down the trail.

Lowering our rifles at the PFs, we motioned them to take the trail. Lafley used the skills at Vietnamese for which he was justly famed. "*Di di,* you sissy bastards. *Di di mau* down that fucking trail, boys, or I swear I'll start bustin' some caps!" The hard, no-bullshit look on our faces probably helped them translate Lafley's instructions. The four slightly built and very frightened Vietnamese stumbled ahead of us to the point in a little throng. Lafley and I urged them along with verbal threats and by brandishing our rifle muzzles. Finally, we passed the huts that lined the riverbank and crossed a fallow field, halting by a huge rice paddy that stretched toward the horizon.

Looking at me with twinkling eyes and a twisted smile, John Lafley asked if I had foreseen his need for our new scouts. "Culbertson, this is the only way to give these little dudes some hands-on training. If there are booby traps or mines in that paddy, these assholes better find 'em. Better them than us! Also, it pisses me off to see them wear our equipment and never use the stuff for anything. If they start to bug out, give 'em a shot 'cross the bow." With a laugh, we motioned the now heavily perspiring Vietnamese soldiers into the paddies and onto the first dikes. After two hundred meters, one PF fell down crying and dropped his rifle in the paddy. Lafley ran ahead, securing the weapon and thrusting it into the PF's muddy hands. Then he put a size-eleven combat boot square in the sissy's butt.

In that way, we Marines negotiated paddy after paddy, connected by slippery mud dikes. Gazing across the immensity of the rice bowl, it appeared like one unbroken paddy, but once we trod into the muck and mud, hundreds of smaller paddies appeared, strung out like pearls in a sparkling necklace.

Suddenly, two of the PFs on my side of the column broke for a tree line fifty meters from the edge of the field.

I raised my rifle and fired a group of snap shots into the water at their ankles. They hit the deck and splashed shit-ridden water and mud all over themselves. I motioned with the barrel of my weapon for them to get moving or I would fire again. Lurching to their feet, the two Vietnamese gave a cry of such horror that I guessed they might just as well be facing the Viet Cong. Of course, that was too generous; the Viet Cong would have eaten those sissy assholes for breakfast.

After several hours slogging through paddies, we labored to a halt in a flat pasture. Lafley pointed toward the nearest village and yelled, "Dismissed, crybabies!" The PFs ran, then fell headlong, cracking their helmet liners against the stacking swivels of their rifles. Rising to their feet, they took off again, spilling food and ammunition out of their packs as they disappeared through the trees. Lafley halted the column, and we broke formation to pull out our canteens and shrug off our haversacks, easing the straps that cut into our shoulders.

Lieutenant Pindel finally made his way up the column to where Lafley and I had crapped out. He jumped our butts for not putting a fire team out on perimeter guard, but we could see all the way to fucking Da Nang across the open paddies. We guessed Pindel never noticed the four PFs that broke trail for us across the fields. If he did see them, he probably thought the idea was sound. Thankfully, he never mentioned it to Lafley or me! Personally, I hated the PFs I met because they wouldn't fight, and the Vietnam War was damn sure their fight. The Marines and the army's 101st Airborne troops had done all the ass-kicking in I Corps since I had been in the country. I had never seen a Vietnamese of any kind, including the ARVN, fire a bullet at a Viet Cong or NVA at any time. But the Marine Corps and those poor 101st Airborne bastards in the A Shau Valley to our north had practically been bled dry.

Lafley, Matarazzi, Woodruff, and Jessmore were as courageous and patriotic as any Marine could be expected to be. Sergeant Wadley, Gedzyk, and Hamilton were heroes in the company. We all risked our hides daily patrolling the Song Thu Bon valleys. We had sympathy for the South Vietnamese peasantry and a kindly disposition toward their safekeeping from the Viet Cong. However, all Marines despised the cowardly local Popular Forces (Vietnamese National Guard), which barely lifted a finger to protect their countrymen or their nation itself. Little Marine emotion was wasted on any PF who got killed or maimed.

Back in America, protesters called for cessation of hostilities. Students and cowards among the American people shirked their duty to guarantee freedom from oppression for our Vietnamese allies from a Communist dictator so heinous and murderous that someone had to see the Viet Cong's handiwork firsthand to believe it. I had seen the decapitated bodies of a whole family of Vietnamese who'd been murdered in a local village because their father was a teacher. The Communists' only hope for the overthrow of South Vietnam's freely elected government was based on the removal of South Vietnam's educated class. It had always been a Communist mandate that rule of the proletariat could only be maintained through constant purging of the educated, professional classes. The classes too smart to buy the nonsense that Communism would or could ever actually work.

Lafley, Woody, and I read about the student protests

back in the States. We were sorry our friends back home couldn't witness the deception of the Viet Cong and the brutality of their North Vietnamese cousins. If only they had learned the truth, the American people would surely have supported our efforts against this most recent Communist threat to a free Vietnam.

CHAPTER TWENTY-EIGHT

Viet Cong Snipers in La Bac 1 and 2

The PFs were long gone. After our short rest, Lafley and I saddled up, breaking trail to the east along the border of the old east-west road running south of the Quan Duy Xuyen River. Flowing northeast away from Phu Loc 6, the Quan Duy Xuyen was a major tributary of the Song Thu Bon. The first village we passed was the heavily fortified Cu Ban 4. During Operation Tuscaloosa, Cu Ban 4 had been one of the Viet Cong's most successfully infiltrated villages. Along with La Bac 1 and 2, Cu Ban 4 had served as a home base and an R & R (rest and relaxation) center for the Viet Cong.

Many of the villagers we encountered during daylight patrols seemed to be hardworking rice farmers. However, those farmers supported the R-20th Main Force Viet Cong Battalion and the increasing number of North Vietnamese troops moving into the Arizona Territory. As a major rice-producing area in South Vietnam, the Arizona Territory served as a food provisioning depot for regular Communist units poised for attack on South Vietnamese–held territory farther south.

As Lafley and I led the column along the main road, the sinuous bends of the Quan Duy Xuyen came into view on our port (left) flank. Thick vegetation and tree lines hugged the river and provided ideal cover and concealment for an ambush. Lafley looked along the ditches and bunkers covered with vines and foliage that provided a commanding view of the river and the myriad exposed sandbars and promontories that jutted into the river.

"Those islands in the river remind me of the sandbar we crossed on Operation Tuscaloosa. Jesus, it was hell crawling through those dunes under VC rifle fire. I can't get that scene out of my head, man." Lafley had hugged his rifle pit for over an hour while Viet Cong machine guns had cut down our friends. Back in January 1967, the Marines of 2/5 had learned what combat was all about, as buddies who had been shot down bled to death with no chance of aid from their fellow troopers due to the deadly curtain of small-arms fire covering the Marine positions.

Shrugging off morbid memories of shattered bodies and screams of dying Marines, I forced my attention back to the trail leading north along the river's breaks, toward the hostile villages of La Bac 1 and 2.

The trail was hard packed in early May, and we glanced through the thickly leaved trees that filtered the harsh sunlight of late spring. The column spread out, searching for mines and booby traps. The main job Lafley and I had was anticipating an ambush ahead. We looked for clumps of bushes and thickets of trees from which the enemy could most easily take the column under fire. Due to our experience walking point together, we felt with all of our senses rather then merely looking for signs of the enemy. Once a Marine had survived several Viet Cong ambushes, strong survival instincts forced him into a supremely sensitive defensive combat mode, the sharp-focus mental concentration needed to detect an imminent ambush. When fighting an experienced and aggressive foe, to fail to sense a threat is to die, and Lafley and I had no intention of dying.

As Lafley strode through the dense foliage along the river's bank, I lost sight of him for a second or two. The trees thinned out, exposing a grove leading to the western edge of La Bac 1. Suddenly, shots rang out and bullets snapped over our heads. I could always tell immediately if we faced Viet Cong regulars instead of the guerrilla units that operated in our area. Main Force VC troops were disciplined and would wait until a patrol was practically on top of their ambush site before opening fire. When we caught a burst of enemy fire that tore over our heads from a hidden ambush position, we knew it was guerrillas firing wildly, spraying the trail, hoping to hit a Marine by chance.

Lafley and Woodruff never did things by chance. A moment after the first volley of Viet Cong bullets passed harmlessly overhead, Lafley led Woodruff at a dead run up the trail, where they threw themselves into firing positions and peppered the clusters of trees and plants to their front. In a flash, John Matarazzi strafed the jungle foliage with deadly grazing fire. The ricochets of the glancing rounds sung as they twisted up into the sky. Matarazzi held his gunsights on the tree line, while Woody and I rushed ahead in short fire team assaults until we reached the spot where the guerrillas had taken us under fire.

The ambush scene was covered with spent brass, crushed banana leaves, and grass where the VC guerrillas had waited for our patrol to come into range. Fortunately, their marksmanship was not up to Marine standards; all their shots had gone high, and they had fled at our first return rounds. If the Viet Cong had continued to trade fire with us, we would have figured the ambushers for regular Viet Cong forces. The remainder of the Marine platoon would have moved into a base of fire, and Lieutenant Pindel would have sent a maneuver element into the attack. As it was, the point scouts and John Matarazzi's machine gun had neutralized the enemy with no problems.

The column dusted itself off and moved cautiously toward La Bac 1. I took the point and, Lafley and Woody backing me, moved slowly across open fields toward the first row of huts just visible through the trees. I understood that the guerrilla fire could have been a sucker's trap for a second, more deadly ambush ahead; sometimes the Viet Cong fired on a patrol and withdrew quickly, hoping to lure the Marines into hot pursuit. When the Marine column strung out trying to catch the first ambushers, a second Viet Cong machine gun would strafe the Marines as they rushed by the real ambush site. It was my practice always to look twice and disregard what I observed the first time. I figured that as big mistakes go, you only got to make one in Vietnam before you got to go home in a body bag. One mistake I never made was thinking the Viet Cong were fools. They didn't kick the living shit out of the French Airborne and Foreign Legion forces at Dien Bien Phu in 1954 because they were foolish or careless. The Viet Cong had impressed the hell out of all of us by then. I was definitely one of the more guarded members of the 3rd Platoon, and I intended to stay cautious and alive. The new troopers could have a shot at earning the Navy Cross by taking extra risks, and they might get to go home early—stiff and cold.

As the first hootch came clearly into view, I noticed several villagers break from the throng watching our approach and slink back into the thickets of bamboo and palm that bordered the huts. Expecting rifle fire, I tensed, but instead was pleasantly greeted by a host of children who came running toward our column. Probing for candy, gum, and C rations, the kids hit our jungle trouser pockets and slapped the sides and backs of our flak jackets. It was little wonder that those innocents might grow into Viet Cong just like their fathers.

The Marine column moved through the village and spread out to search the huts for contraband, rice, and weapons. Nothing was discovered out of place, so Lieutenant Pindel ordered the platoon back into formation to make trail for La Bac 2, two klicks downriver. The men stopped for a moment to fill canteens, while the mamma-sans flashed smiles tainted by reddish betel-nut-stained teeth. The clothes of the residents of La Bac 1 were as primitive as anyplace else we'd been in Vietnam. Black pajama trousers and white cotton smocks soiled with the dirt and sweat of endless toil in the rice fields covered thin, wiry bodies. The villagers looked like they were starving, but in fact exhibited the lean, muscled fitness of tireless workers. Only the aged seemed sickly, with deep eye sockets and toothless grins. I was always amazed at how docile the people seemed, yet they were more than capable of killing.

Lafley and I cut around the last huts in La Bac 1, across a small field, and into a deep thicket of low bamboo. The platoon wound along the trail until our tail-end Charlie was clear of the village. Shots rang out from the huts on both sides of the trail. I was far enough ahead of the platoon's rear guard to miss the action. No one was hit. We guessed that the shooters were the same group of amateurs that had fired on 3rd Platoon during our approach march. The entire column turned about and ran into La Bac 1. I'd seen Marines get pissed off, but nothing like that.

Groups of four and five men took the furnishings from the huts and smashed the tables, chairs, and whatever objects they could find to pieces on the village streets. After the huts were clear, we fired up the village—Marines along the rows of thatched huts used their stainless-steel Zippos to set bundles of roofing straw ablaze. The flames quickly ran up the angled roofs of the one-story dwellings, and the crackling and popping of the firestorm grew until the shouts of the Marines and the sobs and cries of the villagers were drowned out. The first huts burst into balls of flame whose fingers licked along the roof poles. The fire caused air turbulence, and the huts disappeared in a fury of twisting flame that threw off plumes of thick, black smoke that eddied into the sky.

The firestorm had engulfed La Bac 1 so rapidly that most of our men were caught inside the burning compound. Squads of Marines and a stream of villagers flooded into the fields and paddies surrounding the village, which was by then totally engulfed in hellfire. Shards of thatch broke loose from roofs and were tossed into the air by roaring winds that blew smoke and ash across the countryside.

The lieutenant later explained to us that the two villages of La Bac in the old French plantation region along the Song Thu Bon had always been bases for Viet Cong attacks against the Marines who patrolled the river basin searching for contraband rice and weapons. The people of the region, northern Duc Duc Province, were loyal Communist supporters who actively mined roads and trails in an aggressive campaign to hamper Marine operations.

We set out on the long march back to Phu Loc 6. Radio transmission from the platoon commander had alerted the battalion commander and Hotel skipper at An Hoa that the platoon had been ambushed repeatedly and was forced to burn the Viet Cong guerrillas out of their hideouts in La Bac 1. The brass would view the destruction of La Bac 1 as the removal of another thorn in its hide as they tried to pacify the hamlets that sprawled over hundreds of square miles of the Arizona Territory.

By nightfall, after a ten-klick hump to Phu Loc 6, the Marines of Hotel Company's 3rd Platoon dragged their aching asses through the perimeter wire and mounted the hill to their bunkers. Too tired to say much, men headed to the showers in twos and threes. The veterans knew that another fight was brewing along the river. The temperament of the local population in La Bac 1 said a mouthful. The cold stares and forced silence of the old people cloaked a deep hatred for the Americans. The North Vietnamese were their cousins and were pouring into the Arizona in division strength for the first time in the Vietnam War. The NVA troops were as effective as the Main Force Viet Cong we had slaughtered on Tuscaloosa, and there were a hell of a lot more of them.

Fire teams gathered to sip a cup of coffee and burn up a Camel while stories of past combat passed back and forth. In Hotel 2/5, the veterans understood what the 5th Marines stood for. We were the most decorated combat regiment in the history of the Marine Corps. The 5th had fought valiantly in the bloody battles in Vietnam, and we knew we would be called on again when the NVA needed a good ass-whipping. The patrol indicated that day was coming soon. It would be a day for dying, and 2/5 would write another chapter in a history covering nearly two hundred years of blood and gore on battlefields around the world.

CHAPTER TWENTY-NINE

Hotel Returns
to An Hoa for R & R

After the platoon had rested from the river patrol, orders came to the commander at Phu Loc 6. Hotel would be replaced by a rifle platoon from Echo Company and would stand down from its duties as northern sentry for the battalion base at An Hoa. Attempting to control the Communists' activities on Go Noi Island, Echo Company had experienced high casualties in operations to our east in Dai Loc Province. Echo would man the defenses at Phu Loc 6 and run limited patrols south of the river, staying out of the most dangerous regions of the Arizona Territory along the banks of Song Thu Bon and the plain north of the river.

Woodruff and I packed our gear into our seabags and haversacks for the march back to An Hoa. Woody was bending over, lacing his jungle boots over his bare feet. His lower legs were pocked with sores from which oozed pus and blood that ran down into his boots. It seemed a wonder that Woody could withstand the long patrols into the muck and mire of the river valleys. During patrols, our feet and lower legs were constantly immersed in fetid paddies, sometimes for hours at a time.

The undergrowth and vines of the thickly forested hillsides scratched us and punctured our thin utility trousers and jackets and cut and gouged our legs and arms. The untreated wounds festered in the hot humid atmosphere within hours. Grunts who had "beaucoup trigger time" in the Arizona were walking collections of suppurating sores and scars that silently kept score of our forays into the jungle. Woody seemed not to notice the condition of his legs. He finished knotting his laces then stood to strap on his pack.

Looking down at his legs, I spoke. "Jesus, Woodruff, how can you hump back to An Hoa with those gook sores bleeding like that? Man, your calves and shins are all infected. You need to see a corpsman when we get back to the rear."

"Shit, Culbertson, these sores never go away as long as we march through the shit. I've had these deep sores since we fought on the DMZ at Con Thien last fall, back in 1966. Look at your arms, boy, you're starting to scar up and you got a long nasty sore on your elbow."

Pulling my left arm across my abdomen, I stared at the inflamed skin and milky scab that had formed over the shrapnel wounds that had been treated earlier at An Hoa. The skin on my elbow had ruptured when I hit the deck and had been exposed to the germs and human waste that covered the surface of the Arizona's rice fields. Shocked, I frantically searched my torso and legs for more signs of crud and corruption. It was one thing to see sores and terrible wounds on my friends, but it was ten times worse to find them on myself.

My forearms were etched with white scars from old scratches and cuts that stood out starkly through the sun-tanned skin. Sores I had not noticed were clustered on the backs of my forearms and elbows, and I felt a tenderness along my right shin. Tearing the boot blousing springs off my boot tops, I stared at a reddish, puffy line that ran from my ankle up to my right knee. My punji-stake wound was infected, and it bulged out. I started to wonder how either of us would hump the seven klicks back to An Hoa. The main road to An Hoa was Highway 1, and it was mined and booby-trapped every night by Charlie or the local villagers, who showed us much hospitality by day.

The lieutenant walked down from the command bunker to the perimeter bunkers where we gathered our gear. He announced a convoy of six-by-six trucks returning from Da Nang would transport us back to An Hoa. Lieutenant Pindel mentioned that he had radioed the Hotel skipper at An Hoa and requested transport for our platoon because he felt we had gotten sufficient exercise in our last several patrols through the river valleys. He reminded us that he had been an enlisted trooper before, himself, and had not forgotten what "run ragged" meant to field Marines. We all thought, "No shit!" Maybe the new lieutenant would have a dose of common sense. Lieutenant Pindel was the kind of Marine who followed the book to a point, but in combat, he always seemed to put the welfare of his troops first. Pindel was also the most astute officer I had seen when it came to calling in artillery fire missions when the shit really hit the fan. Captain Doherty had been the master in the use of tactical artillery. But Doherty was back in the United States, and we were glad Pindel showed such outstanding leadership qualities.

Lieutenant Pindel also had one "pet" regulation that he kept close tabs on. Night sentry duty. Lieutenant Pindel would sneak up to our bunkers each night around "oh dark thirty hours" and approach some Marine on guard. If the sentry failed to challenge the lieutenant, Pindel would spring into his bunker and startle him to attention and perhaps a court-martial. I had been a guard at a naval weapons station before my transfer to Vietnam. Marine Barracks Fallbrook, California, had provided two platoons of infantry guards to run patrols and bunker watch over the hundreds of square miles of ammunition and naval ordnance housed at the southeast corner of Camp Pendleton. This ammunition depot contained nuclear weapons, mostly warheads for missiles and artillery shells. The guards were specially selected and had to have secret or top-secret clearances. The Marine sentries at NWS Fallbrook were charged with guarding naval munitions. No one was to enter our post except the sergeant of the guard or the officer of the day and live to tell about it. Any duty officer entering a guard sector made certain the sentry was alerted by radio and could easily recognize his vehicle and uniformed presence. That beat the hell out of getting shot by a sentry who was an expert rifleman and might be trigger-happy to boot.

Lieutenant Pindel rightfully feared any sentry dozing at his post, because one Marine who fell asleep at a critical position could compromise the entire platoon. The Viet Cong often probed our lines at night, especially during the early morning hours. They were savvy enough to know that Marines just returned from long patrols were more likely to crap out on watch, so the Viet Cong would launch attacks at a time when sentries on watch were most likely to be asleep or, at least, not be fully alert. Lieutenant Pindel never fell into the error of assuming the lines were secure. In my experience, no other officer had been so faithful to his duty to maintain our combat readiness as Pindel. Personally, because of my experience of over a year of daily sentry duty at NWS Fallbrook under very strict military discipline, I agreed with Lieutenant Pindel's intense supervision of our defenses. It seemed a lot better to get jumped by Lieutenant Pindel than by Charlie, but some of the Marines felt that we would never be attacked on Phu Loc 6 because we had the reputation for being so aggressive and ruthless on patrol. I thought that mentality was really dumb, and I never slept on watch while I served with Hotel Company.

The chug of engines grinding up the rear road to Phu Loc 6 announced the arrival of the truck convoy. The huge trucks lurched to a halt and disgorged cartons of C rations, wooden crates of rifle and machine-gun ammunition, and HE and Willy Peter rounds for the 4.2-inch mortar section. One truck pulled a giant-wheeled water tank we called a water buffalo. It was critical that Phu Loc 6 be supplied regularly and have sufficient ammo reserves to withstand a night attack, because it would take hours to muster a rescue operation from An Hoa if Phu Loc 6 was hit hard. The platoon of Marines that guarded the knobby little hill at the entrance to the Arizona had to stand on its own two feet.

Woody, Lafley, Jessmore, Matarazzi, and the rest of 3rd Platoon's motley crew jumped into the staked rear beds of the trucks. We field Marines jeered the motor transport Marines who stood beside their vehicles in clean jungle utilities and new boots. The motor transport drivers smoked cigarettes and joked with grunts who looked like Caribbean pirates in ragtag utilities bleached almost white. Even 3rd Platoon's rifle stocks showed the dings of constant battering and regular combat action. Finally the motor transport Marines bounded into the cabs of their trucks and the diesel engines caught and came to life. Not one motor transport Marine failed to notice the hard stares and weathered uniforms and bodies of the Marines of the "Fighting Fifth."

Woody lit a cigarette and passed it to me as the convoy sped down to the entrance to Phu Loc 6 and onto the main road. Clouds of dirt kicked up behind the tandem wheels of the trucks and swirled into the beds, covering us in a layer of red clay that plastered our sweat-drenched faces.

"Culbertson, how fucking easy is this duty after all that humping? Man, when we get back to the World, it will be no sweat to work those civilian assholes into the deck. Man, I know we're headed for heaven, 'cause we've already been in hell."

I drew a deep puff on my cigarette and let the smoke exhale naturally. We all felt like that cloud of smoke. Just lazily blowing first this way and then that. No particular place to go. Just drifting, dreamlike. Combat affected men's minds that way. The intensity of mental alertness required to stay alive in battle would be followed by a passive, almost disconnected state of limbo, where the mind and body would rest until another crisis of dangerous proportions would surface. Then, the Marines would scramble like wild animals just to survive. The roller-coaster ride of combat-driven fear and the aftereffects of gloom and depression pushed many nineteen- and twenty-year-old Marines far past the normal tolerance for stress, but the depression never abated entirely. After we returned to America and tried to understand the war of which we had been an integral part, we would pay a lifelong penalty for honoring our nation and serving our Marine Corps.

The hootches of An Hoa came into view, and I snapped out of my daydreaming and collected my gear. Jesus, the thought of a shower and clean clothes sounded better than a piece of ass. It was amazing to me that the strain of constant combat action overshadowed any desire for women or luxury. As the troops jumped from the truck beds, smiles and temporary elation swept over the platoon. We had made it through another month in the Arizona and would eat hot meals and have dry bunks to sleep in. Who could ask for more than that? We were alive and had high hopes of making it all the way through our tours. Thirteen months! Shit, the army only did twelve months, but the Marines always tried to outdo everyone else. Personally, I didn't really give a shit about the length of the tours. I cared more about why we weren't winning the war. We kicked Charlie's ass every time we patrolled the Arizona, but Charlie always came back for more! And there were new reports of massive infiltration into our TAOR (tactical area of responsibility) by North Vietnamese troops who were refitting and taking on rice and resupplies for a push south. Our main job was to stop the infiltration of the Arizona and the valleys to the south. The army's 101st Airborne was up to its ass in alligators in the A Shau Valley to our north in I Corps. Fighting the NVA to the death.

Lafley gave me a knowing glance and said, "Don't worry, Culbertson, we already fought the NVA at Con Thien last fall. I can truthfully tell you that they kicked our asses as much as we kicked theirs. Captain Doherty said the NVA's crack troops are the best jungle fighters in the world. Woody and I hope you learned a lot of good tricks at Sniper School, 'cause the NVA will ambush our asses from so close you can spit on 'em and don't even need a rifle. This fucking war is turning into a nightmare, and it's gonna get worse before it gets any better."

CHAPTER THIRTY

Burns Goes to Bangkok

The platoon hit the sack for the first solid night's sleep in a month before the squad leaders returned to their hootches following a meeting with the platoon commander. The word was soon passed that Hotel would remain in garrison at An Hoa for the month, standing lines and refitting for more duty in the Arizona. Most of the troops had been pushed so hard on patrols that their jungle boots were bleached white as sand, their toes poked through the leather uppers, and their jungle utilities were rotting off their skeletal frames. The grunts of 3rd Platoon had humped the paddies and hills of the Thu Bon River Valley and the tributaries of the Quan Duy Xuyen in a manic search for rice and supplies. Denying the enemy the materiel to continue to promote a Communist takeover was the order of the day. A Viet Cong enemy short of ammo and gear would be forced to limit his activities in I Corps, and the Marines patrolled the hamlets incessantly to interdict Charlie's resupply.

At morning chow, we got another startling revelation. Private Burns had not been dispatched to rear duty by the psychiatrist in Da Nang. On the contrary, the navy doctors, in their infinite wisdom, had presumed Burns to be overwrought by the regular stress of combat patrols along the river. They had recommended a week of rest and relaxation for the big redhead, so Burns had hopped the daily plane south to Saigon and caught a flight to Bangkok, Thailand, for a week of R & R.

Bangkok had already been ravaged by several Hotel grunts on previous R & Rs. Paul Blocker and Alfred McKnight had arrived in Bangkok and been given adjoining rooms. Once they unloaded their bags, they had stretched out on their soft beds to savor some shut-eye without possibility of a mortar attack. But the doors to their suites burst open, and they were flooded with laughing young girls in colorful Thai dress. Blocker swore the girls ringed his bed while the bellboy urged them to pick their favorites for the night or the entire R & R. Blocker said the choice was difficult for him, but it had to be made, so he picked two of them for his first night. They could fight it out to see which one would be his main squeeze.

McKnight was the favorite soul brother of all the troopers in 3rd Platoon. He was a southerner and had fought with Hamilton, Lafley, and Woodruff on the DMZ in '66. McKnight would hang tough in fierce firefights along the Song Thu Bon.

After reports of the events filtered around the platoon when Blocker and McKnight returned, a flood of requests for R & R to Bangkok landed on the first sergeant's desk. As for McKnight and Blocker, they were keeping pretty quiet about their episodes in hopes of a return engagement to an unspoiled Marine's paradise. I felt their attempts at secrecy were fruitless. Anyone knows that when there are booze and women for the taking, there are Marines in hot pursuit and closing fast.

Lafley and I received our assignments for perimeter watch and, after evening chow, headed out to An Hoa airstrip to relieve the sentries in sandbagged fighting holes spread along the flight line. The sun was still hot, and the sky was a soft azure with silky strands of clouds melting into it. It was hard to think about how brutal the war could get after looking across a countryside so green in late spring. But after Hotel Company had rested, taken on replacements, and trained sufficiently, the veterans of Operation Tuscaloosa would return to the river valleys to pry the Communist units from their bunkers and trenches until the Arizona was free of the menace from the north.

CHAPTER THIRTY-ONE

Hotel Is Issued the Black Rifle

Rumors had swirled through Hotel Company regarding the new rifles that were being issued to army troops in the southern sectors of Vietnam. Word had it that a newfangled .22-caliber rifle had been cooked up by the armaments manufacturers back in the United States. The weapon was reputed to be a selective-fire, lightweight, carbine-type rifle that was short and had a polymer stock. More than that, none of us had any inkling other than to protest the commandeering of the trusty M-14s that had served so well in past battles.

Some rumors turn out to be fact, and others just fade away. In the case of the replacement of our M-14s, the scuttlebutt was true. The platoon sergeants passed the word to clean and oil our weapons for inspection prior to turning in our gear—which included magazines, bipods, and magazine pouches—to the armorer's shack. The M-14s were to be fieldstripped and cleaned in GI cans of hot soapy water. When dried, the rifles were to be lightly oiled, and an oily patch run through the bore. The stocks were to be cleaned and rubbed down with a light coat of linseed oil. All web gear was to be washed and scrubbed clean prior to being surveyed by company supply personnel.

Lafley had gone berserk when the announcement was made and formal schedules were issued to the battalion for the retirement of the M-14s. John "Cowboy" Lafley was the senior point scout in Hotel Company, and he had taught me practically everything I knew about walking point for a Marine rifle company. I knew to ask Luther Hamilton, Gary Woodruff, Manny Ybarra, and, of course, Cowboy for guidance any time I negotiated tricky terrain or came upon a village that smelled suspicious. All those veteran troopers had trusted the M-14 rifle since the early days on the DMZ at Con Thien when Captain Doherty had led Hotel in some of the most vicious combat of the war.

Lafley and others vowed not to turn in their M-14s with the reasonable logic that the M-14 rifle had kept them alive so far, and no one saw any reason to fix something that wasn't broke. The M-14 rifle was really an M-1 rifle with reworked gas ports, a shorter operating rod, and a detachable magazine holding twenty rounds rather than the M-1's internal en bloc stamped clip that held only eight rounds. The M-1 and M-14 were practically identical despite the M-14's 7.62mm NATO cartridge; both weapons fired standard .308-caliber bullets weighing 150 grains in the standard ball design. The M-14, like the M-1, could penetrate fairly heavy cover such as was found in the jungles of Vietnam. That capability to penetrate brush, foliage, and the walls of light bunkers was a real advantage to Marines, who usually engaged the Viet Cong from open rice paddies while firing into the enemy bunkers and spider holes. Once an accurate volley of M-14 rifle fire coned into an enemy position, it was only a matter of time before the VC bugged out or stayed to die. All the Marines of Hotel Company were fearful that the new rifle in relatively small .223 caliber would not perform like the M-14 when the real test came in the fields along the Song Thu Bon.

Lafley spoke to the 3rd Platoon, as the men bent over the disassembled parts of M-14s on blankets over their bunks. "I don't know what this new gun is like. I really don't give a shit either. I've killed two dozen Viet Cong with this here M-14 and the son of a bitch has never failed to fire. Culbertson's rifle crapped out on the sandbar on Tuscaloosa 'cause he got sand in the receiver. That never happened again, did it?"

I spoke up from the corner of the hootch by the hatch. "Lafley's right about the M-14s. They're solid weapons. Keep 'em clean, and they keep you alive. On Tuscaloosa, I used the weapon for a shovel to climb that first sandbank. If I had my shit together, I would have slung arms across my back and avoided that mistake."

Gary Woodruff had carried the M-14 up on the DMZ for over three months during intense firefights. He knew that a familiar weapon that was mechanically broken-in was better than any new one. Woody also made the point that once the sights on a rifle were zeroed true, the shooter knew how much Kentucky windage to apply when engaging targets at ranges greater than the two hundred meters battle sights were set for. Overall, I felt the value of a rifle in combat boiled down to a Marine's level of confidence in it. I had shot the M-1 rifle exclusively for a year at the Naval Weapons Station at Fallbrook, California, before coming to Hotel Company in Vietnam. I had gained confidence in the M-1's accuracy as well as in its absolute dependability in all types of harsh conditions. The M-14 was a fine rifle if kept clean, but it was not as tough in a battle-field environment as the M-1. Personally, if I had to pick one battle rifle to stake my life on for a long period in combat without the luxury of cleaning or regular maintenance, the venerable M-1 in caliber 30-06 would be my choice over any rifle ever made. The M-14 was a damn good weapon, but it had to be babied compared to the M-1 Garand.

Soon every trooper in 3rd Platoon had finished cleaning and oiling his weapon for the last time. We formed up in the company street as the platoon sergeants and squad leaders inspected each weapon for dirt or, God save our asses, for rust. A rusty rifle in the Marine Corps is usually worth thirty days' confinement in the brig; on the battle-field a rusty rifle can cost a man his life. We formed a column and marched to the armorer's hootch in the center of An Hoa combat base. As each Marine entered the hootch, several armorers inspected the weapon and logged the piece by serial number on the company roster next to the Marine's name. The Marine signed the roster and the rifle became company property. It was sadder than a divorce to most of the grunts in the line, and nobody seemed very pleased by the prospect of getting his mitts on the new black rifle. When all the M-14s were turned in, the chief armorer stood on the counter of the armory displaying the ugliest rifle ever made by mankind.

"Men, this is the U.S. Rifle, caliber 5.56 millimeter, M-16. It fires a .223-caliber bullet at 3,300 feet per second. The weapon has a selector switch giving the rifle full automatic capability. The weapon is highly accurate out to three hundred meters. The bullet itself is a full metal jacketed 55-grain boattail. This round will kill very effectively at close range, where practically all your firefights take place in the Arizona Territory."

We looked at the puny gray barrel and the black plastic stock with its pistol grip and ventilated front-barrel rib. Groans went up through the ranks, and Marines winced at the sight of the bright new idea from the States.

"Jesus, now that we got this here space gun, is Buck Rogers coming down here to planet Earth to show us how to shoot it?" The voice from the rear of the platoon sounded a lot like Gerald Burns, and it carried over the buzz of voices. I looked over my shoulder. Yep. The big redhead was grinning at me. Burns had gone, and now he had magically reappeared. I was glad Burns was back, but I knew I would have to keep a close eye on him when we went to the field.

The platoon sergeant shouted over the bitching and told everyone that the new weapon was now Marine Corps issue, and we would learn to fight with it whether we liked it or not. It seemed like a reasonable request to me. Why should forty combat veterans have any influence on the selection of a weapon just because their lives depended upon it? Hell, everyone knew the M-14 was better than this measly-looking plastic piece of shit. The troops immediately nicknamed the new M-16 the "Toy Gun" because it was reminiscent of the BB guns we had all shot as children. One small consolation was that the M-60 machine guns, which fired the heavy 7.62-millimeter bullet, would still be fielded by the rifle platoon. Matarazzi, Jessmore, Gedzyk, and Fink would be glad about that little benefit.

One thing that worried me about the new M-16 was that it provided automatic-fire capability to every rifle in the squad. In "the good old days," the only automatic rifles were the M-14s carried by the automatic riflemen like Gary Woodruff and, occasionally, John Lafley. The fire team would have one automatic rifleman; all the other Marines, including the fire team leader, were armed with the semiautomatic M-14. Only the squad leader and the M-60 machine-gun teams carried the .45-caliber pistol in addition to their M-14—and then only if they chose to carry one at all. On Operation Tuscaloosa Gunny Gutierrez had carried his M-14 with the stock cut off at the pistol grip and hung from a jungle sling riding over his shoulder. Each Marine developed his own style of carrying ammunition bandoliers and forming his web sling so that he could carry his weapon in a quick-fire position while on patrol. I almost always carried my weapon hunting style in the crook of my arm, the way my father had taught me back home in Oklahoma. That quail-hunting carry allowed for very fast shouldering of the rifle.

The new M-16 was so lightweight (under six pounds) that it could be carried across the shoulder or held low to the deck by the carrying handle above the receiver, just the way German soldiers had carried Mausers in World War II. The black rifle also allowed the shooter to carry twice the amount of ammunition that he could hump for the M-14. The problem with the new rifle was that each Marine could return the Viet Cong's bullets on full auto. When a patrol is caught in an ambush, the first thought of every trooper is to gain fire superiority and put the enemy soldiers on the defensive. But even the automatic rifleman will admit that full auto fire is hard to aim unless the weapon attaches to a heavy bipod like the M-14. The M-16's lightweight aluminum bipod was more for decoration than combat. I envisioned a situation where a patrol of Marines would be ambushed and pour out full automatic return fire at the Viet Cong. If the Marines got locked into a protracted shoot-out such as happened on Operation Tuscaloosa, which had lasted over nine hours, then the squad would run out of ammunition and be in a world of shit. I knew for a fact that every Marine in Hotel Company loved to shoot Charlie's ass up and, once they got started, fire discipline would go to hell in a handbasket.

At 1st Marine Division Scout Sniper School in March, Gunnery Sergeant Mitchell had harped on strict fire discipline and the need to aim our shots to make a clean kill. Gunny Mitchell joked about troops' shooting on full automatic at the enemy like spraying down a flower bed with a garden hose. Sometimes the shooter could fire a whole magazine without hitting an enemy soldier. A trained marksman picked his target and concentrated on placing one shot at the center mass of the enemy's chest to inflict a killing wound. Spraying lead with an I-don't-give-a-shit-what-I-hit mentality is unprofessional and wasteful of ammo and the opportunity to kill the enemy. Marine line-company snipers in Vietnam averaged an enemy soldier killed for every bullet and a half shot. Regular grunts shot thousands of rounds in combat to produce the same casualty figures. Firing on full automatic would be a moronic method to maintain any fire discipline. Besides the obvious waste of ammunition, the lack of fire concentration would ignore the sound fundamentals of Marine Corps marksmanship training. The scope and quality of Marine Corps rifle training from boot camp through division Sniper School was the main difference between the USMC and other well-trained armies, including the United States Army. Marines had always been rifle marksmen, and any deviation from that really pissed me off.

We of 3rd Platoon took our new rifles back to our hootches. We spent the remainder of the day fieldstripping the weapons and discussing their cyclic rate of fire and the ballistic performance of the .223 cartridge. The M-16 had some inherent advantages over larger caliber weapons in jungle combat: the small round and the large amount of ammo that each grunt could hump. The ammo was also available in small, twenty-round boxes from Lake City Arsenal. I learned to stuff about twenty extra boxes into my haversack when taking the field. The twenty-round magazines for the M-16 I carried in an empty claymore-mine bag over my shoulder. I figured on humping twice as much ammunition for the M-16 as I had for my M-14. My match-grade sniper rifle was stored in the armory and I was ordered to report on the combat functioning of the new M-16.

We finished the cleaning and assembly of our rifles and hung them over our beds on nails hammered into the rafters, with a full magazine inserted, the chamber empty. We never knew when An Hoa could be overrun by the Viet Cong. Hunting around for your rifle and a loaded magazine in the middle of a dark night seemed pretty dumb even for Marines, so we always kept rifles loaded and hung in a handy spot, ready to go into battle.

After evening chow, Hamilton passed the word that we would be making a fifteen-klick reinforced-squad-size patrol north into the Arizona river valleys. We would leave at first light and, hopefully, return by sundown. Everyone would field the new rifles, and we were ordered to take extra ammunition supplies. John Matarazzi would bring his M-60 gun team along, and we would have an M-79 grenadier and two Marines carrying M-72 LAW rockets. The patrol would sweep through a string of villages before heading back to An Hoa over the rice paddy dike systems and trails northwest of Phu Loc 6. I looked up at my rifle hanging on the rafter over my bunk. I prayed the dirt and filth of the paddies would not jam the close tolerances of the receiver group's parts. When I had disassembled the weapon, the polished bolt had seemed tight and would not slide easily out of the receiver. Reassembly was worse and the metal parts stuck, requiring effort to fit up the action. On the M-1 and M-14, the parts in the receiver were made of such tough steel that they hardly wore, and yet they fit easily together. Functional and elegant was the overall design of the Garand by John Garand. The M-16 was a space-age rifle with close tolerances and metal parts that bore upon each other with untested performance. I knew the general design of the M-16 was probably sound, but all new weapons need to be debugged, and none of us wanted to die providing data for engineering improvements.

Before we turned in for the night, Burns had a thought that made pretty fair sense. "You know, Culbertson, me and Lafley already decided that if this piece of shit M-16 don't shoot tomorrow, we're gonna knock some PFs in the head and take their M-1s. I can't figure how the Marine Corps gives a man's rifle like the Garand to some skinny-assed Popular Forces, while we get stuck with Buck Rogers here! The longer I stay in Nam the less all this shit makes sense."

Someone a few bunks down pulled the lanyard and turned off the light in the center of our hootch. A voice yelled out, "Fuck Buck Rogers anyway. Anybody wears a space suit like that is a queer anyhow!" We snuggled under our blankets, and another fun-filled day in Vietnam slipped silently away.

CHAPTER THIRTY-TWO

Combat with the M-16

Day broke over the tin-roof hootches of An Hoa, and 3rd Platoon was saddled up in the company street, haversacks stuffed with C-ration meals and extra cartridges for our new rifles. Matarazzi looked over our squad and smiled in his easy manner. The patrol was no big deal to John Matarazzi, because he still shouldered the big M-60 machine gun that had made him a deadly threat to the Viet Cong every time he and Jessmore took the field. We were relieved Mat and Juice were along with their gun. If we had problems with the new M-16, we knew we could count on the heavy-hitting M-60 to bail our butts out of trouble. I looked along the formation at the hard faces of Hotel's veteran Marines. Lafley was not in sight. Peering through the screen mesh windows of our hootch, I saw no sign of the Montana cowboy. Lafley certainly would be on this patrol as the lead point scout. I always backed him up and took over the point in the afternoon when Lafley needed a break from the intense pressure of looking for booby traps, mines, and the ever-present Viet Cong.

Lieutenant Pindel strode down the column and eyed the men. Pindel was meticulously concerned with every detail of any patrol under his command. That was one of Pindel's strong points. No Marine under his command would ever jeopardize a patrol by failing to hump the required gear, including sufficient C-ration meals and ammunition. Too many horror stories abounded of Marine units that got trapped by the enemy and cut off from reinforcements and supplies. When a unit was trapped, it had to have the ability to sustain itself until help came, or it would die. Lieutenant Pindel checked all the loose ends. If the Viet Cong were going to kill his people, by God, they'd have to fight to the end to do it. In the Marine Corps, the troops will fight to the bloody end, but their officers have the responsibility of seeing that the men are properly armed and supplied. Pindel's pickiness about our equipment and rations was a blessing; 3rd Platoon never got into a scrape in the Arizona Territory that we couldn't handle ourselves, and we had Pindel to thank for his attention to detail.

Hotel had gained a reputation with the Viet Cong troops in the Arizona Territory and among the Communist sympathizers along the river in the villages of La Bac 1 and 2, Cu Ban 4, and Thon Bon 1 and 2. The NVA-led R-20th Main Force Battalion had escaped from the artillery barrages in La Bac 1 and 2 on January 26, 1967, during Operation Tuscaloosa. The surviving NVA and VC had taken over fifty dead and wounded soldiers toward Le Nam 3 through the jungle-clad hills along the Song Thu Bon. The battalion staff of the 2nd Battalion, 5th Marine Regiment, had overestimated their success. The commanding general of the 1st Marine Division had visited the battle area after Operation Tuscaloosa was secured and declared the total destruction of the R-20th Main Force. But intelligence, and rumor, were saying that elements of the R-20th had been refitted and returned to the river valley to disrupt the South Vietnamese government's control over the countryside. Only one impediment remained to the success of a total Communist takeover in the Arizona Territory. That problem was the 2nd Battalion of the Fighting 5th Marines.

We stepped out and wound down the company street and across the airstrip. The perforated steel plate of the runway burnt into the soles of our jungle boots. In addition to 3rd Squad, we had a fire team from 1st Squad and guns and rockets from weapons platoon along for the hunt. The Marine Corps is always offense-minded and only takes defensive postures when forced to do so by an overwhelming enemy attack. This patrol was a hunter/killer patrol designed to recon in force and push any Viet Cong or NVA along the river into a fight. Help would be sent from An Hoa in the form of a Sparrow Hawk reaction platoon to reinforce us in the event we bit off more than we could chew. However, with a dozen grunts and five weapons personnel plus our lieutenant and platoon sergeant, we could chew off a hell of a lot. Unlike the Marine Corps' 1st Division's Force Recon companies, which ran five-man teams, and the heavier teams of 1st Recon Battalion, which could number thirteen men and leaders, Hotel's patrols walked over the enemy, not around him. If there was an enemy unit in the Arizona, we made ourselves available for an afternoon of fun and games each time we entered the river valley. Force Recon and Battalion Recon made their living by going *way* out on patrol and running or sneaking back home when they ran into the shit. Hotel's grunts were armed to the teeth and ordered to find the shit and jump into the middle of it with both boots. We ran from nothin', and nothin' scared us. Just going out in the bush and counting gooks didn't mean shit to us. We went out and killed the bastards, then we counted 'em!

Captain Doherty, Hotel's bravest commander, had once gone out to the Thu Bon River in a monsoon to bring Golf Company in from the far side of the swollen river. Two Golf Marines chose a ford and then stepped off over their heads and drowned. Considering all the gear the troopers of 2/5 carried on patrol, no one wanted to negotiate any unknown streams any time of year. The Golf Company commander radioed the 2/5 battalion commander that he'd lost two troopers and needed reinforcements. Colonel Airheart told him to find his men first and not to come home without them. Airheart said he didn't give a damn if Golf Company searched the river for the rest of the war, they by God better not return to An Hoa without those drowned troopers. The Marine Corps had always been hard like that, and when you were given a job to do you did it. No exceptions allowed and no excuses accepted.

We snaked through the wire defenses of the bunkers along the airstrip and cleared the old French minefield that surrounded the escarpment of An Hoa. Marines can out-hump any army in the world, and we made time in long strides toward Phu Loc 6. Reaching the firebase on An Hoa's northern exposure, the platoon cut a trail to the northeast and rendezvoused with the dismal clusters of the Thu Bon's villages in along the southern bank of the river. Lieutenant Pindel radioed Phu Loc 6 and gave the security platoon commander our checkpoints, advising Phu Loc's section of heavy 4.2-inch mortars to be on call in the event we stepped into trouble. Phu Loc 6 had no heavy artillery, and if Lieutenant Pindel requested big guns, the batteries of 105s, 155s, and 8-inch howitzers at An Hoa would answer the call. Lieutenant Pindel was very careful not to patrol outside the battalion's artillery fan. If 3rd Platoon crossed the river into Antenna Valley, then only the 8-inch self-propelled guns and air support could cover us. It always took time to get air support, and when Charlie slammed the door on one of his L- or U-shaped ambushes, there was no time left.

Suddenly, Lafley joined me at the point. I looked him over like he was a ghost. Lafley just smiled back and lifted his rifle from a low carry under his arm. He held his weapon at high port arms for me to feast my eyeballs on.

"Look what I brung along with me, Culbertson. Bet you wish you still had yours!" Lafley rolled his eyes at me and, nodding at the rifle, began laughing so hard tears ran down his cheeks. I stared at the shiny barrel and roughed-up stock of the rifle Lafley lovingly cradled in his arms. Jesus! Lafley still had his M-14!

"You crazy bastard! Pindel will have you court-martialed when he sees that gun. You are not for real, my brother." I couldn't believe Lafley had the brass to hold on to his M-14 and hide in our hootch while the rest of the platoon surveyed our weapons in the armorer's shack. John Lafley had a big set of balls, or maybe he had just gone crazy. Either way, when Pindel found out Lafley had disobeyed a company order to turn in his weapon, the shit was bound to come down around my partner's ears.

Lafley kept up the silly grin, adding, "Don't sweat the small shit, man. When we run into the gooks up ahead in them villages, all hands will thank the Cowboy for having the sense to bring a gun that'll work. That silly-looking piece of junk you got ain't reliable. The gunny said so hisself. I'll stick with this bad boy right here. This M-14 eats gooks for breakfast!" I thought Lafley might have a point about reliability. The M-16 looked flimsy and felt like a damn toy gun.

We hit the main road and traveled east to La Bac 1. Lafley and I looked sharp along the edge of the huts as more of the village came into view. The peasants were busy tending the rice fields. Huge black buffalo lazily plodded through the muck in half-full paddies bristling with young sheaves of rice. The peasants shot apprehensive glances our way, and the overall mood of the village was foreboding. We stopped the column and broke formation to fill our canteens and have a quick moment to adjust our gear and check our rifles. Lafley watched the villagers with interest because the peasants watched the Marines closely, frequently sending a young boy or girl ahead to tell the Communists our whereabouts and the number in our column.

A group of kids ran through the afternoon sunshine, kicking up small puffs of dust. Their smiling faces and laughter were unsettling. None of us pretended for a minute that the village was friendly to Marines. La Bac 1 and 2, like Cu Ban 4, were hostile and had always been regarded as Indian country by the Marines of 2/5. Nonetheless, we threw gum and cigarettes to the children as we formed up and marched through the village proper, heading for the main road to La Bac 2.

Lafley motioned, with both arms held out parallel to the deck, for the patrol to split and form a staggered column along both sides of the trail. We formed a zigzag file with ten meters or more between troopers and kept our attention outboard, letting the man on the opposite side of the trail watch his own flank. The jungle grew thicker as the column neared the river a klick south of La Bac 1. Finally, La Bac 2 came into view and Lafley stopped the march and knelt down to give the platoon commander time to size up the situation and alter the approach march if he saw fit. Lieutenant Pindel ordered Lafley and me to approach the village, with Woodruff and Burns backing our advance. The rest of the patrol sought what cover they could find and took aim on the huts to our front.

Lafley and I stalked slowly ahead. We kept in the shadows of a deep tree line that ran behind the village. We kept our weapons low to the deck, and moved in twos, rushing together in short ten-meter movements. As we broke out of the tree line, the closest huts erupted with rifle and machine-gun fire. Lafley and I went to ground like one Marine. Woody and Burns were close on our heels. The first prolonged burst of enemy fire cut the small limbs off the trees shading our position, and a cascade of leaves and twigs fell over our helmets, obscuring the enemy position. Figuring that the firing was coming from straight ahead in the village seventy-five meters up the trail, Lafley and I shouldered our weapons and fired low, grazing shots into the village. My rifle was set on full automatic. Lafley hammered away with his M-14. Burns and Woodruff had crawled up to our position and were pouring full auto fire from their M-16s into the village. We shot our first magazines dry and reloaded and fired another burst into the flimsy huts. Suddenly, everything froze up. My M-16 jammed first, a spent round half-seated in the chamber. The extractor had torn the lip off the brass cartridge, and the bolt had continued to the rear of the receiver and stood open. Burns's rifle seized up about the same time as Woody yelled out a profanity and slammed his rifle down at his side, dodging for cover. Lafley's M-14 kept slamming heavy .308 NATO bullets into the village, as John threw in a magazine and went back to work. Behind the point position a half dozen Marines had risen to fire their M-16s over our heads, as we lay scrambling out of sporadic Viet Cong fire that cut into the trees over our heads and kicked up the earth around our buddies in the rear.

When the Viet Cong opened fire, John Matarazzi had thrown his M-60 machine gun off his shoulder. Matarazzi and Jessmore ran toward the point fire team's flank, threw their weapons down behind a clump of trees, and ran a belt into the receiver. Matarazzi listened as John Jessmore identified the incoming fire and pointed out the angle for Mat to aim down. The gun jerked and spent, hot brass tumbled out the ejection port, and the muzzle blast flared out the sides of the flash suppresser. A stream of tracers splashed into the earthworks alongside the enemy's concealed parapets. Clouds of earth and rock lifted into the air with each deadly burst. Matarazzi was a master at his weapon, sweeping along the Viet Cong bunkers and back again, allowing Woodruff and Burns to crawl to the rear under a clutch of trees for safety.

I was stuck like glue to Lafley, who was yelling as he fired round after round into the VC position. "Come on you puny bastards! I still got my rifle, and you don't like that much, do you? Jesus, Culbertson, I wish I had an M-16." Lafley seemed crazed and fired fearlessly ahead as enemy bullets continued to tear into the trees and brush surrounding the Cowboy. I felt naked without a rifle that would function. Remembering my bad luck with my malfunctioning M-14 on the sandbar on Operation Tuscaloosa, I thought twice in this lifetime is too damn much. I never wanted to see another M-16. Matarazzi's machine-gun fire finally coned in on the Viet Cong, ringing them in a deadly beaten zone. The Viet Cong incoming fire slackened—then quit. Sweat was running off my face. Staring to my rear, I saw a Marine stand up and wrap his M-16 around a tree, collapsing the barrel where it threaded into the receiver.

After a moment, Lafley and I got to our feet and walked back into the thick grove of trees and joined the others. In our relief and joy to be alive, both Lafley and I forgot about his still-smoking M-14 rifle. When Lieutenant Pindel saw the gun, he threw his arms into the air and yelled at Lafley.

"Marine, where in hell did you get that rifle? You are to be armed with the M-16 rifle on this patrol. Did that rifle drop from the sky into your thieving hands? Be careful—this is a court-martial offense!"

Lafley smiled at Pindel and swung the M-14 up to port arms, brandishing it like a prize fish before the bewildered eyes of the platoon. "Sir, I know about the M-16 that was issued this week. But, as point scout, I felt I better be sure my rifle worked, sir. That new piece of shit, er, excuse me, sir. That new weapon is obviously unreliable, and since this firefight was not a drill, I am sure you will agree that the M-14 came in handy, sir!" Lafley had a magical way with words. Everyone started laughing and cursing the sorry performance of their M-16s, the Black Rifle!

Lieutenant Pindel had to agree it was nice to have a weapon that functioned. "I suppose if those Viet Cong had been NVA, we might well be dead. Lafley, I will entertain your formal excuse for having that rifle when we return to

An Hoa. For now, good shooting! You might be a combat hero, Mr. Lafley, if you weren't such a shitbird. Burns, that goes for you and Woodruff, too. Start imitating this routine, Culbertson, and I'll slap your butt on tail-end Charlie. Lafley, let's form up and move 'em out to An Hoa. I do not relish spending another second out here with these weapons." Lieutenant Pindel turned on his heel and took up his command slot in the center of the column.

Lafley ran to the point and I followed close behind. The rest of the column tucked inside the roadway and picked up the quick-time march for An Hoa.

Several Marines dragged their rifles in the dirt or used them as walking sticks while holding them by the muzzle. In the Marine Corps we were taught that our rifle is our life, and it had never been clearer to me that the maxim was true. It was an insult to give veteran infantrymen a rifle that would not fire in combat. Our grunts prided themselves on their shooting. I had been one of the top marksmen in the 1st Marine Division Sniper School in Da Nang, and the Sniper School picked the top eighteen shooters out of some twenty thousand in the 1st Marine Division, and I figure I shot in the top half of that group. However, in actual combat, there were no finer shots than Lafley, Woodruff, and, of course, Hamilton, who had picked off a Viet Cong sniper on Tuscaloosa from three hundred yards away on the opposite banks of the Song Thu Bon. John Matarazzi was legendary for his fearless shooting and steady, disciplined fire with the M-60. Except for Private First Class Ivey, Hotel didn't have any grunts who couldn't shoot, and Ivey was hell with the M-72 LAW.

Explaining that we had only one serviceable rifle, one

M-60 machine gun, and three .45-caliber pistols, Lieutenant Pindel radioed Phu Loc 6 for fire support on our hasty return. Hardly enough firepower to hunt turtles in the Song Thu Bon, much less Victor Charlie.

Lafley and I stepped on the gas on point, and by sundown, we had reached Phu Loc 6, where Hotel Company had dispatched another squad-size patrol to lead our weaponless asses back to An Hoa.

CHAPTER THIRTY-THREE

Congressman Ichord
Visits Vietnam

After the patrol returned from the river to An Hoa, a welcoming committee awaited us. The 2/5 battalion commander, Lt. Col. M. C. Jackson, and his staff officers lined Hotel's company street with a team of armorers and clerks. The 3rd Platoon patrol members who had weapon failures, including myself and practically everyone else except John Lafley, marched to the battalion mess hall for a little conversation about the Black Rifle.

Each Marine stood and saluted the colonel and, while standing at ease, held his weapon over a mess table and gave his rendition of exactly what had caused his rifle to jam. Since this was the aftermath of the first field combat for Marines armed with the M-16, company clerks transcribed each man's comments. The armorers asked detailed questions about the cyclic functioning of our weapons and had us empty our magazine pouches on the tables so they could collect live rounds. They also wanted any spent cases that had fallen into pockets or remained in the weapons' chambers. The stories pointed to the M-16's failure to extract spent brass. The reason for that might have been technical, but all the patrol members had to say was that they never wanted to take an M-16 into the field again. The officers looked puzzled. When my turn to speak came, I had a different slant on the trouble with the extraction cycle than the others. I told the colonel that the bolt in my weapon fit so tightly in the receiver that excess friction, coupled with any dirt or sand particles stuck in the oily camming surfaces, would hinder rearward movement of the bolt assembly and cause a failure to extract. I also mentioned that the tolerances were likely so close in the chamber that the cartridge casing—once fired and expanding—could stick inside the chamber. The armorer, Cpl. Billy May, suggested that another lubricant like graphite, which dried as a powder on metal surfaces, would be preferable to a film of liquid oil that would cling to debris. All of us were veterans, so we knew that every patrol would subject our weapons to extreme filth. Excess oil would soak up all kinds of crud on the battlefield. Every Marine who gave a statement asked for his M-14 rifle back, although we knew in our hearts that would never happen. Finally, Colonel Jackson gave us the order to turn in for the night. He praised our courage to stand and fight with weapons that had failed us so miserably. It had been another long day. We figured that Charlie was celebrating the Black Rifle's introduction to the Arizona Territory with glee.

The armorers surveyed our M-16s and wrote our serial numbers next to our weapons' serial numbers where we signed for the rifles. The M-16 would undergo strict tests and the armorers would gauge the bolt and receiver tolerances to mil-spec guidelines. Although the grunts of 3rd Platoon were ignorant of the size and scope of the problem, we eventually found out that the M-16 had failed all over Vietnam.

After a few days, we had rested and returned to the routine of standing lines at the airstrip. It was easy duty, designed to rest platoons that had patrolled for a month and had been mostly in the field. The rotating platoons that served their monthly tour at firebases on Nong Son Mountain and Phu Loc 6 also came home for a month of rest at An Hoa. Everyone got hot chow and showers at An Hoa. In the rear, there was an opportunity to visit the battalion aid station and tend to cuts, wounds, and gook sores that festered on the arms and legs of almost anyone who humped the Arizona river valleys.

Lafley had been lying low. In the excitement of a congressional visit to An Hoa, Lieutenant Pindel had either forgotten about John Lafley's unauthorized use of the M-14 rifle or had decided to drop the subject. Knowing Lieutenant Pindel, I didn't think he had simply forgotten anything. Lafley had the longest time in the country of the company scouts; he was the sharpest point man, and he was a deadly rifle shot. Hotel kept Marines like John Lafley around even when they pulled some nonregulation shit. Luther Hamilton was another Marine who did his own thing. Hamilton had perhaps twice as much courage as the rest of us. On several occasions, I accused Luther of trying to kill himself. Hamilton always said that was his business as long as he didn't take me along with him. Manuel Ybarra was the craziest Marine in Hotel Company and loved to charge enemy machine-gun positions with John Matarazzi and John Jessmore. When I gave the profiles of my comrades some serious thought, I realized that Vietnam could have been very ripe preparation for a psycho ward. I mean, who in hell sends their best troops into combat with rifles that are untested and won't work?

The Marine Corps had troops with balls as big as melons, but some of the divisional staff officers had to have shit for brains to have put us in the middle of the Black Rifle fiasco.

Three days after our first patrol with the M-16, we got the word to report to the battalion mess hall for an interview with a U.S. congressman. I don't think any of us had ever heard of any U.S. congressmen, much less had a chance to meet one personal and up close. Four of us were handpicked, and since we were Marines, the criteria for our selection probably had more to do with military bearing and good looks than brains. After all, the Marines didn't want the congressman to think combat Marines were pussies. For my own part, I desperately wanted to sabotage the M-16, because I thought it was a lousy weapon. Cost considerations and ballistic performance aside, when a rifle wouldn't stand up to filth and abuse on the battlefield any better than the Black Rifle had done for us, then it was no damn good. The M-14 was proven, and any shit-for-brains knows you don't substitute for a winner.

The congressman we came to meet stood in amid a huddle of spit-shined officers who were kissing his ass. When he saw us come in, he could tell we were troopers by our young faces and raggedy jungles. Each of us shook hands with the handsome congressman from the great state of Missouri, Richard Ichord. Congressman Ichord had a tape machine with him and turned it on while he asked us to repeat our experiences with the M-16 rifle. Brainchild of the inventor Eugene Stoner, the M-16 had been pushed into service by Robert McNamara and was licensed and built by Colt Industries. It is amazing what type of gear Marines were ordered to carry into battle. Little did we know that the main consideration for U.S. production of weapons that we would stake our lives on was the industrial interests, which wielded incredible power. They obviously had little concern for us. President Eisenhower had warned against allowing a military industrial complex to make national policy a matter of big business and big-money banking. I figured that with the flak that the M-16 fiasco would generate, grunts would be well served to look after their own asses. That old saying about "Praise the Lord and pass the ammunition!" kept running through my head. I wanted to add "and give us back our M-14s."

Congressman Ichord was polite and gentlemanly. He expressed a keen interest in the men he interviewed that I felt was sincere. He was a member of the Armed Services Committee and would wield real power over appropriations for military hardware when he returned to Washington, D.C. After each of us had answered his questions, the congressman assured us that a mistake such as the issuance of an untested weapon like the M-16 would never threaten young American soldiers and Marines again. Not as long as he served in the House. I believed him, and the Marine brass did, too. We all suspected our commanders were decent people, who would not knowingly send out patrols with malfunctioning gear. Hell, most of the time our officers accompanied us on platoon- or company-size sweeps. No officer in his right mind would want his troops to fail to get him back to An Hoa alive. Captain Doherty had always gone into the field to provide us with excellent artillery support. Lieutenant Pindel had also shown himself to be a brilliant leader—especially in the use of artillery fires. As grunts, our only real need of officers was for their skill in calling in artillery, air support, and medevac for us while we fought our butts off. Our platoon sergeants and staff NCOs like Gutierrez, Huzak, Jones, and Wadley had forgotten about more combat than any officer in the battalion would ever know. For Christ's sake, even if we lost our staff NCOs, we could trust Kirby, Ybarra, Hamilton, or Sergeant Hooley to bring us home alive. The Marines put a great emphasis on NCO training and leadership. Marine NCOs in line companies had to be leaders and had to be able to plan under fire.

No one said much, but I knew everyone's nerves were frayed by the shoot-out at the river. It was about my twentieth firefight at the river. No big deal! Lafley and Hamilton had seen a lot more than I had. We stood to attention as the congressman bid us good-bye and left the mess hall with more officers trailing his butt than there are flies on a dead water buffalo. I just prayed that in their scramble for recognition, our leaders wouldn't forget about the Black Rifle and our reason for talking to the man from Missouri.

CHAPTER THIRTY-FOUR

Hotel Patrols Through Antenna Valley

After four more days in garrison, standing lines at the airstrip, we got the word to pack our gear for a monthlong tour at the Coal Mines at the entrance to Antenna Valley. The pass of Nong Son Mountain, a few miles southeast of the populous river village of Que Son, opened into the North Vietnamese Army stronghold known as Antenna Valley. Nong Son Mountain was a small firebase and observation post guarded by a platoon from 2/5 at the southern bend of the Song Thu Bon. Nong Son firebase was perched about a thousand feet above the river plain, some five miles southeast of An Hoa and twenty-five miles northwest of Tam Ky. There was an abandoned French coal mine near the Marine fortifications on Nong Son Mountain, and the area was interchangeably referred to as the Coal Mines or Nong Son.

Nong Son Mountain and the Marine firebase were reached by foot along the Song Thu Bon from An Hoa until the highway was joined to the southeast. The road led up the mountain in wide, sweeping turns, rising high over the river valley below. The march was so steep after humping from An Hoa that we had to push down on our knees to drive our burning leg muscles up the grade. Once the summit was reached, we found a platform of sand-bagged bunkers dug into the mountainside that was to be our new home for a month. A circle of bunkers and slit trenches ran around the lip of the steep slopes that fell off the mountain. Our fighting holes and bunkers were rein-forced with steel posts and well protected from mortar and rocket attacks.

The southwestern exposure off the crest gave the Ma-rines a picturesque view of the meanders of the Thu Bon River a half mile down the valley. In the early morning and late afternoon, Nong Son firebase was shrouded in low-lying, wispy clouds. The jungle spread north from the river to the huge monolith of Recon Mountain a klick off Nong Son's western flank. On the eastern slope of Recon Mountain, near the summit, stood a small outpost that served as a base of operations for a Marine reconnaissance battalion that ran recon forays into the expanse of Antenna Valley to the southeast of Nong Son.

Antenna Valley was so named because the Viet Cong and the NVA had a network of communication lines throughout the valley. Any Marine patrol that entered the valley would be sighted by NVA pickets guarding the hill-side entrances to the flat expanse of rice fields and plains beyond. To protect their supply bases along the river, the NVA soldiers were quick to engage the Marines, sniping at the officers and their radio operators.

The amount of weapons, munitions, and personnel moving down the Thu Bon River and its tributaries to supply the North Vietnamese buildup in the Arizona Ter-ritory was immense. When Marine patrols threatened the

Communist supply lines, as had occurred on Operation Tuscaloosa, the Viet Cong and NVA would fight a pitched battle to defend their territory. Since January 1967, the North Vietnamese had streamed into the Arizona Territory and Antenna Valley in battalion strength. The most recent reconnaissance provided by 1st Recon Battalion had identified the crack NVA 21st Regiment's movement into Antenna Valley southeast of An Hoa. The bad news was not only that the soldiers of the NVA 21st Regiment were battle-proven, hard-core fighters with plenty of experience fighting along the DMZ, but the Marines of 1st Recon Battalion had snatched several prisoners and gotten their statements. That intelligence placed the NVA 21st Regiment in a garrison status with operational control of all Viet Cong forces in the Arizona Territory. The obvious long-term objective of the NVA 21st was to draw the Marines of 2/5 into a series of pitched battles in the hostile valleys southeast along the river.

By late May 1967, the Communist high command had learned that civil unrest in American colleges and on the streets in large cities promised an opportunity to bring the Vietnam War to a speedy conclusion by forcing a political retreat by the Americans. Once the Americans had gone, and taken their vastly superior war machine with them, the North Vietnamese could turn south and deal with the pathetic remnant of the Army of South Vietnam. It had long been believed by Gen. Giap Vo Nuygen and other North Vietnamese leaders that the Saigon regime was a puppet to the United States government. The real fear harbored by the North Vietnamese was the possibility that the highly trained, mobile U.S. Army would send its airborne divisions to invade Hanoi. The North Vietnamese military strategists realized that an all-out U.S. Army invasion, coupled with a Marine divisional-strength, seaborne attack from the coast could catch North Vietnamese Army forces in a pincer movement and grind the Communist armies to pieces. So the North Vietnamese sought the answer to winning the war in a political solution. The American Army divisions in the south, and the 101st Airborne Division, along with two Marine divisions in the north, in I Corps, had destroyed the best regiments that the Communist command could throw into battle. American forces had killed over half a million Viet Cong and NVA troops, and the true number would never be known due to the devastation left in the wake of American air power.

Third Platoon's commanders informed the troops about the fundamental shift in power from the Viet Cong to North Vietnamese officers in our TAOR (tactical area of responsibility). The discovery of the NVA 21st Regiment by the scouts of 1st Recon Battalion was the first indication that the war was changing. The remainder of 1967 and all of 1968 would witness the bloodiest fighting of the Vietnam War.

The Marines of Hotel's 3rd Platoon were ready for battle, and sitting around a firebase up in the clouds was not our idea of combat. The 5th Marines had spearheaded the attacks at Belleau Wood and Château-Thierry in World War I, Guadalcanal and Peleliu in World War II, and Chosin Reservoir in Korea, and our battle record had already earned two Presidential Unit Citations in Vietnam, in 1966 and 1967. It seemed like the month prior to Operation Tuscaloosa all over again. The Marines were gearing up for a fight. This time it would be against the NVA 21st Regiment. The electricity of anticipation ran up and down our spines. Hotel Company would be ready to fight, and none of us felt for a moment that the NVA 21st would hesitate. This is what the "game of combat" was all about. The two biggest dogs on the block finally meet in an alley with no quarter asked and none given. Marines like that type of confrontation! Two veteran infantry units, armed to the teeth and locked in combat to the death. The greatest satisfaction for the victors is hearing the groans of defeat from their enemies and witnessing the fear and respect in the eyes of the villagers on the first patrol after the battle.

Our M-16s had been refurbished by the battalion armorers. The bolts had been lightly polished and the chambers had been honed to make the functioning smooth without excessive friction. The weapons had been test-fired before we left An Hoa and showed no glitches. The use of graphite instead of oil as a lubricant also kept debris from sticking in the chamber. We felt more confident in the weapons, and still had our M-60 machine guns, M-79 grenade launchers, and M-72 LAWs in each rifle platoon. When the time came to face the NVA, we would be ready. I thought Lafley and Burns were ready even when they slept. Burns swore that a good night's sleep always included a lengthy dream from a war movie. His favorite was *Custer's Last Stand*, but in his dream, all his Marine pals were painted and dressed up as Indians. If the 21st NVA had known about

Woodruff, Burns, Lafley, and Ybarra, they would probably have packed up their shit and headed back to North Vietnam.

CHAPTER THIRTY-FIVE

The NVA Twenty-first Regiment Throws Down the Gauntlet

Third Platoon settled into a routine at the Nong Son firebase. Due to the almost vertical slopes on three sides of the mountain, the Marines of Hotel stood four-hour sentry watches from widely spread bunkers guarding the summit's perimeter. Only the northwestern exposure, which dropped gradually to the floodplain of the Thu Bon River, presented a clear danger for enemy infiltration. The officers of the battalion had positioned an M-60 machine gun to fire down the main trail leading off Nong Son in the event of an enemy attack. The logic was sound, but a defensive corridor held by a single machine gun was vulnerable to attack by mortars followed by an infantry assault or by a coordinated sapper attack employing RPGs (rocket-propelled grenades). The road to Nong Son rose abruptly at the entrance to the firebase, and the field of fire covered by the M-60 position was twenty meters wide but not over fifty meters deep. A quick-moving assault following a mortar or grenade attack could penetrate the Marine lines in under thirty seconds if the lone M-60 were destroyed or its gunner wounded too severely to continue firing. Brush and loose rocks along the other sides of the firebase made a vertical assault seem ridiculous to the

Marine planners who had designed the defenses to be impregnable.

Sergeant Harold Wadley along with Gunncry Sergeants Gutierrez and Jones had fought for ten straight days in Korea in 1952 on Operation Nevada Hills. One battle, for Outpost Vegas, had been defended by Sergeant Wadley's Hotel Company 2/5. In Korea, in order to survive the vastly superior numbers of Chinese attackers, the Marines had become expert in aligning their defensive bunkers' automatic weapons and rifle fire. The cross fires and interlocking machine gun firing lanes had been designed so carefully that a gnat couldn't have flown into a Marine position at night if it had hid inside a Chinaman's ass. Any gap in the lines was immediately plugged by a reserve platoon that had just come off the firing lines. Mortars and rifle grenadiers covered the most likely avenues of approach to Outpost Vegas.

It was easy for Sergeant Wadley and his buddies to pick out the most likely avenues of approach for the Chinese infantrymen. All Harold Wadley had to do was sight his crew-served weapons on the frozen corpses that clogged the approaches to the defensive earthworks. As Sergeant Wadley observed, it didn't require a hell of a lot of brains to predict that the Commies would send their next wave over the same ground as the previous attack. The Marines had gleefully strafed Chinese hordes yelling wildly as their silhouetted forms appeared in the muzzle flashes of Marine BARs (heavy .30-caliber automatic rifles) and .30-caliber Browning machine guns set up on tripods. The main fear Harold Wadley had on Outpost Vegas was of not receiving the daily ammunition resupply or of burning out the barrel of his Browning automatic rifle in the furious action that would come after a chorus of Chinese bugle blasts in the middle of the night.

Sergeant Harold Wadley walked along the perimeter on Nong Son Mountain, shaking his head—trying to stifle a laugh. The officers who had flown out to inspect the defenses the preceding week had been 1st Marine Division staff officers, and one of the team had been a general officer with several full-bull (i.e., O-6 colonels as opposed to O-5 lieutenant colonels) colonels in tow. Confidence in the fighting abilities of 2/5's Marines or foolish reliance on the fact that Nong Son firebase had never been attacked in force had led the inspection staff to agree that the defensive bunkers were soundly and tactically placed. Nong Son firebase also had several 106-millimeter recoilless rifles mounted on tripods and upon strange-looking four-wheel-drive Marine utility vehicles called Mules. There was also a section of long-range 4.2-inch mortars emplaced along the top of the hill where they could fire missiles along the river or pivot to fire into Antenna Valley.

Sergeant Wadley grabbed Luther Hamilton and myself. We walked the ground along the approach to the M-60. Due to the severity of the slopes on the mountain's other flanks, this was obviously the easiest avenue along which an attack could be made

"Hamilton, the general's staff is a lot more confident in that M-60 bunker than I am. A strong rush at night or early morning could take that gun out, especially if NVA sappers crawl within grenade-throwing distance."

Luther Hamilton and I looked at the solitary bunker on the right side of the trail. The field of fire was good enough, but if the gunner and loader got hit with grenades or an RPG, that would be all she wrote. The NVA would rush a platoon into the base under grazing AK-47 fire, and any Marine who came out of his bunker to join the fight wouldn't stand a chance.

Wadley scratched his chin and pointed at a small knoll twenty meters to the rear of the M-60 bunker. "Suppose the gooks already know where that gun position is? I reckon we can move it a ways back without one of the general's staff being any the wiser. Then the gun has a longer lane to fire down, plus that knoll gives the gunner and loader real cover. It's a hell of a lot stouter than the sandbag bunker. What do ya think, Luther?"

"If I got to man that machine-gun bunker, there ain't time to change belts if we get hit hard. Maybe we ought to put two guns on each side of the road, and if the gooks come on we can really tear up some butt." Hamilton had a wide grin on his face; two guns would produce a cross fire that no one could get through.

Wadley smiled at his young pupils. "You youngsters are starting to get the idea. You know, Culbertson, it ain't like I never laid out a defensive perimeter before. All that Officer Basic School bullshit ain't worth a nickel compared to the real thing."

Hamilton looked off into the jungle, where clouds covered the approaches to Nong Son Firebase. "On Tuscaloosa, if it hadn't been for Gunny Husak and Gunny Gutierrez's leadership, Captain Doherty would've never pulled off the miracle that got us off that beach. I still can't believe we lived through that. Culbertson and Lafley had so many bullet holes through their jungles and 782 gear they looked like Swiss cheese. Woodruff and Jessmore looked worse than that."

Wadley stared away for a moment. Then, looking Luther

Hamilton and me in the eyes, he told us the real skinny on Marine combat operations. "You know, boys, all the planning in the world isn't worth shit if the planners haven't tested their theory in battle. The only school that's worth anything is right here facing the enemy. That blackboard approach is fine for training, but combat instincts develop when you put your ass on the line in battle. You boys stick with old Sergeant Wadley. I know tricks the gooks ain't even heard about!"

Sergeant Wadley put a hand on Luther Hamilton's shoulder, and the two walked back to their bunkers.

CHAPTER THIRTY-SIX

The NVA Hit
Recon Mountain

After Hotel had run a few short patrols off the firebase along the river and through the big villages at the mouth of Antenna Valley, Lieutenant Pindel reported to battalion headquarters that a serious buildup was continuing to our southeast. Villagers had reported to Lafley and me that uniformed Communist soldiers had entered their hamlets to secure rice and water supplies. The villagers were caught in the middle of the mess, and I felt they would not be completely truthful in reporting the NVA's actions and whereabouts. Lieutenant Pindel had sensed that we were not as secure in our mountaintop lair as the 1st Division S-3 colonels imagined. Pindel had us polish our defensive tactics and add additional layers of bags to our bunkers. Lafley, Woodruff, and I put two new layers of bags on the roof of our large sleeping bunker. We replaced and repaired the sandbags along the perimeter but left the cover off so we could see and hear better. We climbed down the side of the slope and hung cans and bottles on the wire that wrapped around the hilltop. I suggested making a wide firing ledge in the outboard lip of our slit trenches to put grenades and extra magazines on in the event we were hit hard. There ain't no such thing as too much ammo and grenades in battle.

Lieutenant Pindel walked the perimeter with Wadley and encouraged us to stay prepared. Pindel was the most thorough officer I had served under. On defense, when the shit hit the fan, thoroughness was about half the battle. Wadley made his comments sparingly, pointing out areas of weakness and suggesting finishing touches to our efforts. Pindel listened to Wadley, which showed that his prior enlisted service had endowed him with that most basic of qualities for a leader—common sense.

I opened a can of ham and limas and lit the heat tablet inside the crimped can. Nobody liked to eat ham and mothers, but I was in Vietnam to kill NVA and VC, not to become a cook. Even as a kid, food never meant much to me. I always wanted to hit the ball hard, and I slid into base with the hope of grinding my spikes into the third baseman's shins. The Marines were a lot like real-life Little League baseball in a way; after the game was over, the only thing that counted was winning. Hamilton squatted next to me and laid out hot sauce, jelly, and catsup. He liked to switch ingredients and come up with new creations. That was Hamilton's bag. Lafley and I just wanted to kill somebody.

Suddenly, explosions and the sound of rifle fire broke out along the slope of Recon Mountain. We watched green tracers arc up the flanks of the jungled mountain toward the OP held by a twelve-man team from 1st Reconnaissance Battalion. Slowly, the firing inched up the side of the mountain. A broken line of invaders poked out of the thick foliage for a brief moment only to be swallowed up in the clumps of vegetation ringing the outpost.

Lieutenant Pindel had his binoculars trained on the slopes.

He yelled to Sergeant Wadley that preset firing coordinates were dialed into the 4.2 mortar section at the top of our hill. Pindel told Wadley to start walking the mortar rounds *up* the mountain from the base of the slope to be safe. He also got one of our 106-millimeter recoilless rifles into action. The huge backblast of the 106 was deafening, but the powerful explosion hurled deadly rounds point-blank across the gorge from Nong Son to Recon Mountain.

I watched the exploding round slam into the hillside, tearing clumps of jungle from bare rock. Debris hung in a cloud under the slowly advancing NVA assault line that wavered on the higher slopes. All of us wished we had our M-14s. The .223 bullets of our rifles would carry the klick or so distance to Recon Mountain, but I doubted that the 55-grain bullets would retain much energy at that distance. Even so, maybe we could shake up the dinks enough to make them break off their attack. We commenced firing on the Communist soldiers and lobbed bullets into their formation.

John Matarazzi and Stephen Gedzyk had set up their M-60s and were hosing down the slopes with a steady stream of tracers. The hard-hitting 7.62-millimeter rounds from the MGs kicked up grass, dirt, and chips of rock as they whacked into the mountain's flank. The tracers ricocheted high into the late afternoon haze. After an hour of hectic shooting, Hotel's 3rd Platoon put down their weapons when 1st Recon radioed that the NVA had broken off the attack. The Recon boys gave us thanks and praise. All of us felt it was apparent who the real gunslingers were in the 5th Marines. None of us wanted to join a recon team, although many of us had opportunities to volunteer. I personally felt that recon was a little light in the ass when the combat monster came calling. I liked a lot of friendly bodies around me, since my overall plan was to go home alive. The recon boys could have all the medals they wanted.

Lieutenant Pindel and Sergeant Wadley had done a righteous job defending Recon Mountain. I appreciated the target practice, even with the sorry-assed M-16 rifle. One thing was positive: our rifles hadn't jammed. I thought the firing would help wear the actions in better. When and if the NVA came up our mountain, I damn sure wanted my rifle to "Hong Kong" spit out some lead.

CHAPTER THIRTY-SEVEN

The NVA Twenty-first Regiment Pays Hotel a Visit

After the dust and smoke settled over Recon Mountain, and the 1st Recon boys had radioed "situation clear," I could spot no trace of the NVA assault line that had threatened the OP minutes before, but large gouges were visible along the mountain face where the 106-millimeter recoilless rounds had slammed home. The 106s fired almost point-blank at that range and had torn through the heavy vegetation all the way to bedrock. Doubtless, some NVA casualties had resulted from shrapnel or concussion, because the Communist assault wave had floundered near the summit then abruptly broken and vanished under the intense incoming fire from Hotel. First Recon had huddled together near the top in their bunkers and had allowed Hotel's marksmen to deal with the invaders.

My gaze swept over the slopes of Recon Mountain's summit and down over the road leading to the river. A large shape came into view and lifted into the valley beside our firebase. The *whump, whump, whump* of the chopper blades biting into the humid, late afternoon sky reached my ears. Finally, I could make out the fat, rounded belly of a Marine Sikorsky H-34 skimming over the rising slopes toward Nong Son. The chopper settled in a rush of wind and clouds of blowing dust behind our bunker at the top of the hill. Our "command staff," Lieutenant Pindel, Sergeant Wadley, Sergeant Ybarra, and Sergeant McDonald, rushed to the idling helo. Huge crates of mortar shells, grenades, and rifle ammunition were passed from the cargo bay by the chopper crew to the working party of grunts below. After the munitions were secured in Hotel's ammunition pit, a dozen olive-drab metal cases were gently transferred to the waiting hands of our men. The lieutenant gave a thumbs-up to the pilots, and the 34 throttled up and lifted off, pitching its nose down the mountain as it fell, gaining speed before rising into the setting sun over the river. The lieutenant called the platoon together.

"Men, the supply chopper has brought good and bad news for us. First, these aluminum cases hold a banquet of steaks, hot mashed potatoes, gravy, and ice cream for Hotel's evening chow." As Lieutenant Pindel rubbed his glasses and looked at his bewildered men, I thought I would faint. A hot meal! My mouth watered. Hot mashed potatoes and gravy were a dream come true. I began to check my uniform for bullet holes in case I had been shot dead and gone to heaven. The lieutenant told us to fetch our mess tins and ordered the NCOs to break out the chow. We lined up along the slope to the command bunker and were dished out large steaks and piping hot spoonfuls of potatoes with hot, brown gravy just like my mom used to fix back home. The ice cream would come last, as we sat mutely in squads and dug into our feasts. The aluminum knife and fork combo that came with our mess kits wasn't sharp, and half the grunts had to slice their meat with K-bars and used the knife point to flip chunks of beef into their mouths.

Burns was never modest; he announced, "The chopper boys could have sent us a couple a beers. Some of these bastards don't have no idea that only a bunch of sissies would want a steak with no beer. If I drink water, it'll give me gas." No one wanted Burns to have gas.

As we finished the steaks and went back for seconds on potatoes and gravy, Lieutenant Pindel said he had saved the bad news until we had finished our meal.

"Boys, the recon team across the pass radioed back to An Hoa that they have been probed by a platoon from the NVA 21st Regiment. They believe that the main body of enemy infantry will move against our outpost tonight. The NVA have moved into the Antenna Valley and are harassing Marine patrols as far south as Tam Ky. We stand in the way of their linkup with NVA units in the Arizona Territory to the northeast. They will likely try to take over our outpost and consolidate control over the high ground and mountain passes leading north of An Hoa. We have received extra mortar rounds, grenades, and rifle ammunition. I want each bunker to be well supplied for a defensive battle. Tonight every man is to be in flak gear and helmet. We will assume 100 percent alert status at dark. Squad leaders, man your bunkers and set out aiming stakes and claymores if you haven't already done so. That is all."

I almost threw up my steak and potatoes. Jesus, was the bad news always worse than the good news was good? The 21st Regiment of the North Vietnamese Army was four full infantry battalions with a sapper company, a scout or communications company, and a supply company. About thirty-five hundred men. We were fucking outnumbered a hundred to one. I started saying my prayers. That always happened when I needed God really bad. I knew that I always needed God, but some times were worse than others. It was hard to think about God and a juicy steak at the same time, especially when Burns was running his big mouth about beer and everything.

Shit, I knew I needed to pull myself together, because one thing was a fact: Hotel's 3rd Platoon was not going to let the gooks climb up and take our hilltop without a fight! I looked at Lafley and Burns, who were tearing into a wooden case of grenades. All along the parapet of the firebase's outer defenses, Marines were loading magazines and laying out dozens of grenades on the ammo ledges of their bunkers. The feet of a Marine kicked dirt into my hole, and Tom Jiminez landed beside me with his M-79 and a crate of HE rounds. Matarazzi and Jessmore had emplaced their M-60 on its bipod so they could lift the gun's stock and receiver and shoot along the slanting slopes of our position. Gedzyk had his M-60 in a bunker off the main road, where Sergeant Wadley had moved him to the rear and left of the old position.

Sergeant Ybarra had Marvin Redeye and Vic Peterson covering the backside to Nong Son, where the water mule and latrines were dug into our hilltop. Lieutenant Pindel was painstakingly moving from bunker to fighting hole, checking weapons emplacements and aiming stakes. It was critical to maintain interlocking fires from each position. The approaches to the mountain must be covered in depth if a large attacking force is to be stopped cold.

The mortar section at the top of the hill raised the tubes

of their weapons almost vertical to provide a cordon of defensive fire and shoot illumination to expose the enemy positions.

By the time dusk had set in, every Marine was in his flak jacket and helmet. We were buttoned up in our fire team bunkers, but men were hanging over the lip of the perimeter listening for the crackle of branches or the sounds of sliding rocks that would announce the enemy's approach. I sat silent with Lafley and Woodruff, pulling the safety pins out of our pile of grenades and, after straightening the pins, reinserting them into the M-26 firing assemblies. We had about fifty twenty-round magazines loaded with two-ball to one tracer round to the top. Burns had set his entrenching tool's spade at a ninety-degree angle. The Marine entrenching tool was good for lots of things besides digging a shitter. In World War II and Korea, the Marines had occasionally been overwhelmed by Japanese banzai attacks and by human waves of Chinese. When the enemy came too close to use rifle fire without endangering other Marines, the old salts had used their E-tools like baseball bats. To their joy, the Leathernecks discovered that an entrenching tool will decapitate an attacker, and if you miss his head, the E-tool is damn destructive to chests and backs. Needless to say, it's hard to get a battle dressing to cover a wound that is ten inches wide and a foot deep.

If Gerald Burns was noted for anything, it was his combat practicality. John Lafley and I broke out our E-tools and set the blades perpendicular to the handle. Lafley glanced in my direction and smiled. His teeth were covered with tobacco juice, and he spat into the dirt at my feet. I always knew when Hotel was ready to do some killing, because Lafley, Burns, and Woodruff perked up. Those three were the epitome of the combat Marine, cold-blooded killing machines who relished their work. I was sure I wasn't that way, but as I looked over my pile of grenades, rifle magazines, and my cocked entrenching tool, I knew I was just bullshitting myself. I had crossed the line the day after Operation Tuscaloosa, and I would never be whole again. Let the fucking NVA climb on up Nong Son firebase! The bastards would have to do some serious dying to overrun my ass. There were only about forty Marines in our tight perimeter, but we were seriously armed and every man a veteran.

We sat in fire teams and watched and waited. The evening sky was nearly black, the only illumination came from the stars twinkling at us.

An hour passed as the tension built along our perimeter. Lieutenant Pindel, always observant, made his rounds, checking the alertness of his troops and encouraging us to remain vigilant no matter how secure we might feel. Pindel admonished us that the NVA would likely strike when we least expected, probably in the early morning darkness. Sergeants Wadley and McDonald spent a few minutes in each bunker to bolster our confidence. Wadley told us that the hard part of defending a hill was the waiting. Once the action started, we'd be having too much fun to be bored.

Frankly, I was scared shitless. I massaged the stock of my rifle and kept removing the magazine to check the seating of the rounds. Sweat ran down my face, and the collar of my utilities was lined with the clammy perspiration that fear produces. Hell, I was a shooter. Probably the best in our battalion. I liked to see the enemy in my sights and pick him off in daylight. But the eerie nighttime quiet was terrifying. All we heard was clicking insects and the cries of monkeys high in the jungled canopy. The NVA soldiers would be coming. Moving like army ants up our mountain, higher and higher, until I would blink and one would be standing over me with his bayonet poised at my throat; a smiling North Vietnamese killer that felt no pain, no mercy, no conscience. They were coming, and there wasn't a damn thing I could do but wait.

Suddenly, brush snapped a hundred meters down to my left. A couple of cans jingled on the wire apron spread along the bottom of the firebreak that had been blasted by the Seabees when Nong Son firebase was constructed. I gripped the stock of my M-16, placing it on the sandbag firing ledge. I grasped a grenade and eased the pin halfway out of the firing assembly. Lafley, Burns, and Woodruff had their grenades armed and held tight to their chests, ready to hurl down the slope if an attack was confirmed.

Corporal Kirby and some other fire teams had passed the word to the lieutenant that the sounds of sticks breaking and stones scraping were audible at the firebreak. Lieutenant Pindel wasted no time in ordering the 4.2-inch mortar section to fire a single illumination high over the lip of our defenses. The round thumped out of the tube's fiery mouth and arced high overhead. On its downward trajectory, the round burst and disgorged its phosphorus filament, which spun suspended on a parachute, bathing the hillside in white light. The NVA point element was slow to freeze on the steep incline. As the Communist sappers and riflemen went to ground, Lafley, Burns, Woody, and I threw grenades downslope at them. The spoons popped loudly a third of the way down as the tumbling, live grenades fell among the NVA. Sharp flashes of red and orange burst, and then were engulfed by the dark of the night. We armed a second group of grenades and let fly. More flashes, and groans and stifled moans could be heard from the firebreak.

John Matarazzi cut loose with his M-60, sending flights of red projectiles slashing across the Communist assault wave. Bodies kicked and pitched out into the darkness. Twisting, screaming forms launched themselves into the blackness and fell from the mountain. We could hear commanding voices as new soldiers clawed over the dead and took up the assault. I started pulling pins on my stack of M-26 grenades and tossing the grenade bodies over the lip of our hill. As fast as one grenade fell, I tossed another. A chaotic barrage of flashes lit the base of our firing zone, silhouetting the NVA as they pulled back into the protective cover of the jungle. Hoping to kill or wound any soldier who tarried behind his comrades, we shouldered our rifles and fired burst after burst on full automatic into the surrounding brush.

On the other side of the perimeter, Sergeant Wadley had heard the first team of NVA sappers creep up the dirt trail toward the old machine-gun position. Stephen Gedzyk and his loader, Private First Class Fink, had earlier moved back under Wadley's supervision to a more defensible position. As the sappers crept slowly into view under the weight of haversacks loaded with satchel charges, Sergeant Wadley commenced firing his rifle into the attackers. Taking his cue from the sergeant, Gedzyk squeezed off a long burst of M-60 fire which raked the line of sappers as they raced toward our lines, knocking several onto their backs, where they lay silent. Others did not catch killing rounds, but were stitched by ricochets and low grazing fire that tore through legs and knees. The wounded men screamed and flopped about in fits of agony, as Stephen Gedzyk made another pass with his gun to complete the work. A dozen bodies lay tattered and torn. Gedzyk watched the smoke spiral off the barrel, while his loader ran another belt into the breech and waited for the second wave of infantry. After ten minutes with their hearts in their chests, Gedzyk and Fink relaxed as Wadley and two riflemen joined their position to reinforce the backside of Nong Son Mountain.

Lieutenant Pindel had gone from slit trench to bunker during the fighting. He estimated that his troopers had killed fifty enemy sappers and infantry in the first fifteen minutes of the engagement. Pindel knew that reconnaissance said a regiment was headed our way. Maybe the first sappers were probing our lines to determine the Marine automatic weapons positions and the real assault could come at any time. Pindel had made several sitreps (situation reports) to battalion at An Hoa and informed the S-3 operations officer that Nong Son was under attack. Lieutenant Pindel requested an overflight and fire support from one of the U.S. Air Force AC-130 Spectre gunships— better known to the grunts as "Puff the Magic Dragon." The air force scrambled a crew, and within twenty minutes, we had Puff on station, circling a thousand feet over the bald crest of Nong Son firebase.

I sat reloading my spent magazines and readying my pile of grenades for the next NVA push. It was 2000 hours or thereabouts. The night had grown inky, and we couldn't see a yard in front of our sandbags. I heard the engine's high-pitched whine as Puff overflew our firebase and banked to come around in a tight orbit about two hundred meters out from our wire. The lieutenant illuminated our position with a red flashlight, and Puff banked hard, coming in close for a strafing run.

The gunship's Vulcan minigun was perched in the cargo bay of the ship, with many thousands of rounds of ammo in hard-cased belts. The six-barreled gun jutted out the left gun port behind the wing. As Puff came across our perimeter, the gun fired some six thousand rounds per minute down into the flanks of our mountain. Each barrel rotated as the Gatling gun fired, reducing the overheating of the barrels. Technically, the Spectre gunship could put a round into each square foot of a football field–size target in one pass. No attacking force could run the gauntlet through that kind of fire and survive.

The sound of the gun's firing gave off a *hrruumm* sound that throbbed in the night air. The tracers flowed down from the plane's gun mount like a stream of lava coating the hillside with fire. Puff made several passes, firing into the flanks of the mountain, then she continued to circle, waiting for any return ground fire. When no NVA tracers arced toward the Spectre, the pilot received permission from Lieutenant Pindel to leave the station and return to Da Nang. The Puff crew radioed their base that they were returning after a successful fire mission. A Spectre gunship would remain on call through the long night ahead, and could return and engage the enemy inside of twenty minutes.

We hated to see the gunship leave, but the odds were the NVA had seen enough of Gatling gunnery for a lifetime. Puff had put out as much firepower as an entire company of Marines firing on line together. Those of us who have seen the devastation that a Marine rifle company can dispense know that the Spectre gunship was one bad machine. Burns and Lafley started imitating the gunship's humming gun passes. If that shit went on all night, I was going to add another two bodies to the line of dead littering the firebreak.

I will state this reality, however, that after any Marine infantryman survives the heavy strain of battle, the first fresh breath of cool night air is sweet as honey and intoxicating. When you've already figured yourself a goner, being alive is better than sex.

In the morning, we rose like zombies from our bunkers. We stared a hundred meters down the slopes at the piles of sprawled bodies, arms and legs headed everywhere. Some NVA corpses had limbs shot away, no doubt by the fire from the Vulcan aboard Puff. Others, ribs and joints bursting through the skin, looked like fresh beef covered with *thrumming* hoards of flies.

"God, Lafley, we gotta eat chow right away!" Burns said. "By noon those dudes will start to rot, and the smell will be horrible. Remember how Culbertson threw up when we crossed the VC trenches after the assault on Tuscaloosa? These gooks down the hill are gonna smell lots worse. Those afternoon breezes that fan the slopes will bring all the flies, blood, and shit up here. I hate it when Culbertson pukes all over everything."

I stared at Burns and took my K-bar from my hip sheath. I just pointed the knife at him and smiled. He smiled back, but he also shut his mouth. I moved back from the cliff and broke out my canteen. I sat alone, looking off into the green hills that tapered away to the river. Everything could seem so peaceful in Vietnam. Then, combat would begin, and the world would turn ugly, desperate. I was starting to get pretty sick of Vietnam. I remembered what Captain Jerry Doherty looked like as he walked up Phu Loc 6 to the waiting helicopter. Six feet four inches and only one hundred and forty pounds. I understood how the strain of regular action stressed out the officers and NCOs who had to worry about our lives, not just their own. Lieutenant Pindel was tight on discipline, but I was still alive, and that meant we thought our officers and NCOs were doing a good job.

CHAPTER THIRTY-EIGHT

Foxtrot Tackles the NVA Twenty-first Regiment in the Que Son Valley

The following day, 3rd Platoon received word that we would be rotated back to An Hoa to rest and refit. Late in the afternoon, a dusty column from Golf Company wound its way up the road to our firebase. Hotel was saddled up and marched to the foot of the mountain, where we climbed aboard a small convoy of six-by-six trucks and began the journey to the rear. The red dust blew about the staked cargo beds as the big diesel transports churned up the roadbed. An hour later, we off-loaded at the airstrip and humped back to our company area.

Most of the grunts hit the showers, but some of us made sick call and were treated for cuts and bruises suffered during the NVA's aborted infiltration of Nong Son firebase. I was relieved to be alive, and hit the mess hall doors with Lafley and Woodruff. The hot meal of chicken-fried steaks and mashed potatoes hit the spot. Most of the grunts in Hotel were around nineteen or twenty, our officers weren't over twenty-five, and even the staff NCOs were shy of thirty. The Marine Corps fielded some of the finest and best-trained light infantry in the world, but the physical demands and training were extreme. Thinking about our latest combat action, I was certain who the other best-trained light infantry were. The NVA 21st Regiment got my vote—hands down.

We played cards and wrote letters home until lights out. Taps sounded over the PA system and faded into the night chill as we huddled in our blankets. Sleep was often fitful for the young Marines who humped the paddies of the Arizona Territory and Que Son Valley. Several times, I startled awake as visions of brutal combat assaults or desperate defensive battles played out in my head. Sometimes, one of my friends would awaken from his latest nightmare, sitting up abruptly in his cot, fear contorting his face and a drenched T-shirt clinging to his heaving chest. The trauma of combat had permeated our ranks, and the officers and staff NCOs had their share of problems just like the rest of us.

Morning was always a welcome sight. It meant two things: we were still alive, and chow awaited. Mornings were cool until about 0900 hours, when the summer sun would first flare into our hootch. By 1000 hours, everyone had removed his utility jacket and went around in green T-shirts. By 1200 hours, the T-shirts showed big sweat rings at the necks and armpits and the sun burned mercilessly through a bird's-egg-blue sky. An Hoa was hotter than the rice paddies, where a man could catch a friendly breeze on occasion. The hard-packed streets of An Hoa combat base radiated the heat into our boot soles like a furnace.

After noon chow, we got the word that Foxtrot Company had hit the NVA in the Que Son Valley. Foxtrot had joined two companies of the 1st Battalion, 5th Marines, on Operation Union II in the rice fields ten miles east of Nong

Son. The word was that Foxtrot was pinned down by a numerically superior enemy, and Hotel would be Sparrow Hawked into combat to rescue them. We ran to our hootches and shrugged off the aching fatigue of two sleepless nights. Back in our flak vests and helmets, we grabbed our rifles and machine guns and formed up in the company street.

A working party from Supply was bringing up cases of ammunition, grenades, and M-72 rockets for us. We marched quick-time to the strip and sat in rifle squads along the PSP of the runway. By 1300 hours, choppers arrived and lined up along the strip to ferry us into battle. I prayed that I would make it through again. Glancing about, I marveled at the tenacity of our men; their faces were creased with fatigue, worry, and tension, yet the Marines joked and bullshitted each other as they loaded magazines and adjusted web gear.

At 1400 hours, we got word that Foxtrot had been pinned down by two NVA heavy machine guns and had taken beaucoup casualties but didn't get any concrete information. Tempers flared, and Lafley and Burns started bitching about not getting into the fight. By that time, we had waited two hours, and the choppers still sat mutely.

At 1500 hours, we heard that Cap. James A. Graham, who had fought with us on Operation Tuscaloosa, had assaulted one of the gook positions and taken over a machine gun, turning it on the enemy. Then we were standing by in squads as the Sikorskys ran up their engines to take us into battle. Half the company had loaded into the H-34s when word came down that Captain Graham had been killed defending his machine-gun position. Foxtrot's

Marines had shot their way into a perimeter and were desperately fighting an entire NVA battalion that was determined to destroy them.

Why weren't we already there fighting alongside our brothers? Nobody knew the straight facts, but everyone bitched as the order came to dismount the choppers and return to our company area. We had fought side by side with the Marines of Foxtrot on Operation Tuscaloosa and they had taken out a mortar team that was cutting Hotel to ribbons. Foxtrot's attack on La Bac 2 on January 26, 1967, had turned the tide of battle in our favor and screened Hotel's assault on the hostile village of La Bac 1. Captain Graham had fought gallantly under the skilled leadership of Hotel's Captain Doherty. Now, the heroes of Foxtrot lay wounded and dying in a tight perimeter, assaulted by overwhelming enemy infantry with mortars and machine guns, and we weren't allowed to help. I didn't know for certain what kind of leadership that type of strategy represented, but none of us wanted any part of it. Foxtrot and Hotel Companies of the 2nd Battalion, 5th Marine Regiment, were two of the finest battle-tested infantry rifle companies in Vietnam. The logic of letting one sister company get chewed to pieces by a vastly superior force while the other company sat on its butt, dressed for the dance but not allowed to waltz, was insane. That was a glaring example of failure to plan and coordinate by senior leaders. One of the first maxims taught by Clausewitz or Heinz Guderian for that matter, is never to initiate an attack until the enemy is analyzed and defined as to troop strength and supporting arms. It didn't take a fortune-teller to discover that the NVA were well-armed, elite soldiers. To my mind, sacrificing a platoon of crack Marine troops that are forced to fight when badly outnumbered was the height of incompetence. I thought we were in Vietnam to win the war and drive the enemy back across the DMZ. The Marine Corps seemed to glory in fighting battles with the odds strongly in the enemy's favor. I thought it might be wise to prove how smart we fought, not how many uphill battles we could win.

Later, we were to learn from our buddies in Foxtrot that they had been trapped all day by a crack NVA rifle battalion with heavy machine guns and mortars. The NVA had caught Foxtrot's 2nd Platoon in a cross fire between two machine-gun positions. Cpl. Vic Ditchkoff and Melvin Long were the point element that maneuvered around the first machine gun. Ditchkoff and Long led their Marines between the first NVA gun, which had Captain Graham's headquarters section pinned down, and a second NVA machine-gun position that held its fire until the Marines entered the kill zone. When the second gun opened fire, Corporal Ditchkoff and Melvin Long were past the trap and returned fire on the NVA manning the second gun. Many men in Foxtrot's 2nd Platoon were caught in the cross fire and killed. Vic Ditchkoff continued to rally his squad, and under harrowing fire, retreated back along the path of their advance.

Corporal Ditchkoff led his squad into position, providing supporting fire, while Captain Graham rallied his men and assaulted the NVA gun position. After Graham silenced and overtook the NVA in the first position, he concentrated his fire on the second machine gun. Corporal Ditchkoff's squad, with Melvin Long backing his action, continued to creep forward and direct accurate fire on the enemy. But the NVA reinforced their machine-gun nest and assaulted Captain Graham and his dying radioman. Graham turned the firepower of his commandeered machine gun on the enemy attackers, which he described by radio as around twenty-five NVA. Corporal Ditchkoff and his men continued to pour fire on the enemy, but Captain Graham was cut down as he stood firing his machine gun point-blank into the enemy, killing fifteen men. Falling into the rear of his bunker, he shielded his severely wounded radioman with his own bullet-riddled body. Then he was repeatedly bayoneted by the NVA.

Captain Graham had ordered John Lafley and me into the river on Operation Tuscaloosa as we led the 3rd Platoon into battle. I knew James Graham as a fearless leader and stubborn disciplinarian. While Captain Graham did not possess Capt. Jerry Doherty's combat instincts and experience, Captain Graham made up for his lack of time in the field with a brilliant mind and courageous heart. Captain Graham was a true combat hero of the 5th Marines, along with NCOs like Vic Ditchkoff and Melvin Long.

Lafley and Burns were still playing cards. I sat on my bunk and held my head in my hands. Marines aren't supposed to cry, but I did that day. Our battalion was losing too many good men. America was losing future leaders, and for what? America had to get off the dime and fight the war to its proper conclusion. But how could we honor the memory of our fallen brothers without all Americans giving the struggle their best efforts? I knew in my heart that we had the will to win in us, but by the summer of 1967, we had lost many Marines who could never be replaced.

Capt. James A. Graham was one of those men, and America and the Marine Corps would dearly miss him.

This book is dedicated to Captain Graham, the Marines of Foxtrot and Hotel, and their fighting spirit as Americans and Marines. Semper Fidelis to my brothers in arms.

Appendix

THE PRESIDENT OF THE UNITED STATES IN THE
NAME OF THE CONGRESS TAKES PRIDE IN
PRESENTING THE MEDAL OF HONOR
POSTHUMOUSLY TO:

CAPTAIN JAMES A. GRAHAM
UNITED STATES MARINE CORPS

ENCLOSURES: PRESIDENTIAL CITATION
OFFICIAL SUPPORTING STATEMENTS

The President of the United States in the name of The Congress takes pride in presenting the MEDAL OF HONOR post-humously to

CAPTAIN JAMES A. GRAHAM
UNITED STATES MARINE CORPS

for service as set forth in the following

CITATION:

For conspicuous gallantry and intrepidity at the risk of his life above and beyond the call of duty as Commanding Officer, Company F, Second Battalion, Fifth Marines, First Marine Division, in the Republic of Vietnam on 2 June 1967. During Operation UNION II, the First Battalion, Fifth Marines, consisting of Companies A and D, with Captain Graham's company attached launched an attack against an enemy occupied position, with two companies assaulting and one in reserve. Company F, a leading company, was proceeding across a clear paddy area one thousand meters wide, attacking toward the assigned objective, when it came under heavy fire from mortars and small arms which immediately inflicted a large number of casualties. Hardest hit by the enemy fire was the second platoon of Company F, which was pinned down in the open paddy area by intense fire from two concealed machineguns. Forming an assault unit from members of his small company headquarters, Captain Graham boldly led a fierce assault through the second platoon's position, forcing the enemy to abandon the first machinegun position, thereby relieving some of the pressure on his second platoon, and enabling evacuation of the wounded to a more secure area. Resolute to silence the second machinegun, which continued its devastating fire, Captain Graham's small force stood steadfast in its hard won enclave. Subsequently, during the afternoon's fierce fighting, he suffered two minor wounds while personally accounting for an estimated fifteen enemy killed. With the enemy position remaining invincible upon each attempt to silence it and with their supply of ammunition exhausted, Captain Graham ordered those remaining in the small force to withdraw to friendly lines, and although knowing that he had no chance of survival, he chose to remain with one man who could not be moved due to the seriousness of his wounds. The last radio transmission from Captain Graham reported that he was being assaulted by a force of twenty-five enemy; he died while protecting himself

and the wounded man he chose not to abandon. Captain
Graham's actions throughout the day were a series of
heroic achievements. His outstanding courage, superb
leadership and indomitable fighting spirit undoubtedly
saved the second platoon from annihilation and reflected
great credit upon himself, the Marine Corps, and the
United States Naval Service. He gallantly gave his
life for his country.

STATEMENT OF LIEUTENANT COLONEL PETER L. HILGARTNER 051942 USMC
COMMANDING OFFICER, 1ST BATTALION, 5TH MARINES

7 June 1967

On 2 June 1967, I was Commanding Officer of 1st Battalion, 5th
Marines, during Operation UNION II. My Battalion was directed to take
an area known as "Objective "F", a piece of terrain centered around coordinates BT 090320. About 1130 on 2 June, Companies D and F had passed
their intermediate objective and were launching the attack on "Objective
F". Company D, on the right of Company F, was committed first and met
the first resistance. Company F launched their attack across a 1000
meter paddy field and were met by a tremendous barrage of mortars and
small arms. This barrage succeeded in stopping Company F's assault,
killing and wounding a large number of Marines. It was now apparent
that both companies had hit a sizable force, consequently, Company A,
the reserve company, was committed to the attack on the left of Company F. Company A and Company D, both made attempts to flank the enemy
but were unsuccessful. During this period, Captain GRAHAM, Commanding
Officer, of Company F reported that he was receiving very heavy fire
from two machine guns, which should be knocked out. He also reported
that he was trying to re-organize his company. At this time I tried to
get Company F to slide either right or left, but the enemy fire was
evidently too intense and they were unsuccessful. Around 1500, I
tried to tried to get Captain GRAHAM on the radio and was told by his
First Sergeant that he was organizing an assault group to try to take
out the machine guns. Later, I reestablished communications with Captain
GRAHAM and he reported that he had made it across the paddy field and
was occupying a portion of "Objective F". He reported that he had six
wounded and only four effectives with him. He requested help. Again,
we tried to maneuver Company A or Company D to aid him, but were unsuccessful. From his position, Captain GRAHAM was adjusting close air
support and calling fire into the enemy positions. The battalion also
delivered mortar fire in his support. At about 1700, I had my last radio
communication with Captain GRAHAM, at which time he announced that about
twenty-five of the enemy were making an assault on his position. He died
there, trying to defend his wounded and to maintain a toehold for the
Battalion, on "Objective F". His action constituted the most significant
penetration of the enemy lines during the battle.

P. HILGARTNER
LtCol   USMC

TRANSMISSION:
Capt. W. S. BAKER
010076

4229

STATEMENT OF FIRST SERGEANT CLEO EDWIN LEE 1023519 USMC

4 June 1967

On 2 June 1967, I was First Sergeant of Company F, Second Battalion, Fifth Marines during Operation UNION II. We had three objectives for the day. The first, we took with no resistance, on the second we received a little sniper fire and killed 3 enemy soldiers. We were advancing toward the third when Company D, on our right flank, was hit pretty hard. Company F was rushed in to take some of the pressure off Company D. It wasn't long before all three of our platoons were engaged in a fight for their lives. The 1st and 3rd platoons were being hit from the high ground on our left while the 2nd platoon was pinned down by a hail of automatic weapons fire from the right and from the front. Captain GRAHAM used all the mortar rounds we had and air and artillery. The air strikes were effective but they couldn't seem to hit the area from where the 2nd platoon was getting all the automatic weapons fire. Finally the Captain got the Gunnery Sergeant and most of the headquarters group and started to fire and maneuver towards the tree line where all the fire was coming from. He managed to knock out one machine gun position then radioed back to me to send him more men. I sent the last five men from the headquarters group but they were cut down before they got half way. Captain GRAHAM kept trying to get help on the radio until finally I didn't hear him any more. His determination, courage and assurance throughout the action kept the rest of us going and his action in taking on that machine gun saved the 2nd platoon from complete annihilation. In twenty-two years of military service, he is the finest officer I ever knew.

Cleo E. Lee
CLEO E. LEE
1STSGT USMC

WITNESSED:
Capt. W. S. PARKER
080976   USMC

STATEMENT OF GUNNERY SERGEANT JOHN SHERMAN GREEN 1275527 USMC

4 June 1967

On 2 June 1967, I was Gunnery Sergeant of Company F, Second Battalion, Fifth Marines, during Operation UNION II. We were advancing towards our third assigned objective for the day, when Company D, on our right flank was hit hard by a large force of well dug-in North Vietnamese soldiers. Company F was ordered up to assault the enemy force and relieve the pressure on Company D. We moved out with the 2nd platoon on the right, the 1st platoon on the left and the 3rd platoon in reserve. It wasn't long before the 2nd platoon was pinned down by heavy automatic weapons fire from our right front. The most damaging fire was from a machine gun at the vicinity of coordinates BT 00931S. This gun was set up in the remains of a house and there was a tree line running right in front of it and perpendicular to the line of fire. The 3 platoon was ordered to take the high ground to our left, but it soon became evident that they were going to have to fight their way in because the enemy was dug-in there too. The 1st platoon tried to go to the aid of the 2nd platoon, but they began to take too many casualties. The Platoon Commander was killed and the remainder of the platoon managed to link up with the 3rd platoon. The 2nd platoon was pinned down in an open paddy field and was really getting hurt. Meanwhile, Captain GRAHAM had the command group take cover in a ditch some distance to the rear of the 2nd platoon. He continually exposed himself to a hail of fire in order to ascertain the situation, give guidance and encouragement to his platoons and adjust air and artillery strikes. The air strikes were coming, but they couldn't seem to get their bombs close enough. Finally Captain GRAHAM decided he had to do something about the machine gun which was hurting the 2nd platoon so badly. He called in all available riflemen to form an assault group. He put me in charge of three men and took three plus the corpsman. He pointed out our objective and we began to advance by fire and maneuver through the 2nd platoon towards the machine gun. We assaulted the machine gun position and forced the enemy to withdraw. During this assault, the Captain was hit and slightly wounded. We consolidated our position and formed a hasty defensive perimeter, all the while continuing to fire at enemy soldiers. At sometime during this period, the 2nd platoon commander and about seven of his men joined us. Captain GRAHAM had him take a force on an enveloping movement against a second machine gun emplacement while the rest of us laid down a base of fire. They never made it and only one man that I know of was able to make it back. During all this time, Captain GRAHAM tended the wounded, tried to get help on the radio and fired his weapon at the enemy. By his spirit, he kept the rest of us going. He personally accounted for between 12 and 15 enemy dead. He was also hit and slightly wounded a second time during this part of the action. Finally, we ran completely out of ammunition and it became apparent

that if we stayed there we would be overrun. The Captain ordered all
of us who could to leave and make our way back to the area. Captain
GRAHAM stayed behind to care for the last wounded man who couldn't
be moved. Had it not been for Captain GRAHAM's action in assaulting
that machine gun, there would be no surviors of the 2nd platoon. He
was the bravest man and the finest officer I've ever known.

JOHN S. GREEN
GYSGT   USMC

WITNESSED:
Capt. W. S. PARKER
080976   USMC

4229   ENCLOSURE (4)

STATEMENT OF CORPORAL DARYL JAMES SOUKUP 2163585 USMC

4 June 1967

On 2 June 1967, I was Right Guide of the 2nd platoon, Company F, Second Battalion, Fifth Marines during Operation UNION II. Our platoon was advancing on the right flank of the company when we were caught in the middle of a paddy field by a storm of automatic weapons fire about two hundred meters to our front. The platoon tried to advance but was quickly pinned down by the intense fire. I was delegated to take care of the wounded. Company D, on our right, was evidently pinned down and unable to move also. The jets were making air strikes but they never seemed to hit the right place. We were taking heavy casualties but there didn't seem to be much we could do about it. We had been there what seemed like two hours when Captain GRAHAM came through with some people from the headquarters group. He stopped to check on the wounded and to give us all words of encouragement and then I could see him lead his group by fire and maneuver and finally assault the machine gun which had been giving us the most trouble. I couldn't see the action, but that machine gun didn't bother us any more. I never saw the Captain alive again.

Daryl J Soukup

DARYL J. SOUKUP
CPL   USMC

WITNESSED:
Capt. W. S. PARKER
030976   USMC

4229   ENCLOSURE (5)

STATEMENT OF PRIVATE FIRST CLASS THOMAS PHILLIP LABARBERA 2207330 USMC

4 June 1967

On 2 June 1967, I was a clerk attached to Company F, Second Battalion, Fifth Marines during Operation UNION II. When Company D got hit, Company F moved forward to try to take the pressure off Company D. I was with the headquarters group. We heard over the radio that the 2nd platoon was pinned down. Captain GRAHAM moved us to a position in the rear of the 2nd platoon and continually exposed himself to enemy fire while he tried to get air and artillery in on the people who had the 2nd platoon pinned down. It didn't seem to do much good so Captain GRAHAM decided to assault the enemy position. He formed an assault unit from personnel of the headquarters group and we made our way by fire and manuever to a position from which we finally overran an enemy machine gun position. We formed a hasty defensive perimeter and the 2nd platoon commander and some of his men joined us. Captain GRAHAM ordered the Lieutenant to take an enveloping force against another machine gun position while the rest laid down a base of fire. I went with the enveloping force. The Lieutenant and most of the others were killed before we could reach our objective. Somehow, I made it back to Captain GRAHAM's position. All the while I was there Captain GRAHAM kept working the radios, trying to get help, trying to get air and artillery. He also found times to tend the wounded and fire his own weapon at the enemy. He personally accounted for between 8 and 12 enemy dead. Finally we ran out of ammunition and could see the enemy advancing toward us. Captain GRAHAM ordered all of us to leave but there was one man who was wounded too bad to be moved. The Captain and I tried to move him but he screamed with pain. Captain GRAHAM ordered me to leave and he stayed with the wounded man.

Thomas P. La Barbera

THOMAS P. LABARBERA
PFC   USMC

WITNESSED:
Capt. W. S. PARKER
080976   USMC

4229   ENCLOSURE (6)

DEAR MOM
A Sniper's Vietnam

By Joseph T. Ward

The U.S. Marine scout snipers were among the most highly trained soldiers in Vietnam. With their unparalleled skill, freedom of movement, and deadly accurate long-range Remington 700 bolt rifles, the scout snipers were sought by every Marine unit—and so feared by the enemy that the VC bounty on the scout snipers was higher than on any other elite American unit.

Joseph Ward's letters home reveal a side of the war seldom seen. Whether under nightly mortar attack in An Hoa, with a Marine company in the bullet-scarred jungle, on secret missions to Laos, or on dangerous two-man hunter-kills, Ward lived the war in a way few men did.

Published by Ivy Books.
Available at bookstores everywhere.

INSIDE THE CROSSHAIRS
Snipers in Vietnam

By Michael Lee Lanning

At the start of the war in Vietnam, the United States had no snipers; by the end of the war, Marine and army precision marksmen had killed more than 10,000 NVA and VC soldiers—the equivalent of an entire division—at the cost of under 20,000 bullets. Now noted military historian Michael Lee Lanning shows how U.S. snipers in Vietnam—combining modern technology in weapons, ammunition, and telescopes—used the experience and traditions of centuries of expert shooters to perfect their craft.

Lanning interviewed men with combat trigger time, as well as their instructors, the founders of the Marine and U.S. Army sniper programs, and the generals to whom they reported. The author demonstrates how the skills of these one-shot killers honed in the jungles of Vietnam provided an indelible legacy that helped save American lives in Grenada, the Gulf War, Somalia, and Bosnia.

Published by Ivy Books.
Available at bookstores everywhere.

DON'T MISS THE MOST AUTHENTIC
THRILLER OF THE DECADE!

REMOTE CONTROL
by Andy McNab

A former member of the Special Air Service crack elite force, Andy McNab has seen action on all five continents. In January 1991, he commanded the eight-man SAS squad that went behind Iraqi lines to destroy Saddam's scuds. McNab eventually became the British army's most highly decorated serving soldier and remains closely involved with intelligence communities on both sides of the Atlantic.

Now, in his explosive fiction debut, he has drawn on his seventeen years of active service to create a thriller of high-stakes intrigue and relentless action. With chillingly authentic operational detail never before seen in thrillers, REMOTE CONTROL is a novel so real and suspenseful it sets a new standard for the genre.

Available in hardcover in May 1999 from Ballantine Books at a special introductory price of $19.95.